Yakov Alpert, a pioneer in several fields of radio and space plasma physics, participated in *Sputnik I* and many other Soviet satellite projects in the 1960s and 1970s. He hosted the officially banned refusnik scientific seminars in Moscow in the 1980s and emigrated to the United States in 1987. He is now senior scientist at the Harvard-Smithsonian Center for Astrophysics.

Making Waves

Yakov Lvovich Alpert, drawn at the academicians' resort Uzkoe, near Moscow, on 12 February 1945 by Victor A. Vesnin, architect and member of the Academy of Sciences of the U.S.S.R.

YAKOV ALPERT

Making Waves

STORIES FROM MY LIFE

Yale University Press
New Haven &
London

Set in Sabon type by Keystone Typesetting, Inc., Orwigsburg, Pennsylvania.
Printed in the United States of America.

Library of Congress Cataloging-in-Publication Data

Al'pert, IA. L. (IAkov L'vovich)
    Making waves : stories from my life / Yakov Alpert.
      p. cm.
    Includes index.
    ISBN 0–300–07821–8 (alk. paper)
    1. Alş'ert, ëi. L. (ëikov Lş'ovich)   2. Physicists — Russia (Federation) —
Biography.   I. Title.

QC16.A342 A3
530'.092 — dc21
[B]   00–035918

A catalogue record for this book is available from the British Library.

10 9 8 7 6 5 4 3 2 1

The best mountains are the mountains you have never climbed.
The world has no peaks which cannot be captured.

— *Vladimir Vysotsky*

Contents

Foreword

How much can a single human being pack into a lifetime? By any measure, Yakov Alpert's must stand as truly remarkable. Consider the eras his life has spanned. Beginning before the Soviet Union itself, his memoir encompasses its postrevolutionary era, Stalin, wartime, Khrushchev, Gorbachev, and its demise. Through his eyes, we see this epic drama unfold from a unique vantage point. His professional life not only stretches across much of fundamental science but intersects the space race, nuclear weapons, and environmental concerns. A firsthand witness to the interaction of Soviet science with the policies of the Soviet state, Alpert offers in this chronicle of his life day-to-day insights into one of the twentieth century's most remarkable stories.

The town of his birth could well have served as a real-life set for *Fiddler on the Roof*. Here we glimpse the generations-old traditions of Jews in Russia emerging from a time when the tsars still ruled. But not for long. As war and revolution swept away the old regime, a new one emerged: the Union of Soviet Socialist Republics.

Normalcy amid chaos. Growing up in an era of civil war, economic devastation, and political turmoil, young Yakov struggled to find a place for himself. Yet he also found time to exercise his lively curiosity. He began tinkering with bits of electrical equipment salvaged from local junkyards while still in elementary school — early evidence of the passionate spirit of inquiry that has marked his entire life. Another sign of things to come emerged as well: conflict with arbitrary authority. The young high school student organized a strike against an incompetent instructor, found himself expelled, and was then reinstated. Brilliant in his work, but too much of a maverick to play along with the system.

Brilliance won out in those early years. Through a combination of native intelligence, hard work, and sheer audacity, he gained entry into the USSR's fledgling radio industry — and the scientific establishment being created to support it. As an avid amateur radio operator, he immersed himself in what was then an infant technology, one based more on arcane art than on what we now regard as modern science. Stretched across eleven time zones and covering more than eight million square miles, the Soviet Union depended upon so-called short wave radio for much of its communications. Since electromagnetic theory tells us that radio waves travel along straight paths, however, one might expect the curvature of the earth to limit radio communication to something like one hundred miles or less. But nature gives short wave radio a key bit of extra help. For these waves, the earth's ionosphere acts as a huge curved mirror. Instead of flowing out into deep space, therefore, short waves are deflected downward toward the earth's surface. That surface also acts as a mirror for these waves, resulting in multiple bounces covering thousands of miles.

Unlike most of his contemporaries — who regarded the vagaries of this multi-hop phenomenon as a nuisance — Yakov Alpert saw it as an opportunity for deeper understanding. An independent thinker from first to last, he chose to devote his life to the study of radio physics. An audacious choice for someone officially trained as a cabinetmaker and assigned to manual labor. But Yakov's knack for taking matters into his own hands won out in the end. And so a distinguished career began. Joining the Lebedev Institute just a year after its founding, he embarked on a series of investigations that established him as a leading expert on the ionosphere and related physical phenomena.

Through ingenious use of the limited experimental tools then available and powerful theoretical analysis, he gained important insights into the thin layers of ionized gas — or *plasmas* — that lie between the earth's atmosphere and the vast emptiness of outer space. A new picture emerged. Disruptive forces — such as ionizing energy from the sun's radiation or lightning — contended with the holding power of the earth's magnetic field. The result: an elastic medium prone to oscillations (or to *make waves*).

Important from a scientific and even a commercial standpoint, the physics of space plasmas seemed unlikely to attract much outside attention. But a new revolution soon changed matters. This time, a revolution in technology. With the end of World War II, Soviet scientists began to take their first steps toward a space program using captured German rockets. Unanswered scientific questions abounded, and Alpert soon became involved. With the dawn of the space age at hand, ionospheric radio propagation moved to center stage.

This heightened profile proved a mixed blessing. On one hand, official interest brought additional resources for experimentation and the likelihood of career advancement. On the other, it also meant heightened attention from the KGB. And "attention," of course, meant cooperate or face the consequences.

Self-described resistance to KGB pressure abounds in post-Soviet autobiographic literature. Virtually everyone able to pick up a pen these days seems to have bravely defied authority. But consequences speak louder than words. While the careers of less-distinguished scientists continued to flourish, Yakov Alpert quickly found himself stripped of his much-needed security clearance, fired from his job, and barred from further employment in his field.

Reinstated because of a continuing need for his talents, Alpert found that the ups and downs of his conflicts with authority continued — and culminated in his decision to apply for emigration. In doing so, he became a refusnik. Never one to choose an easier path for the sake of convenience, he participated as activist and observer in the historic confrontation between a handful of scientists and the massive power of the Soviet state.

In all this and much else, Yakov Alpert's continuing sense of moral indignation affords him a clarity of vision not given to those who got along by going along. Fortunately, he has lived to tell the tale, and he now shares it with us.

Arno Penzias

Acknowledgments

It is my pleasure to express my great gratitude to many people who helped me to realize this project. I am especially indebted to Pierre Hohenberg and Arno Penzias for their unfailing enthusiasm and essential support. This book would not exist without the help and labor-intensive work of Svetlana Alpert, who read, corrected, and prepared many drafts of the manuscript. Elie Wiesel's perceptive comments were very important for me as I revised the book. Sidney Siskin and Kevin Klose also read the manuscript and gave me many valuable comments and suggestions. I would like to thank Dr. Eugene Mallove for his interest in the book and some fruitful discussions at the early stage of my writing. I am grateful to Hilary Hinzmann for his deep and thorough editing of the book. And I want to thank Jean Thomson Black and Jonathan Brent of Yale University Press for their patient interest, guidance, and support as this book took shape.

Lines from Eve Shapiro's translation of Bulat Okudzhava's "The Black Tomcat" are used by kind permission of Ardis Publishers.

Instead of an Introduction: Being in America

In my eightieth year, on my birthday in March 1991, the prestigious New York Academy of Sciences held a special reception and invited me to speak before its members as well as dozens of other guests. This speech embodied many of the thoughts and feelings I have about life and the development of my scientific career. It is as good a place as any to begin this collection of reminiscences. This is how it went.

I began with a philosophy: to tell about one's life is not merely to relate what happened yesterday and what is happening today and to predict what may happen tomorrow. Nor can it or should it be simply a chronological story. Life is, instead, a chain of interconnected events. To understand the deep pattern of our lives, we must discover the connections between past events and what happened before and after. If one believes in God, one might even say that all the connections of cause and effect in one's life are preordained, that God has foreseen them. Here I relate some of the stories of my life that seem to illuminate these connections, and in the process to reveal the logic of my life as a man who lived and worked in the Soviet Union for about seventy years.

In talking so much about myself I am afraid that I may at times seem rather immodest. If I do indeed seem to be immodest, please forgive me. My greatest boast is that I am and always have been a toiler, a person whose most profound love and pleasure is scientific work. What happened to me as a scientist in the Soviet Union happened, in different combinations of circumstances, to other people, too. And often much worse! My principal aim here is to tell about the experience of the men and women of my generation who devoted their lives to research. What is most important to realize is that in these shared circumstances in the Soviet Union, the KGB — that most terrible and dangerous part of the Soviet regime — often played a commanding role.

When I gave my speech before the New York Academy of Sciences it was the third time in my life that I had spoken in public on my birthday. The first time was at my bar mitzvah, at the age of thirteen. For the occasion I had written a *drosho,* which is an essay in Hebrew, on sixteen yellow pages of a school exercise book. It was a lavish expenditure of paper for a family that was not rich in writing materials. But I did not follow that carefully written text when it came time for me to speak. I spoke extemporaneously with my text as an occasional guide. I cannot now recall what I said. But I must have spoken about the life I hoped to lead and the ideals I would strive to follow.

I do remember that my father, Lev, and my paternal grandfather, Moishe, were very proud of me on that day. Even at that age I believed that it would be best for me to devote my life to the search for unique laws of nature. Many years later I understood that it is one's duty to share freely with others the fruits of one's research, without thought of prizes or profit. After all, if one has any scientific talent that is simply a gift of nature in the first place. In the course of my career I have known many excellent scientists who envenomed their lives because they were obsessed with prizes and honors, especially the glorious Nobel Prize.

I wish I could refresh my memory of that day long ago by consulting my drosho, but the ultimate fate of those sixteen yellow pages was tragic, as was the horrific death of my grandfather. But I am getting ahead of myself. We will encounter these stories later.

My second birthday speech came decades later, in 1961, at the Institute of the Earth's Magnetism, Ionosphere, and the Propagation of Radio Waves (IZMIRAN) of the Academy of Sciences of the USSR. I was then fifty years old and was being honored for my scientific work. At the time of my other birthdays I usually left Moscow for the mountains to ski and hike.

The director of IZMIRAN at that time was the well-known geophysicist Nikolai Pushkov, a person of goodwill and satisfactory moral standards but nonetheless an orthodox Communist, with all that that implies. On that day I received congratulatory cables from different institutions, the president of the Academy of Sciences, and various private citizens. It was especially gratifying to receive cables from Lev Landau, Eugene Lifshitz, and Peter Kapitsa, all prominent and respected scientists. I also received congratulations from many visitors from other institutes, from Nikolai Pushkov and my colleagues, and from many young assistants. Yet despite these honors I was in many ways already persona non grata in the USSR. I was firmly set, even if I didn't know it, on a course that led to years in "refusal" and ultimately to leaving my homeland.

When I think over how that happened and how inevitable it now seems, I see that the answer lies deep in my own character and deep in the character of the Soviet regime. To reveal those two characters, I will have to tell you some stories.

What Happened in the Prime of My Life

Imagine the evening of 1 March 1951, the day I turned forty, the day that utterly changed my life. Winter still held Moscow in its grip, but even a pessimist could begin to think of spring as a fact and not merely a dream. My first wife, Irina Chernysheva, and I were at home waiting for a visit from three of our best friends, the well-known physicists Semyon Belenky, Boris Geilekman, and Vitaly Ginzburg. A friendship had blazed up in the mid-1930s between Semyon (Syoma to his friends), Boris (Borya), Vitaly (Vitya), and me (Yasha) and had continued strongly through all the intervening years.

We met as idealistic young men, newly minted physicists eager to make great discoveries. We spent time together every week, often every day, and enthusiastically discussed the problems of humankind as we walked along the streets, in parks, and in the surroundings of Moscow. We happily thought of ourselves as the Indissoluble Four, and others also saw us that way. Even after we all had married, for many years we took it in turns every week hosting a gathering of our families.

I was never so open and frank with anyone as I was with Vitya Ginzburg. He was the same with me. For many years we lived in the same building. One morning when I went from my fourth-floor apartment to his on the second floor, he opened the door and greeted me by saying, "Yasha, you are the only one who can be as frank as Jean-Jacques Rousseau in his *Confessions*," which he was just then reading. My relations with Borya Geilekman and his wife, Natasha, were the most intimate and cordial. Yet the friend with whom I shared a mutual understanding most was Syoma Belenky. We were quick to pick up on each other's meaning. The Four declared that among them Syoma was the wisest, Borya the most handsome, Vitya the most talented, and that I was the best human being. This is how we lived in friendship, with humor and irony.

On that birthday in 1951 Borya gave me a rare book bought at a second-hand bookstore. Its title was *The Hellene's Culture*. In it Borya wrote, "To Dear Yasha, who is always seething and boiling up and is never boiling over." Syoma and Vitya also gave me presents. It was quite something to have such fine friends, all established physicists who were devoted to science. I cherish the gifts they gave me, and I have kept them to this day.

Up until that day the Soviet system smiled on me, too, for the most part. In 1951 I was a senior scientist and head of a small research group at the prestigious P. N. Lebedev Institute of Physics (PhIAN) of the Academy of Sciences of the USSR. I enthusiastically worked in my laboratory ten to twelve hours a day. I had worked there since 2 January 1935, shortly after the institute's inception in 1934, when the Academy of Sciences moved the headquarters of its vast network of basic research institutes from Leningrad to Moscow.

During that time I had been lucky in my research. I had published three books, and I had developed special devices to research the nature of the ionosphere. In 1940 I was unanimously nominated and elected, along with two other young scientists, to receive the inaugural Stalin Prize in Physics. The chair of the prize committee on physics, the famous physicist and academician (in Russian parlance, a member of the Academy of Sciences) Abram Fyodorovich Ioffe, who played a great part in the development of physics research in the USSR in the 1930s and later, quietly told colleagues of the decision. The prize committee must have chosen young scientists as a matter of policy, because some of our senior colleagues deserved the highest awards far more than we did. As it happened, Stalin canceled those 1940 prizes the night before they were to be given. But I shall tell about that in Chapter 7.

During World War II many Russian scientists, like their counterparts in England and the United States, had joined projects to help the military. As a radio physicist I took part in research and development of improved radio communication and radio navigation technology. Although I had long had misgivings about the Soviet leadership—in 1938, for example, I wrote a letter to the newspaper *Pravda* protesting Soviet cooperation with Hitler—I believed in the ideals of socialism and continued to hope that Russia would make progress toward achieving them. I was also glad to take part when, later in the

1940s, the talented Russian rocket creator Sergei Korolyov asked me to perform experiments for the first launch in the USSR of the captured German rocket FAU (Freie Arbeiterinnen Union). To make the radio sets for these experiments, a design group was formed in a special engineering bureau of the Radio Ministry.

My recent tenure at PhIAN had been particularly fruitful and congenial. Sometime in 1949–50, during a talk between colleagues about the upcoming nominations for membership in the Academy of Sciences, an activity that always excited people, I was astonished to learn that one of the most accomplished and influential middle-aged members of PhIAN, Vladimir Veksler, had said, "Among us the first who will be elected to the Academy is Alpert." Veksler's contribution at that point was much greater than mine was. In 1944 he had invented the synchrotron, a new type of elemental particle accelerator. This invention became a milestone in the physics of high energy because it allowed the discovery of new elementary particles. The American physicist Edwin McMillan, who independently invented the same method of particle acceleration, shared the Nobel Prize for chemistry with Glenn Seaborg for the discovery of transuranium elements using this method. Because physics was "closed," or top secret, in the USSR, no one in the West at that time knew of Veksler's work, and he was never considered for the Nobel. But in 1958 he did become a member of the Academy of Sciences, which incidentally proved his prediction about me to be wrong.

My achievements at PhIAN between 1948 and 1951 owed a great debt to the leadership of two distinguished physicists, Sergei Ivanovich Vavilov, academician and director of PhIAN, and Mikhail Alexandrovitch Leontovich, also an academician and at that time director of PhIAN's laboratory of oscillations, in which my research group was based. Let me now say a little about these distinguished human beings.

Mikhail Leontovich was one of the earliest disciples of the academician Leonid Isaakovich Mandelshtam, the guru of the most brilliant group of physicists in the Soviet Union. Mandelshtam's legacy, as I discuss later, was a vital force at PhIAN, for directly or indirectly many of us were influenced by his example and his ideas. As a scientist and as the head of a laboratory, Leontovich was a worthy pupil of his great master. Beyond this, he was a noble person, a true humanist. He took many positive steps against the sluggish bureaucracy in the academy; he helped many people through difficult times; and he never turned his back on dissidents or the so-called refusniks, the Jewish people who were perennially refused exit from the Soviet Union.

Sergei Ivanovich Vavilov, who greatly admired Mandelshtam, was also an extraordinary person and scientist. He was directly responsible for one of the most important discoveries in physics in the early decades of the twentieth century. In 1933 Vavilov asked his postgraduate student Pavel Cherenkov to research the luminescence of a solution of natural uranium salts under the influence of gamma-ray radiation. The fine and delicate experimental method Cherenkov used, developed under Vavilov's guidance, permitted the finding that there was a unique kind of luminescence. Its characteristics radically differed from those of any other luminescence phenomenon known at that time. In most luminescent bodies, the luminescence occurs as a spherically symmetrical emission around the whole body. But Cherenkov's experiments revealed that when uranium atoms were bombarded by gamma rays, the luminescence occurred as a cone of emission that projected out ahead of the body. Vavilov immediately understood that this new kind of luminescence was caused by the radiation of the free fast electrons produced in the uranium salts by the gamma rays. An important property of nature had been discovered.

In Russia this is called the Vavilov-Cherenkov effect. Vavilov's insight and Cherenkov's experimental data were the fundamental starting points of the theory of luminescent phenomena developed by PhIAN physicists Igor Tamm and Ilya Frank. In 1958 the discovery and the theory were honored with the Nobel Prize. But Vavilov had died in the interim and could not share the prize, which is never awarded posthumously, with Cherenkov, Tamm, and Frank. Sadly, scientists in the West are not even aware of Vavilov's role in the discovery of what they call Cherenkov radiation.

Vavilov was also the one who, together with his pupil Vadim Levshin, discovered the first nonlinear optical effect in 1923. Vavilov saw that nonlinear optical phenomena were a rich field of study. But the necessary experiments could only be realized after the discovery of lasers in 1960.

Vavilov was not just a brilliant scientist. He was also an accomplished biographer and a historian of science who wrote important works on Galileo, Newton, and the great seventeenth-century Russian scientist and thinker Mikhail Lomonosov. I think that Vavilov must have felt a special admiration for Lomonosov, a fisherman's son from the north of Russia who became a true Renaissance man. Lomonosov not only discovered a wide range of natural phenomena; he was also a poet, a painter, and a historian. That was the range of interests Vavilov himself had.[1]

He also possessed a magnetic personality, one that conveyed equal measures of strength and gentleness. He had a fine, handsome face and soulful eyes. Most important of all, Vavilov's heart was in the right place. He helped many people and took special care of his colleagues at PhIAN. He fought for what was right

1. Vavilov's works have not been translated into English, and his name does not even appear in American dictionaries and encyclopedias. The same is true of Mandelshtam.

even after his brother Nikolai, a biologist who was himself an academician and who did groundbreaking research on selection in plants, fell victim to Stalin's terror in the 1930s. Nikolai Vavilov opposed the lunatic science of the agronomist Trofim Lysenko, who had Stalin's ear. History proved Nikolai Vavilov right, as Lysenko's policies strangled biological research in Russia. But in the short term, Lysenko was responsible for the tragic fate of Nikolai Vavilov.

What a remarkable family the Vavilovs were. I was told that one of Sergei Vavilov's conversations with Joseph Stalin helped prevent research in physics in the USSR from crashing as biological research had crashed because of Lysenko's ideas. For Sergei Vavilov to try to turn a man as strong-willed, unpredictable, and capricious as Stalin away from one of his schemes, and to do so despite Nikolai Vavilov's political murder, took great courage and great cleverness. It must be said that Sergei Vavilov was a master at manipulating the Soviet system, and that this earned him many enemies. Vavilov died in middle age, and many people thought that sorrow over the tragic fate of his brother Nikolai shortened his own life. Whether or not that is so, the strain of carrying out his responsibilities under Stalin's dictatorship certainly exacted a severe personal toll.

One day in 1945 I had an appointment with Vavilov, but when I went to his office at PhIAN, his secretary and assistant, Anna Stroganova, said that he had suddenly been summoned to appear before Stalin. She asked me to return later that day. Although Vavilov returned to the institute in the late afternoon, he canceled all his remaining appointments. He remained shut up in his office for hours, Stroganova told me the next day, smoking one harsh Kazbek papirosa after another. At one point Stroganova had to bring him a fresh pack from the emergency supply she kept for him.

Only many years later did I learn what happened that day between Vavilov and Stalin. The dictator Joseph Stalin told Vavilov that "they," the members of the Politburo of the Communist Party, had decided to install a new president of the Academy of Sciences of the USSR. There were two final candidates, Vavilov and Andrei Vishinsky, then the chief prosecutor of the USSR. In the show trials of 1937–38 and throughout the worst of Stalin's terror, Vishinsky had served the state loyally and effectively as chief inquisitor.

What was Vavilov to do? To accept the presidency of the Academy of Sciences would multiply many times the dilemmas and strains he suffered as an honorable scientist and administrator in a corrupt, inhumane system. To decline the post would be to resign Soviet science to the lackeys of that system. Either decision might ultimately lead to an arrest and sordid death of the kind his own brother had suffered. We can only imagine his mood after that meeting with Stalin. But we know the result. In 1945, Vavilov was elected president of the Academy of Sciences of the USSR, a post he held while continuing to serve as director of PhIAN.

In those dual posts Vavilov continued to act toward his colleagues and assistants with unwavering kindness and humanity and to exert his remarkable political skills on their behalf. It was a great privilege and pleasure for me to do research in an institute directed by such a man and scientist as Sergei Ivanovich. I fondly remember his pride when I showed to a packed scientific meeting in the large hall of our institute a film that recorded the reflection of the entire sequence of radio wave impulses from the ionosphere with a resolution of 1/50 second. This was a new kind of physics experiment at that time, several months before my fortieth birthday on 1 March 1951.

Personally and professionally, then, I had many reasons to be happy with my position in life as I looked forward to celebrating my birthday with Syoma Belenky, Borya Geilekman, and Vitya Ginzburg. My work was going well and I had already achieved the pinnacle of ambition for Muscovites, the possession of a good private apartment for my wife and me and for my wife's son, including three separate rooms in addition to a kitchen and bathroom. There was plenty of space and privacy, the greatest and scarcest luxury in Russia, for a joyful party with my friends. Except that earlier in the day, as I told Syoma, Borya, and Vitya that evening, General Fyodor Pavlovich Malyshev, the KGB's representative and chief watcher at PhIAN, had given some chilling news to Mikhail Leontovich: I had lost my security clearance and could no longer work at PhIAN![2]

Why and how had this happened? I never had the least contact with Malyshev, except to see him in the lobby and at meetings of the institute, dressed always in his KGB uniform. Some researchers at PhIAN periodically visited Malyshev to demonstrate their solidarity with him and with the system. I never did so.

It seems that Malyshev delighted in these meetings, and it must be understood that his behavior was that of a likable man. He did not impose himself on anyone. On the contrary, he had a smile for everyone and a ready laugh. He was an artist with people.

In fact, I had visited Malyshev in his office once, two or three months before my birthday. This came about because of my meeting with the academician Igor Kurchatov, the head of the atom bomb project in the USSR. He was the Russian Oppenheimer, if you will, and a very powerful person. It was common knowledge that none of the government ministers was as influential in the

2. The Soviet secret police became known as the KGB (Committee for State Security) in 1954. For convenience, this narrative also refers to the secret police in earlier years as the KGB.

leadership of the USSR as Kurchatov. I sought a meeting with him to relate some of my ideas about the effect of atmospheric nuclear explosions on the environment. I told Kurchatov that I could help solve the problem of detecting the location of an atom bomb explosion, which was a critical requirement for intelligence purposes and for the military.

To do this work, a theory of the propagation of very low frequency electromagnetic signals in the spherical earth-ionosphere wave guide had to be developed. You see, the earth-ionosphere system acts as a complex channeling device for electromagnetic signals. If you know the characteristics of that system, you can determine the shape of packets of waves recorded at different distances from their source. My proposal was to conduct appropriate experiments and theoretical research. Mind you, most of us at research institutes wanted to help Soviet efforts in the atom bomb project at that time, believing that this work was in the best interest of our homeland and of world peace. We did not believe that we were engaged in immoral efforts that would endanger human civilization. In his memoirs Andrei Sakharov speaks of his excitement at joining the atom bomb project. This excitement was widely shared.

Igor Kurchatov was apparently impressed with my ideas, for he instructed me to ask General Malyshev to obtain a security clearance for me of the highest secrecy status (known as O.V., for *Osoboy Vazhnosti,* "of exclusive importance"). This had to occur before the project could go forward. Thus it was that I finally entered Malyshev's huge office at PhIAN, even larger and better appointed than the office of the director of the institute, Sergei Vavilov.

When I told the general that Kurchatov wanted me to have an O.V. clearance, Malyshev asked, "What did you speak about with Kurchatov?"

"That is a secret," I answered. "Kurchatov instructed me that no one should know what we discussed." With that I left the general to stew in his magnificent office.

All would probably have been well with me, despite my evasive and even insolent reply, except that Sergei Ivanovich Vavilov was then very ill. Shortly afterward, on 25 January 1951, he died. By an unfortunate turn of circumstances, his post as director of PhIAN remained vacant for a time. The person chosen to replace Vavilov, the physicist and academician Dimitri Skobeltsyn, was then in the United States. He was there as the chair of the USSR's delegation to a meeting of the Baruch Committee on atom bomb affairs. The vicedirector of the institute, Vadim Lyevshin, was a weak person who would never oppose the authority of the KGB. So Malyshev had a clear field. Slyly, he waited about a month to spring an attack. Then, on my birthday, as I have already noted, he told Mikhail Leontovich that I no longer had security clearance. But that was a lie!

To get a security clearance in the former Soviet Union, one had to sign a special confidentiality agreement, promising to maintain secrecy and to abide by all the appropriate rules and precautions for safeguarding classified information. When it became known that General Malyshev was throwing me out of the institute, a senior scientist at PhIAN came to talk to me in private. This was none other than the future Nobel laureate Pavel Cherenkov, whose laboratory was close to my own. He told me that the security department of the institute had asked him to sign a document for final approval of his O.V. security clearance. In reading the document before signing it, Cherenkov saw that it included an O.V. clearance for me. Yet I was never asked to sign the document. It seemed that the denial of my security clearance and my expulsion from the institute were the work of General Malyshev alone and not the result of an order from higher up in the KGB command. But who could know these things for sure?

Why Malyshev did not go further and arrange for my arrest is a wonder to me to this day. It could not have been because of any achievement or any contribution to the state. The cases of Sergei Korolyov and many others, before and after him, show that plainly.

Korolyov began to work on rocket technology in 1929, when he was twenty-two years old. In fact, he was one of the pioneers of the cosmonautic-astronautic era. Yet he did not avoid the fate of many talented engineers and scientists in the USSR (about twenty-five hundred people) who were arrested and spent many years in the Gulag. These people were held in the special prisons that Alexander Solzhenitsyn called *sharashki*. They worked in the prisons on many problems in different fields, including military technology, biology, and geology. Korolyov was in a *sharashka* from 1938 to 1944. He was sentenced to ten years but was discharged four years early, during the war. Eventually he became the chief director and organizer of the Sputnik satellites and of many other satellite and rocket projects in the USSR. One of the most distinguished physicists of our time, Lev Landau, spent a year under investigation in prison. He later received the Nobel Prize. Yuly Rumer, a very talented physicist, who was arrested on the same night as Landau, was in the Gulag for ten years. And not everyone, by any means, survived such imprisonment.

Stalin's Anti-Semitic Affairs, 1947–1953

In 1951 I only lost my job. I got off cheap, as they say, especially in light of the anti-Semitic policy then being pursued by Stalin. In 1947 Stalin had initiated a series of anti-Semitic actions by causing accusations of "cosmopolitanism" to be made against Jews in many different fields. For the supposed crime of "groveling to the West," people accused of being "cosmopolites," or "cosmopolitans, without kith or kin," often lost their jobs, their careers, their freedom, and even their lives.

Toward the end of 1947, the charge of cosmopolitanism was made against me in connection with my first book, *The Propagation of Radio Waves in the Ionosphere,* which had just been published by GostechIzdat. As part of the normal procedure for publishing scholarly books, the publisher had asked Professor V. N. Kessenikh, dean of the Department of Physics of Moscow State University, for his opinion of the book. Kessenikh praised the book and supported its publication, and GostechIzdat showed me his comments shortly before the book appeared. But after the book came out, Kessenikh wrote a newspaper article condemning it and branding me a cosmopolite. I was guilty of cosmopolitanism because in the book I referred more to Western scientists than to Russian ones. I did so because at that time the majority of the papers published in the relevant branch of radio physics were by German, English, and American researchers. Although scientifically the achievements of Russian researchers, and especially their theoretical works, were at the least not lower — often they were much higher — than the achievements of scientists in the West, many of their results were not published or were published only with a delay because they were classified by the Soviet censors.

At the same time, two of my colleagues at PhIAN, Semyon Khaikin and my close friend Vitaly Ginzburg, were also accused of being cosmopolites, although not by Kessenikh. Usually in such cases cosmopolites were at a minimum dismissed from their positions. But the Communist Party secretary at PhIAN, who was responsible for taking such actions, chose another course. This man was not a physicist but a party activist assigned to his post by the party leadership of the Moscow region that included PhIAN. I have forgotten his name. I remember that he was a clever man in his late forties and also a decent fellow. During the war he had lost a hand, and I have always wondered if that experience played a role in his decision about us cosmopolites. I have also wondered what mitigating influence the director of PhIAN, Sergei Vavilov, had on this man. In any event, instead of dismissing us from our jobs, he organized a hearing in the largest conference room at PhIAN, attended by nearly all the researchers and employees of the institute. Khaikin, Ginzburg, and I were severely criticized, and some people at the hearing abused us verbally. But we kept our jobs and continued our research.

Shortly after this show trial in miniature, so to speak, I defended my dissertation for the degree of doctor of physics and mathematics before PhIAN's Council of Science. In Russia, as in France and Germany, the Ph.D., which we call the "candidate of science" degree and which I received in 1941, is not the highest academic degree but the second highest. The highest degree is that of doctor of sciences, and specifically in my field doctor of physics and mathematics. So long as they were employed, doctors of science in the Soviet Union received a special salary, and they never had to write proposals for research funding.

The chair of the Council of Science, Sergei Vavilov, asked me who should review my dissertation for this degree. I gave him only one name: Kessenikh. Vavilov was astonished. But I reasoned that it was better to see the enemy face to face than to let him stab me in the back. The other reviewers, the distinguished physicist and academician Vladimir Fock and the radio engineer and academician Alexander Shchuckin, were chosen by the council, perhaps recommended by Leontovich. During my dissertation defense, Kessenikh opposed my study and argued that I did not merit the doctoral degree in physics. Alexander Shchuckin refuted him quietly and convincingly. After I completed my defense, the reviewers voted by secret ballot, and there was one vote against me. Everyone understood whose vote that was, and the other members of the council were indignant.

One morning several months later I asked for a meeting with Sergei Vavilov. His secretary informed me that Vavilov had arrived at his office early in the morning in a rush, canceled all meetings at PhIAN, and asked that the meetings at his office as president of the Academy of Sciences also be canceled. He was going to a session of the All-Union Attestation Commission of the Ministry of Education of the USSR, because at that session my degree of doctor of physics and mathematics would be officially approved or rejected. Vavilov told his secretary that he had to be there in case there were attacks against me.

It was lucky for me that Vavilov was willing to fight so publicly for what was right during this period of heightened anti-Semitism. Many people were not so fortunate. And Stalin's anti-Jewish policy became ever more dangerous. In 1952, more than one hundred people were arrested in connection with state investigations of the Jewish Anti-Fascism Committee (JAC). After a sham trial, ten members of the JAC were convicted of antistate activity and executed.

The Jewish Anti-Fascism Committee grew out of the Jewish Anti-Semitism Committee, which the Kremlin formed in 1942 to raise funds in America to support the Russian war effort. As head of that committee, the Kremlin picked Solomon Mikhoels, the distinguished actor and producer who led the famed Jewish Theater of Moscow. Many articles about that theater appeared in Russian and Western newspapers. Russian and foreign tourists, even those who did not know Yiddish, flocked to the theater to see Mikhoels play the leading roles in Sholem Aleichem's *Tevje the Milkman* (the source for *Fiddler on the Roof*) and Shakespeare's *King Lear*. I saw both productions and I suspected that the critics did not exaggerate when they called Mikhoels the best Lear in the world.

In 1946 the Kremlin awarded Mikhoels the State Prize of the USSR. Two years later, he died in a staged car accident in Minsk, the capital of Belorussia (now Belarus). So Mikhoels did not live to see his close friends and associates executed on trumped-up charges. But Stalin resourcefully cast him in a role even after his death. In 1953 the Kremlin claimed that a conspiracy of Jewish physicians had been discovered. These "physician murderers" allegedly planned to assassinate leading Soviet personnel. They were said to be acting on the instructions of Solomon Mikhoels, who had then been dead for five years, and Boris Shimelovich, who was one of the ten JAC members executed in 1952.

In denouncing the Jewish physicians, the Kremlin meant to prepare the public to accept a program of action against all the Jews of Russia. Less than a decade after the end of World War II, with the memory of the German concentration camps still fresh in the world's mind, Stalin planned to deport Soviet Jews to Siberia. Barracks in Siberia were readied, a schedule of rail transport was drawn up, and long lists of Jews were prepared. The propaganda arm of the Kremlin arranged for prominent people in the USSR to write letters justifying the deportation, to be published as the Jews were being rounded up. And a member of the Central Committee of the Communist Party wrote a polemical tract, "Why Is It Necessary to Deport the Jews from the Industrial Regions of the Country?"

Everything was in readiness to implement this plan when Stalin suffered a stroke on the night of 1 March 1953. His death four days later freed humankind from a great evil.

I have talked about Mikhoels because he figured so prominently in Stalin's anti-Semitic policies. As with Korolyov, Landau, and other distinguished people, Mikhoel's great achievements and undoubted patriotism could not save him from the caprices of a repressive state. For me and for many others, such examples raised disturbing questions. Why were we not arrested and imprisoned? Such questions arose for me at several points in my life. Of course, it is inconvenient for the state to arrest everyone. And an atmosphere in which arrests are as random as lightning strikes can be a useful tool for maintaining a system of oppression.

In any case it was lucky that I was only fired from my job in 1951 and not arrested. Perhaps the answer lies buried deep in a KGB file. In any event, General Malyshev had his revenge for my refusal to curry favor with him. On 6 March 1951 PhIAN order number 6 announced curtly, "Ya. L. Alpert, Doctor of Physics and Mathematics, was dismissed from the institute on 5

March 1951 owing to a reorganization of the laboratory." A little more than a year and a half later, officialdom spoke more harshly. On 16 October 1952, a report from the vice-director of PhIAN, Vadim Lyevshin, stated, "In 1951–52 Ya. L. Alpert . . . [was] dismissed from the institute because . . . [he was] found to be unsuitable."[3]

The statement that I was unsuitable followed many actions to the same effect. For example, shortly after I was fired, I received an official letter from PhIAN asking me to make one of the rooms in my apartment available for an employee of PhIAN and his wife. The living space for my family (forty-seven square meters) was in an apartment house built specifically for senior scientists, professors, and so on. When we moved there, our old living space was given to a young employee of the institute and, following Soviet law, the new apartment became ours. At that time in Moscow and other large cities of the USSR, it was common for two, three, or more families to occupy a single apartment with one kitchen and one bathroom for all.

Of course, I rejected the institute's demand that we give up space in our apartment. A long wrangle ensued. Then, on 17 December 1951, the institute appealed to the People's Court of the Leninsky section of Moscow, where we lived, asking them "to help the institute evict Ya. L. Alpert from his apartment or at least to free one room for another family." Irina and I hoped that the court would decide in our favor, but we could not be confident that it would do so. The institute argued that my firing meant that I no longer had the rank of senior scientist and thus no longer merited such a large living space. Luckily for us, Irina, whose field was German lexicology and stylistics, had the rank of professor. And forty-seven square meters was just under the minimum living area that professors were supposed to receive. On this basis the court rejected PhIAN's appeal on 12 January 1952, and the institute did not trouble us anymore. Whatever else happened, we still had our apartment.

But, like a bolt out of the blue, at age forty I was unemployed. I still had to earn my living, and as an experimental physicist I needed a laboratory to work in. The physicist Pavel Peshkov, the Academy of Sciences' scientific secretary for physics, told me that I would never again find work at the academy, especially in Moscow. Soon afterward I asked for a meeting with the head of the Science Department of the Central Committee of the Communist Party. It was the only method I could think of to try to improve my situation. At that time

3. I learned of these two official statements about me from file copies of the Russian Academy of Sciences (file ARAN 532-1-198) and the Institute of Physics (file F.411, Op. 39 D49 L.47), which Gennady Gorelik, a Russian physicist and historian, brought me from Moscow.

the head of the department was the chemist Yuri Zhdanov, the son of Andrei Zhdanov, a marshal of the Soviet army and a member of the politburo of the Central Committee of the Communist Party. Among other actions, Andrei Zhdanov was known for having criticized Dimitri Shostakovich for composing "anti-Soviet" music.

To my astonishment, my appointment with Yuri Zhdanov was immediately approved. Ordinarily, people had to wait many, many days for such appointments. Yuri Zhdanov met me courteously. He rose from the table to greet me, shook my hand, and said that he had recently read my latest paper, a lengthy review that had been published in the *Journal of Advanced Physics* (Uspekhi physicheskikh nauk). When he finished talking, I told him about my problem. All of a sudden his courtesy and respectfulness changed, and he fell silent. It was as if the man disappeared and a grim doppelgänger instantly took his place. Clearly he had not known about General Malyshev's action. When I saw this, I took my leave.

In October 1951 I handed a four-page letter for Joseph Stalin to the Communist Party Central Committee. I wrote about my circumstances and my research, emphasizing in particular projects that had interested Marshal Alexander Vasilevsky, the first deputy minister of defense of the USSR. I asked Stalin to help me return to my work.

It was not until two years later, on 29 October 1953, in a letter signed by the head of the Committee of Atomic Energy, corresponding member of the Academy of Sciences' Vasiliy Yemelyanov, that I received an answer to my letter to Stalin. "Regarding your letter to M. G. Malenkov of August 1953 [*sic*]," Yemelyanov wrote, "I inform you: Your evaluation of the state of the investigations of the ionosphere is wrong. There is no reason to renew your work at the Lebedev Institute of Physics." It was obvious that the name of the addressee, Joseph Stalin, had been changed to Malenkov, who at that time was the chair of the Council of Ministers of the USSR.

Meanwhile, I made many requests to become a full professor at other institutes. In Russia scientific work was centered not in the universities but in institutes, especially those of the Academy of Sciences. Members of these institutes were not expected to teach but to devote their time to research. When I was interviewed the reaction in each case was positive and offered hope for work. But soon the final answers came, and they were uniformly, "There are no open positions." The personnel departments of these institutes, always under intense supervision by the KGB, were informed about my "circumstances." Leontovich made great efforts to find a position for me at other institutes within the Academy of Sciences, but all his efforts were unsuccessful. He offered me money, and I borrowed some.

During this period the Academy of Sciences did try to place me in one position. Two to three months after I was fired from PhIAN, I was invited to the Department of Physics of the Presidium of the Academy of Sciences and urged to look for a job outside Moscow. There might be an appropriate post, I was told, at Vilnius University in Vilnius, Lithuania.

The academy bought me air tickets, reserved a hotel room, and gave me money for traveling expenses. I went to Vilnius, where I had never been before, and met a representative of the university. He offered me the position of chair of the Physics Department and said that I could soon be elected to the Lithuanian Academy of Sciences. He also showed me the large apartment that I would have, with two bedrooms and two toilets, no less! For an ordinary citizen of the USSR, having two bedrooms and two toilets was unimaginable. I said that I had to think about the job and would reply on returning to Moscow. Instead I was asked to stay on in Vilnius, although I was not told why.

For several days I walked the streets of that beautiful city, visiting museums and churches and other sites. Then the university called. A car picked me up at the hotel and took me to the office of the Communist Party chief of Lithuania, Antanas Snechkus. He was a well-known political figure in the USSR and had been a member of the Communist Party since 1920, when Lithuania was still a "bourgeois republic." In 1951 he was a member of the Central Committee of the Communist Party of the USSR. We spoke about the position at Vilnius University, and then his main question popped out: "Yakov Lvovich, why are you not a member of the Communist Party?"

I immediately replied, "You know, I am an active person. I devote my life to research, to science. I cannot at the same time be a member of the Communist Party." I reminded him that the late president of the Academy of Sciences of the USSR, Sergei Vavilov, had never joined the party. Snechkus shot back, "But he was much older than you!" Our meeting ended.

The next day I sent a cable from Moscow declining the Vilnius offer. No doubt Snechkus expected me to say that I would become a member of the party, that it was a "misunderstanding that I was not yet a member," and so on. At that time in the USSR that would have been the answer from most citizens who found themselves in my predicament, without any hope for a job, without an income, and targeted by the KGB.

In all fairness, I must say that General Malyshev did not refer to my "cosmopolitanism" when he withdrew my security clearance in 1951. But it may well have been part of what the KGB told the institutes where I applied for work. Certainly I could never have been accused of that "sin" without the involvement of the KGB.

The Thick Book of the Cosmopolites

As it happened, the first person to accuse me of being a cosmopolite, V. N. Kessenikh, was not done with me. While I was looking for a job, I was also trying to get another book published. In 1949, I proposed to Vitaly Ginzburg and Eugene Feinberg, both colleagues at PhIAN, that we collaborate on a book of three independent parts. One part would be by Feinberg on the theory of the propagation of radio waves along an inhomogeneous surface of the earth, not taking into account its curvature or the influence of the ionosphere; the second part would be by Ginzburg on the theory of the propagation of radio waves in the ionosphere; and the third part would be by me and would review the methods and results of experimental and theoretical investigations of the propagation of radio waves in the ionosphere. This book, *The Propagation of Radio Waves,* was ready in 1951, at the time I became unemployed. We submitted it to the publishing house GostechIzdat in June 1951. The press asked Kessenikh to review the book, and his review was negative. Over the next several months the press tried to get the book cleared for publication but could not overcome Kessenikh's opposition. Because of Kessenikh's influential position as dean of the physics department at Moscow State University and his having long served as the press's chief reviewer for books in radio physics, GostechIzdat did not feel it could ignore him. Then the chairman of the Council of Radio Science of the Academy, Axel Berg, intervened.

Axel Berg knew the capriciousness of the Soviet system firsthand. His career began in Leningrad (now St. Petersburg) in various branches of the navy. In 1937–39, the years of Stalin's terror, he was arrested and sent to the Gulag. After the beginning of World War II, however, he was taken from prison and brought directly to Stalin's office. Berg related the event to my second wife, Svetlana, and me when we were walking with him near the resort of the Academy of Sciences, Uzkoye, in Moscow in 1980. "An officer entered the prison cell," Berg said," asked me to change into the clothes he had brought, and took me by car to the Kremlin." There Joseph Stalin told Berg that he had been chosen for the vital task of developing the USSR's radio location technology. Berg soon organized a large institute devoted to that problem, gathering together many physicists, engineers, and theoreticians. I sometimes went to that institute for various discussions organized by Berg, and I first met him there.

These discussions could be quite wide-ranging. Despite his recent imprisonment, Berg was willing to address difficult political questions. When a philosopher named Maximov began to write during the war that certain ideas in physics, such as quantum mechanics, violated the principles of Marxism-Leninism and were anti-Soviet, Berg invited many scientists to his institute to consider responses to this attack on science.

Years later, Berg also became chair of the Cybernetic Council of the Academy of Sciences, and for several years he was the USSR's deputy military minister of science. He was recognized with many Soviet orders and received the naval rank of admiral engineer.

In 1952, Berg convened a special board meeting of the Radio Council of the academy to discuss the book I had written with Ginzburg and Feinberg. A person who attended the meeting later told me what happened. Kessenikh held the rank of lieutenant colonel engineer, and he came to the meeting in his military uniform. Berg familiarized the meeting with the circumstances of our book, stressing Kessenikh's review and the pressure he exerted to keep Gostechizdat from publishing it. Not too long after, following a different kind of discussion among the members of the council, Berg stood up — he also was in his military uniform — and briefly summarized the opinions the members had expressed. Then he reprimanded Kessenikh for his activity against the book. When Berg stood up, Kessenikh, being of lower military rank, was obliged to stand facing the admiral and salute him. Kessenikh did this. It must have been an impressive spectacle! Shortly thereafter the positive recommendations of the council were sent to the publisher, and our book was approved for publication by GostechIzdat. It was printed in 1953, but it was never translated into English. The nickname of the book among professionals was *The Thick Book of the Cosmopolites*. It really was a thick book — about nine hundred pages.

About a year before publication of the book, at the beginning of February 1952, Nikolai Pushkov contacted me. He offered me a position at the geosciences institute that he had organized and now directed. It was a brave and noble step for Pushkov to offer me a position, for it could have caused him great personal difficulty. At that time the institute was part of the Hydro-Meteorological Service of the USSR. Years later, when I served briefly as vice-director of the institute, now known as IZMIRAN, it became at my instigation part of the Academy of Sciences of the USSR. But before I can tell you about my work at IZMIRAN, I must share a few other stories.

2

Seven Years Later
Lightning, Atom Bombs, and a Chopped-Off Head

When General Malyshev told Mikhail Leontovich that I could no longer work at PhIAN, Leontovich made, as he told me, many efforts to reason with him. He even told the general, "An important branch of physics in the USSR will be backpedaled. Yakov is foremost in his field."

"There will soon be others who will do the same work," Malyshev replied.

Leontovich went to Igor Kurchatov to ask him to intercede for me. But Kurchatov would do nothing. The situation was complicated. Kurchatov was in a tough position. He could not argue to the KGB that my security clearance should be reinstated without weighing the possible consequences to him. Of course, Kurchatov had a powerful position. But to exercise power in the USSR always carried some risk, especially in the time of Stalin.

When Igor Kurchatov died in 1960, he was only fifty-eight years old and still in hard harness, daily managing the large scientific and technological operations of Russia's atom bomb development. That was a vital contribution to Russia's defense, but at what personal cost?

I once talked with a mathematician, the academician Mikhail Lavrentiev, about his support for a misguided project. I was driving him to Moscow from IZMIRAN, where we had discussed the project in person with Axel Berg and the vice-minister of communications for the USSR and by telephone with the president of the Academy of Sciences. Lavrentiev was very frank with me; he said, "Yakov Lvovich, you are right. But if I fight them, I won't be able to do my job." At that time he was organizing a new physics research center comprising many different institutes, in Novosibirsk in southern Siberia. He did a very good job, indeed, and the center made a significant contribution to the science of the USSR. So he saved himself to do that patriotic and worthwhile thing for his country. Was it not the same with Kurchatov?

In contrast there was sometimes the conduct of people such as Sergei Vavilov. He served the system, but he also often took risks to help people who came into conflict with it. Many people resented what they saw as Vavilov's ability to manipulate the system. But he had to accept many compromises. In the Soviet system, what else could he do? We have to remember that Vavilov, too, died young, and that many people thought that his brother's death and the strains of his job had much to do with that.

I have to note here that Leontovich was exasperated when he learned about my meeting with Kurchatov. "Yakov has gone and confused Kurchatov," he complained. Leontovich did not understand why I had gone to see Kurchatov in the first place. Kurchatov did not enlighten him, and I obeyed Kurchatov's order to keep our discussion secret. Leontovich could not imagine what I, a radio physicist pursuing radio wave propagation and ionospheric research, could have to do, as he thought, with creating better atom bomb explosions. Nothing, in fact; he was absolutely right about that. But it turned out that I found an effective method to locate atom bomb explosions. What is a little bit interesting is that I learned to do this with research on lightning.

Locating Atom Bomb Explosions

One evening in 1958, I came home from IZMIRAN, the institute where I found a job after being fired from PhIAN, and learned from my first wife, Irina, that there had been many calls for me from the offices of various ministers and also from the office of Igor Kurchatov. He wanted to see me. Later that evening, one of Kurchatov's chief collaborators, Professor Mikhail Millionshchikov, came to my home. (Years later Millionshchikov became an academician and eventually the president of the Supreme Soviet of Russia.) He asked me to come to the committee on atom bomb affairs the next day and gave me the address.

Committee III, as the committee on atom bomb affairs was known, was not housed in the Kurchatov Institute, where I had visited Kurchatov at the end of 1950, but in a building of its own in another part of Moscow. The great boss Kurchatov himself was waiting to greet me. "Yakov," he said, "you have become a famous man. We need your help." He used the familiar "ty" form of the pronoun *you,* which is generally reserved for one's family, friends, and close associates.

At that moment I realized that Kurchatov's eagerness to see me was connected with a meeting then going on at the United Nations in Geneva. Representative commissions of English, Russian, and American scientists and technical advisers were discussing different aspects of detecting atom bomb explosions made on the earth's surface. The main question was whether the explosions could be located by observing packets of waves, very low frequency electromagnetic signals, created by the explosions and recorded at different distances from the source.

To interpret these signals required an understanding of how these packets of waves changed their shape as they were propagated in the ionosphere, the earth's wave guide. This was the basic idea of the research and method of locating the atom bomb explosions that I had proposed to Kurchatov seven years earlier. Independent of that conversation, when I went to work at IZMIRAN in 1952 I began to study the propagation of very low frequency electromagnetic waves in the earth-ionosphere, both experimentally and by means of some theoretical calculations. The source of these waves was lightning bursts. Because IZMIRAN was a geosciences institute, there were already researchers there who were interested in locating lightning, mainly in order to gain knowledge for weather prediction. Before I arrived at the institute, a talented engineer named Vladimir Kashprovsky designed and built a sensitive set of apparatus that could record the waves from lightning bursts and could estimate the distance from the source of those very low frequency electromagnetic waves.

I immediately saw that Kashprovsky's experiments could be expanded to obtain data not only to locate lightning bursts but also to learn the propagation of the electromagnetic waves created by lightning and even their velocities and the changes in their shape as they traveled from the lightning to the observer in the earth-ionosphere wave guide. Using Kashprovsky's apparatus with some modifications, and employing theoretical calculations of the spectra of so-called atmospherics, the packets of electromagnetic waves created by lightning, we began a study that lasted a couple of years.

The treatment of the experimental data we obtained demanded a good deal of mathematics. I performed a complex Fourier analysis of the atmospherics — that is, I calculated their spectra, estimating not only the amplitudes but also the phases of the recorded waves. To do that I used numerical calculations, simple mathematical methods, not the elegant mathematics of professional mathematicians.

I published the results of that comprehensive study in a small monograph in

1955. The next year an English translation was published in the United States by the American government's National Bureau of Standards. An American theoretician in that field, Professor James Wait, published an extensive book on the subject in 1962. In 1967 I also published, together with Dora Fliegel, a comprehensive book on the subject. That book was the first to present results of calculations of the shape of signals propagating in the wave guide produced by the earth and the ionosphere. It was translated into English and published in the United States by Consultants Bureau in 1970. The English translation was edited by Professor Wait.

At the United Nations conference in Geneva in 1958, at least some members of the American scientific team apparently knew of my 1955 book. When the problem of locating atom bomb explosions was discussed, they assumed that I was involved on the Russian side behind the scenes. In Moscow, after the conference was over, Igor Tamm, a member of the Russian delegation, showed me a copy of a confidential letter from an American scientist to the president of the United States, Dwight David Eisenhower. The letter said that in this field American scientists were following my lead. How Tamm obtained a copy of this letter I do not know.

Kurchatov asked me if I could send to Geneva data that would show how to locate atom bomb explosions from records of electromagnetic signals. I said that I could, and I asked for two computer systems and people to help me with the calculations. I asked for two computer systems because I anticipated programming problems. Such problems arose. At the Mathematical Center of the Academy of Sciences I immediately recognized that the results obtained on its computer were wrong. The spectra calculated by the computer were not close to what my earlier research with lightning led me to expect. Yet those working with me would not concede the possibility of a mistake on their part. Therefore I left this group to work only with the second group at the Mstislav Keldysh Institute. We worked day and night, and in three to four days I finished the study, obtained the necessary results, and prepared recommendations for the Russian commission at the United Nations. I learned how the shape of the electromagnetic signals produced by atom bomb explosions and their spectra could change over distance. For these calculations I used the records of the electromagnetic signals produced by atom bomb explosions at locations near the explosions. My recommendations were reported at the United Nations in Geneva by Professor Yevsey Leipunsky, who noted that I had prepared them.

A look at some of the records from my study at IZMIRAN may make the essence of the problem clearer. Even with the naked eye one can see in figures 1 and 2 how the shape of the electromagnetic signals produced by lightning bursts changes with distance. By studying the main features of the signals and their spectra, therefore, we can estimate the approximate distance between the observer and the source of the electromagnetic waves. The same process applies whether the waves are triggered by a natural explosion or an unnatural one, although the shape of the waves will be different in each case. It often happens that we cannot predict how purely scientific problems can lead to technological breakthroughs. Of course, atom bomb explosions are not pleasant technological devices.

Soon after the results of this assignment were sent to Geneva, I was asked to see one of the heads of the committee on atom bomb affairs, a man named Efremov. When I went to his office, he was speaking to a physicist named Rozhdestvensky, a member of the Physics Department of the Presidium of the Academy of Sciences. I don't remember their first names. Rozhdestvensky was going to Geneva with some records of electromagnetic wave signals for the Soviet commission. Efremov wanted me to look at these signals. I saw that some of the recorded signals were produced by lightning and some were produced by atom bomb explosions. I roughly estimated the distances from the sources by eye. Efremov was impressed. No doubt he knew very well where the atom bombs had been detonated and where the signals had been recorded. "How do you know this?" he asked.

"One has to know physics," I replied.

Subsequently a member of the Russian delegation in Geneva, a Red Army colonel who shared responsibility for researching methods to detect atom bomb explosions, told me that Efremov and other leaders of the committee on atom bomb affairs were enormously excited by what I told them. The colonel also said that for many years he and other military personnel had recommended that I be invited to work on detecting atom bomb explosions. The military had often consulted me on radio navigation and radio propagation problems.

A special atom bomb location group existed, but it had never included me. The scientific leader of this group was a well-known radio physicist, an academician, and the head of a department of the Radio Technical Institute of the Academy of Sciences of the USSR. Unlike my small team at IZMIRAN, this group had the latest technical equipment and special airplanes for experiments. Yet they could not find the necessary algorithm for interpreting the electromagnetic signals produced by atom bomb explosions. Every time the military staff suggested that I be brought into the project, the answer was no, no, and no. Certainly this was a KGB decision. Perhaps the same General Malyshev who stopped my experiments at PhIAN seven years earlier was ultimately responsible for this decision.

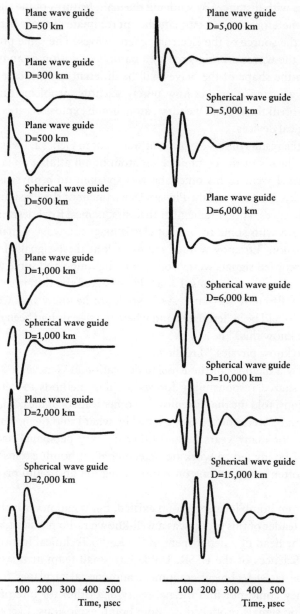

1. Theoretically calculated electromagnetic signals simulating atmospherics, propagating at distances of 50 to 15,000 kilometers from their sources (lightning bursts) in the earth-iono-sphere wave guide

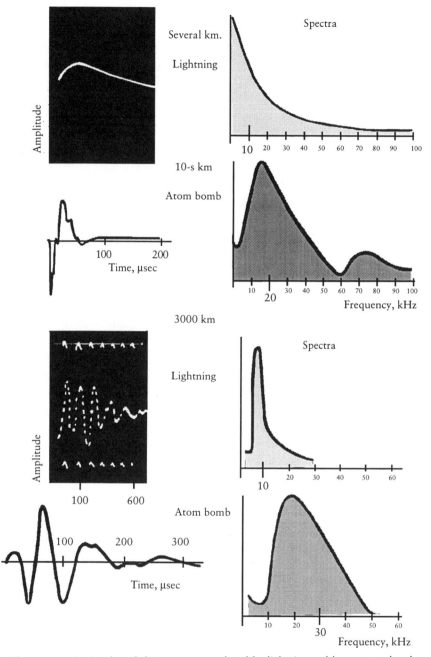

2. Electromagnetic signals and their spectra, produced by lightning and by an atom bomb explosion

High-Altitude Atom Bomb Explosions

The atom bomb explosions I have spoken about were those produced close to the surface of the earth in the low part of the atmosphere, the troposphere, at altitudes of less than twenty to thirty kilometers. They are especially terrible for humankind. Their energy is captured in the atmosphere, and the destructive power of such explosions is comparable to, if not larger than, thousands of millions of horsepower. Even at a distance of about ten kilometers, the radiation produced by fast ß-electrons emitted by the bomb is deadly. The light flash of the explosion is brighter than the light of the sun and is blinding to animals and humans. The electromagnetic signals generated by the explosions are, in a sense, similar to the electromagnetic signals produced by thunderstorms and have been recorded by radio receivers at many thousands of kilometers from the explosion. The shock waves of the explosion create seismic waves, which have been observed at ten thousand kilometers and even farther from their source. The fast electrons produced at such distances create artificial auroras.

Further artificial phenomena and a choking of the environment by alien formations, radiation, and matter are created by atom bomb explosions at altitudes of about forty to sixty kilometers and higher above the earth's surface. During such high-altitude explosions the density of the atmosphere does not impede the free flow of the fast electrons produced by the decay of uranium fragments and does not hinder X-ray radiation emanating far outside the explosion region. These components of the explosion disturb the ionosphere — that is, the ionized part of the atmosphere where free electrons and ions are produced — and are responsible for many disturbances in the propagation of radio waves close to the region of the explosion, far from it around the earth, and even at the antipode of the explosion site.

It follows from this that atom bomb explosions can greatly complicate basic scientific research into the environment's natural phenomena. The disturbances the explosions cause distort efforts to record and interpret a wide range of environmental data.

The artificial phenomena I have mentioned here were in fact observed after the five atom bomb explosions made by the United States in 1958. Two of them, in an experiment named Hardtack, occurred in the middle of the Pacific Ocean at altitudes of about thirty to forty kilometers above the coral atoll island Johnston on 1 and 12 August. The power of these one-megaton explosions was extremely high. Three other explosions known as Argus I, II, and III — each one with about five hundred to one thousand times less power —

were detonated in the South Atlantic, between South America and Africa, at much higher altitudes of about five hundred kilometers. One explosion was above the Tristan da Cunha islands on 27 August, and the other two took place farther to the south on 30 August and 6 September.

After the explosions at Johnston Island, ionospheric and radio wave propagation disturbances were recorded on Maui, Hawaii, at 1,300 kilometers from the explosion site, and on Raratonga Island, in the Cook Islands off Australia, which is 3,000 kilometers from Maui and 4,500 kilometers south of Johnston. These phenomena were observed there for six to ten days after the explosions. Similar effects were observed after the Argus explosions, even at distances of 5,000 kilometers. The large distortion of the ionosphere at the explosion region lasted for five hours.

Many optical effects were also observed in different places. The light flash at Johnston lasted for fifteen minutes, and an aurora luminescence lasted for seventeen minutes at the Fiji and Samoa islands — 4,000 kilometers from Johnston. Photographs taken during that explosion illustrate the evolution of the heated cloud after the explosion and then the expansion of its envelope and of the radiance at one, two, and three minutes. Very strong artificial auroras were recorded after the Argus explosions in a five-hundred-to-one-thousand-kilometer region. These lasted for about half an hour at the Azores. The fast electrons guided by the magnetic field lines of the earth cause such effects. Many other kinds of phenomena were observed. For example, after the Johnston explosion aligned particles of lithium roved the atmosphere above the earth for many days.

The Door to the West Opens

Soon after the Argus and Johnston high-altitude atom bomb explosions by the United States, I was invited to take part in discussions of the consequences of these explosions. My interest was in the disturbances produced by these explosions in the ionosphere and the magnetosphere. Many rumors concerning these phenomena appeared in the American press at that time. For the most part these rumors were incorrect. For example, some journalists mistakenly wrote that these explosions can completely destroy radio communication lines.

Among those who participated in our discussions were the well-known physicists and astrophysicists Vitaly Ginzburg, Yevsey Leipunsky, Yuri Raiser, Joseph Shklovsky, and Sergei Vernov. I am not sure who organized the meeting; it may have been the committee on atom bomb affairs. The discussions were held in preparation for the joint Russian, English, and American Conference on the Discontinuance of Nuclear Weapon Tests, which was to take place at the United Nations in Geneva in June 1959.

In the course of these discussions in 1958 I was asked to present a special report, "Ionospheric and Other Geophysics Effects Created by High-Altitude Atom Bomb Explosions" (see appendix A). This report, in the form of a thirty-eight page memorandum, together with two other papers I wrote later regarding low-atmospheric and high-altitude atom bomb explosions, I did not publish until recently. I also presented a talk about this work at the Ministry of Defense, at a special meeting organized by Axel Berg, the vice-minister of defense in charge of scientific matters. Dozens of powerful generals and scientists attended that meeting. Soon I was again invited to see Efremov. He informed me that I had been made a member of the Russian delegation to the June conference in Geneva. Thus the KGB opened the door to the West for me.

Together with other members of the delegation, I flew to Geneva on 19 June 1959 in the official airplane of Foreign Minister Andrei Gromyko, who was then in Geneva and about to return to Moscow. The plane was a specially outfitted Tupolev passenger liner, with a cabin divided into several compartments. The other scientists and I were all sitting together in one compartment in normal airplane seats. It would be interesting to know what the rest of that plane looked like, or if it carried any additional passengers or cargo on that flight.

At the United Nations I presented a long paper on the physics of high-altitude atom bomb explosions. The head of the American delegation, the famous physicist Wolfgang Panofsky, then director of the High Energy Physics Laboratory at Stanford University, was most enthusiastic about my talk. When I finished speaking, Panofsky, a small, excitable man, jumped up from his seat, ran to the podium, and embraced me.

It was interesting to see the official roster of the different delegations (see appendix B). The Americans sent the largest group, nine men, but only Panofsky and Professor Kenneth Watson of the University of California at Berkeley were well known in their fields. The English sent three men, all technical advisers from Great Britain's Ministry of Defense. The Russian delegation, six men, included several scientists with international reputations, headed by the physicist Eugene Fyodorov, a corresponding member of the Academy of Sciences of the USSR. The roster of the delegations, which was prepared in Geneva, listed me as a corresponding member of the academy. Later Sergei Vernov joined us.

The U.S. delegation included one military man, a colonel from the Pentagon. The Russian delegation also included a colonel, the man I mentioned above, but he was not announced as such and he appeared in Geneva only in the guise of a civilian scientist on the staff of the Academy of Sciences.

Certainly the roundtable discussions at Geneva were not to be purely scientific. The chair of each group had obviously been given instructions on the politics involved. But I think it is fair to say that the Russian delegation was better prepared than the others for the scientific discussions. In our talks in Moscow beforehand, we considered only the scientific aspects of the matter. And perhaps the purely scientific nature of my talk is what astonished Panofsky. I could not say the same about all of his talks. During one session I was struck by the blatant political nature of Panofsky's remarks, and I opposed him strongly. I knew that as the head of his delegation he had a political as well as a scientific role. Still, I told him, "My colleagues in Moscow and I have studied only the physical aspects of the problem, and I am here only for such discussions, not to speculate politically on the subject." Later Sergei Tsarapkin, the Soviet ambassador in Geneva and the vice-minister of foreign affairs of the USSR at that time, told me that the U.S. ambassador had spoken to him about me. He valued my participation highly because of my plain speaking. And it was also surprising that the head of our delegation, Fyodorov, did not condemn me for my spontaneous outburst, which disregarded the instruction that all remarks must be cleared with the head of our delegation. Certainly everything we said and did in Geneva was carefully watched by the KGB.

At least Professor Panofsky did not hold my remarks against me. In August 1998, I wrote Panofsky an e-mail about an article he published in that month's issue of Physics Today. In his e-mail response the next day he wrote, "I remember well your constructive and objective participation in the technical working group in Geneva."

Upon returning to Moscow I was asked by the famous physicist Peter Kapitsa, director of the Institute of Problems in Physics and later a Nobel Prize winner, to present a talk about the physics of high-altitude atom bomb explosions at his Wednesday evening seminars. When I talked about the Argus and Johnston explosions, I referred to Argus, the many-eyed giant in Greek mythology. Perhaps the Argus atom bomb operation was so named because of the manifold destructive phenomena created by that explosion. In that case, I wondered, was it not up to the scientific community to play the role of Hermes, who lulled Argus to sleep by playing a flute and then killed him? In Greek mythology, Hermes was the god of travelers, luck, music, and commerce, and in Egypt he was identified with the god of art and science. If we scientists could not stop the military from detonating atom bomb explosions, we could carefully document and report their effects. I spoke about this in my presentation at Kapitsa's seminar, and I wrote about it in a paper, "High-Altitude Atom Bomb

Explosions," published in August 1962 in the popular Russian scientific journal *Priroda* ("Nature").

. . . and Closes

During the years of Soviet rule the door to the West was open for only a few scientists. That I traveled to Geneva for some weeks was an uncommon and unexpected event in my life. My friends and colleagues were very much struck by the fact that the KGB allowed me to do so.

All of us in the delegation enjoyed that time in Geneva. We never felt under any constraint when we were not on duty at the conference. We stayed in a good hotel near Lake Geneva and took pleasure in exploring the city and its environs. In the evenings we often went to movies, because movies from the West were not then commonly shown in Moscow. After being in Geneva for a few days I began to recall the French I taught myself in childhood, and I was able to translate some of the dialogue in the movies for my colleagues. On Sundays we went to exhibitions or took excursions to see historic sites, such as the route of Julius Caesar's visit at the head of a Roman army. One of my colleagues even went skiing in the high Alps. And one day I had the fun of seeing Oona Chaplin, thirty-seven years younger than Charlie, walking by the lake with her children.

It was invigorating to breathe the air of the West, but not everything in the West pleased me. For example, in Moscow I never saw such a gulf between rich and poor, and so many poor people on the street, as I did in Geneva. So although I enjoyed very much that visit to the West, I was also glad to return home to Moscow at the end of the conference. But at that point, the door to the West was again firmly closed to me for nearly thirty years!

From the early 1950s on, I was frequently invited to the West to give lectures and chair sessions at conferences, to become a visiting professor, and even to take part in an international conference session dedicated to my own research. Of course I was flattered to receive such invitations, and I wanted to travel and see the world, but I do not mention them solely out of egotism. These invitations, none of which I was allowed to accept, constitute so many lost opportunities to discuss interesting science and even to stimulate new ideas. The progress of science in both Russia and the West suffered enormously because the Soviet regime allowed only a few scientists, and often not the best ones, to travel to the West or even to correspond and exchange ideas with scientists from other countries. Here let me mention just a few instances that involve me.

On 18 November 1943 I mailed a letter to Edward Appleton, who would share the 1947 Nobel Prize for physics for his "investigations of the physics of the upper atmosphere, especially for the discovery of a new layer in the ionosphere above the so-called E-layer at altitudes of 100–130 kilometers." Appleton made that discovery by investigating the propagation characteristics of the radio waves from radio stations. In his paper "The Existence of More Than One Ionized Layer in the Upper Atmosphere," published in *Nature* in 1927, Appleton showed that the radio waves were reflected in the atmosphere not only at altitudes of 100 kilometers but even at altitudes above 260 kilometers. This region of the ionosophere at altitudes of 220–300 kilometers, otherwise known as the F-2 layer, became known as the Appleton layer. But in 1923, the Russian radio engineer, physicist, and academician Mikhail Shuleikin discovered that layer in the course of a military research project, also by investigation of the propagation of radio waves. Shuleikin's results, however, were not known even to most Russian scientists, including me. I learned of them only in 1956. Until then, the results had been kept secret by the military and could only be found in their archives.

To write to Appleton and to try to collaborate with a scientist in the West was a risky step, especially in 1943, during the war. In that letter I asked Appleton to send me reprints of his work. I was then preparing a new type of experiment to investigate what I later called the statistically inhomogeneous nature of the ionosphere, and I did not want to miss any data that might help in that effort. My letter reached Appleton after almost a year's delay, and he mailed me his answer on 2 October 1944. Owing, no doubt, to the actions of the KGB, Appleton apparently received only one other letter from me, although I wrote him several times. This was in 1947, as I discuss below. And I did not receive another letter from Appleton until 1956. He wrote me then about my book *The Propagation of Radio Waves in the Ionosphere*, which had been published in Russian about ten years earlier. In the years that followed I received letters from him only from time to time. The last one was in 1961, four years before he died. I recount the history of my correspondence with Appleton because it shows how difficult it was, even impossible, for Russian scientists to come to any regular fruitful collaboration with colleagues in the West.

In 1953 I was invited to attend the opening of the Environmental Research Laboratories of the National Oceanic and Atmospheric Administration (NOAA) in Boulder, Colorado, and to spend several weeks in research collaboration there. It must have been a great event in the United States, because President Dwight Eisenhower was at the opening ceremony of this large and interesting scientific and technical center on 14 September 1954. I was not allowed to accept the invitation, but a year later I received a copy of the president's speech along with other material describing the NOAA's many different laboratories for research in astronomy, radio wave propagation, the ionosphere, forecast systems, and even superconductivity. Forty years later, in

1992, I was finally able to visit the NOAA's space environmental laboratory. During my discussions there I learned that several researchers at that laboratory were trying to establish the fine structure of the phase and amplitude of the electromagnetic field in the near zone of a radiating antenna. It is a delicate problem indeed, both theoretically and experimentally. Yet I had published the results of such a comprehensive study fifty years earlier, in 1940–41, as part of my Ph.D. thesis. Just think of the progress American and Russian scientists might have made if only we had been free to talk to each other.

Soon after my trip to Geneva at the end of 1959, I was invited to take up a visiting professorship at the famous Cavendish Laboratories in Cambridge, England. The invitation came from Professor Neville Mott, who would share the 1979 Nobel Prize for physics. It was initiated by the radio physicist John Ratcliffe, who was president of the Physics Society of England, and by the astrophysicist Martin Ryle, who would win the 1974 Nobel Prize for physics. When I spoke about the organization of my trip with the head of the Department of Foreign Affairs of the Academy of Sciences, KGB general Sergei Korneyev, his only question to me was, "Why have they offered you such a high honorarium as £500? Only members of the highest level of the Academy get such high honorariums."

My immediate reaction was sarcastic: "It is because they want me to tell them about our confidential affairs." I understood from the start that the KGB would not allow me to go to England. In fact, I did go to Cambridge and to the Cavendish Laboratory, but not until 1988!

In August 1962 John Ratcliffe came to Moscow to visit me. This was an unexpected but pleasant event for me, and I was honored by it. Upon his arrival Ratcliffe declared, "Since it was not possible for you to come to us, I have come to you."

During our discussions, he asked me, "How many Alperts — other physicists working in your field — are there in your country?" This question referred to the diversity of my research in the propagation of radio waves and the ionosphere. Researchers in the West generally deal only with narrow branches of their fields. When Ratcliffe returned to England he wrote me, "I am anxious, if it is possible, that you should come and visit us here in England sometime." Well, dozens of years later it happened that I was able go to England. Unfortunately, it was after Ratcliffe had died.

In 1960 I was invited to give a lecture at the Electronic Conference in Chicago. The distinguished professor of physics Semyon Khaikin, of Moscow University, and the astronomer and director of the Crimean Astrophysics Observatory, Andrei Severny, who became an academician in 1968, had also been invited from the USSR. In connection with these two and other invitations to the United States of about thirty to forty years ago, it is appropriate here to recount the following.

As we will see, during a solar eclipse in Brazil in 1947 Khaikin became the first to observe the radio emission of the Sun's corona. He was one of the creators of experimental radio astronomy. Together with two other notable physicists, Alexander Witt and Alexander Andronov, Khaikin wrote the classic *Theory of Oscillations*.[1] The publisher deleted Alexander Witt's name for political reasons, however, yet another example of the Soviet reality. These scientists were among the most distinguished members of the school of Leonid Mandelshtam. Under the influence of the scientific spirit he inspired, they founded the theory of nonlinear oscillations and in particular the theory of "auto-oscillations" and "automatic regulation" by Andronov. The results of those studies became a fundamental part of our knowledge of the physical phenomena of nature as a whole.

These three highly accomplished scientists were never permitted to attend any conference or symposium in the West. They never enjoyed the fruits of a visiting professorship outside the USSR. Witt, who was an exceptional researcher, became a victim of Stalin's terror. Arrested in 1937, he was "lost" in 1938 in prison when he was only thirty-six years old. Khaikin never got his just deserts. He was severely criticized for his excellent book *Mechanics*. That monograph of pure physics was considered to be against the materialistic ideology of Marxism-Leninism and thus anti-Soviet. Khaikin was denied election to the Academy of Sciences as either an academician or a corresponding member. Andronov's fate was better. He founded a highly productive scientific school as part of the Technical Institute of Physics in Gorky, the research city on the Volga. He became an academician in 1946, when he was forty-five years old. And the people of Gorky elected him to be their representative on the Supreme Soviet Council of the USSR, although he never joined the Communist Party.

I did not know Andronov well. He was an older, more established scientist; he lived in Gorky and I lived in Moscow. But once I went to Andronov's institute in Gorky to serve as a reviewer during a young physicist's dissertation defense. Andronov was not a reviewer, but he observed the defense as a member of the institute. We finished late in the evening. Andronov and I then went for a walk along the streets of Gorky that lasted to about 1 A.M. We spoke to each other very frankly about politics, and I learned that Andronov suffered much because of the rules of the Soviet system. Although he did not say so in

1. Semyon Khaikin, Alexander Witt, and Alexander Andronov, *Theory of Oscillations* (Leningrad: ONTI Publishing House, 1937).

so many words, I could understand from what he told me that Andronov had become a member of the Supreme Soviet Council not from a desire for power but as the act of a good citizen. He tried to help people, to lessen their suffering at the hands of the system, and his responsibilities weighed on him heavily.

Of course, we also discussed science. We worked in different fields, and I told him about my research ideas. Later he spoke of our long conversation to Vitaly Ginzburg, who was then living temporarily in Gorky, and said, "Alpert deserves not one but two, three institutes to realize his ideas." I was glad to hear this from Ginzburg.

During that conversation on the dark streets of Gorky, Andronov stopped speaking whenever we saw another person. At one point we came to an apartment house with balconies. Andronov suddenly lowered his voice.

"We must follow the Rule of Wigner," he whispered. "Where there may be ears, we must interrupt our talk." Wigner was a mathematician in the research city of Saratov. It was good of Andronov to tell me all he did, and not least to teach me Wigner's Rule. A brilliant scientist and a direct and eminent human being, Andronov died in 1952 when he was only fifty-one years old.

It seems to me that Wigner's Rule reflects the paranoia of the Soviet system in an interesting way. Because the regime saw a potential threat to its security both in every conversation with the West and in every conversation between its citizens, it had to have ears everywhere. In the conspiracy of silence that the regime inflicted on us, following Wigner's Rule was a self-protective act. But it was also a small act of resistance, because implicit in Wigner's Rule is the necessity to speak again, when the state cannot overhear.[2]

Of course, this begs the question of when it is necessary to speak openly, even defiantly, to the state. The years to come would bring many hard lessons in answering that question both for Russia as a whole and for Russian scientists.

A Chopped-Off Head and Other Mournful Events

My stay in Geneva lasted from 19 June until 12 July. As soon as I got back to Moscow, I called my elderly parents to see how they were. Several years after my going to Moscow as a young man in 1929 my parents had moved there to be closer to me. They left everything they had established in Zhitomir, Ukraine, especially their good friends and relatives. In Moscow they lived in a single room of a two-bedroom apartment. Another room was occupied by a couple with their daughter. Today it is the same; many families occupy a common apartment with one kitchen, one closet, and one bathroom.

2. I am not sure that I have spelled the name correctly: it may have been Wagner.

Large apartments may be occupied by three families or more. My parents never moved in with Irina and me, because Irina's son already lived with us and there was not enough room.

Over the course of a few hours I telephoned my parents several times, but there was no answer. I began to be concerned, and I immediately drove over to their apartment. When I entered their room, it was almost empty. The neighbors then told me that both of my parents had fallen ill and died while I was in Geneva.

Only after the rapid decay of my mother's organs had begun, I later learned, did the clinic that was responsible for her care discover her deep-seated cancer. Nothing could help her. The same thing happened with my father. Only at the last moment did they find his uremia. In the USSR there were often such manifestations of free medical care. Much later I learned that the life of my father could have been saved. In the hospital they had not used the appropriate medicine, which did exist at that time and was available in the USSR.

But this was not the fault of the doctors. New medicines were not used in the treatment of free-of-charge patients. It was forbidden for the doctors even to mention that such medicines existed, and individuals who did know about them were not able to buy them. Such medicines were accessible only to people under the care of special clinics, in particular the so-called Kremlin hospitals and clinics. There were also many people like me who were under the care of a special clinic and hospital, in my case those of the Academy of Sciences, yet could not buy special medicines. In the clinic and hospital of the academy these medicines were accessible only to academicians and the most powerful bureaucrats. For other employees, including senior scientists, only a decision of a special committee of the academy could authorize a person to buy the full course of a medicine recommended by the doctors. Many times I received the necessary medicine after such decisions because I was a doctor of sciences and chief of a department in an institute of the Academy of Sciences.

One can imagine my shock and sorrow as I stood in my parents' empty room. After I had been there for a while I began to wonder what had happened to all of their things, including some of my childhood belongings that my father had saved. These included two thick books in Hebrew. One was a collection of the poems and rhymes of Chaim Byalik, a big red book of this outstanding poet, and the other was a large children's anthology, *Abikurim*, that I had delighted in as a young boy. In addition, my father had saved some of my childhood notes, my bar mitzvah drosho, and many other things. But the two closets and my parents' bookshelves were empty. Someone had taken everything in their apartment. Who had done this?

I was particularly disappointed at not finding the drosho. To this day I am sorry not to have it: what a program of my future I had scheduled at thirteen years of age! My father kept the drosho as one would a relic. He reread it many times and cited it often during our spirited discussions about the Soviet regime. He understood the terrible nature of that regime many years before I did. To my regret, I never read my drosho again after 1929, when I left Zhitomir for Moscow.

As I thought of my parents and my drosho, I also thought of my grandfather. It was really the pride and pleasure that my father and grandfather took in my drosho that made those yellow pages so special to me.

During my childhood my parents and I lived at times in my grandparents' house. It seems to me that that lasted until I was six or seven years old. My grandparents had a big apartment on two floors with many bedrooms and one huge living room with a long table. At least fifteen to twenty people could sit at that table. The respect and admiration everyone in our big family had for my grandfather was particularly expressed by there being a special chair in the room that was never used by anyone else.

Grandfather Moishe was a modest man with a long beard who smoked a great deal. He was the owner of a small gristmill and was a respected person in the city. At precisely the same time in the middle of every night, he would awaken. He would then cough slightly and smoke a cigarette. You could check the time by his cough, just as people checked the time in Göttingen when the great philosopher Immanuel Kant walked the streets. The doctors insisted on grandfather's not smoking, so he stopped. He was a person of great strength of mind.

My grandmother Shendel was even more popular in the city. In accordance with Jewish tradition, she always covered her head with a wig. The people of Zhitomir celebrated her because of her wisdom. They visited her for advice just as Jewish people go to a rabbi. This very small woman gave birth to thirteen children, though I remember only seven of them, four boys and three girls. Perhaps the others died before I was even thought of. Grandmother died some years before my bar mitzvah. At that time we did not live in my grandparents' house. Her funeral was the first of the saddest days in my life. Her burial made a profound impression on me, and on that day I vowed never again to go to a burial. Unfortunately, life did not let me keep that vow.

The apartment building where my grandfather lived was located at the front of a long yard. There were root cellars at one side of the yard, and there was a well in the middle. On the other side of the yard there was a small house where the groundskeeper lived. As I remember, he was a thickset man who was on good terms with my grandfather. After the revolution it was a hard, unstable time, a time of hunger and misery, and my grandfather helped the groundskeeper a great deal.

The last time I saw my grandfather was in Moscow at the beginning of 1931. At that time I lived in the apartment of his daughter, my aunt, Lisa Meyerovich. She was married to Nathan Meyerovich, who had come to Zhitomir on business. They fell in love, and she moved to Moscow with him. Grandfather, who had never before been in Moscow, came to see me. What was very touching, too, was that he brought me a package of fresh home-baked buns. He knew that I loved them.

We knew that my grandfather died during World War II, when the Germans occupied Zhitomir, but for some time we did not know precisely what had happened to him. Around 1950–51, my parents received a letter from Zhitomir. The letter revealed that the day after the German fascist troops marched into Zhitomir in 1942, someone knocked on the door of my grandfather's apartment. I do not know whether anyone lived with him at that time. The groundskeeper was at the door with an ax in his hands. He chopped off the head of that old Jew, my grandfather.

I try to recollect my grandfather Moishe now, to remember his joyful eyes when I presented my long drosho in Hebrew. I do not have a photograph of him. And I ask myself again, who emptied my father's bookshelves? Who had any interest in taking his Hebrew books and the sheets of paper handwritten in Hebrew? Undoubtedly, it was a man from the KGB or a KGB informer, for that house in Moscow, like every house and every institution in Soviet Russia, had at least one such observer.

Bulat Okudzhava wrote an expressive song, "The Black Tomcat," about those watchers. The black tomcat lives in a doorway "as if on an estate," and

> He hides a grin behind his whiskers,
> darkness is his shield.
> All other cats sing and sob —
> this black cat stays silent.

> He doesn't nag, he doesn't beg,
> his yellow eyes just burn,
> each one of us brings him something —
> and thanks him for the honor.

> He doesn't utter a sound,
> simply eats and drinks,
> clawing the filthy floor
> as if he were clawing throats.

> You know, somehow it's no fun
> living in his house;
> we should put in a light back there —
> we can't be bothered to raise the dough.

Certainly, for all the years when I was at the academy, and especially during my trip to the United Nations in Geneva, I was under the watchful eyes of the KGB. Maybe my drosho is at this moment lying somewhere in the files of that most terrible creation of the October revolution. But let me tell you a little about the KGB later on in this book. Now I want to tell you more about my family and my early life.

3

My Early Childhood
The Pogroms, 1915–1919

Imagination may well distort our earliest memories. But I trust a vivid recollection — one of the earliest I have — of lying on the kitchen floor in Zhitomir at about three or four years of age, my face covered with blood from having bitten my tongue half off when I fell trying to reach the jars of delicious homemade jam my mother, Gittle, stored on the highest shelf, just beneath the ceiling. When my mother came in and found me very shortly afterward, she instantly picked me up in her arms and ran with me to the doctor.

This episode entered our family's history and was often retold. Perhaps I remember it so well because of hearing my elders recount it again and again. But I do retain a vivid visual memory of the incident, and my other strong early recollections also date from around this time.

I have no memory of my birthplace, which was a shtetl, a small Jewish village, called Ivnitsy, about a dozen kilometers from Zhitomir. My father met and fell in love with my mother there, during his travels to buy hops for the brewery that employed him. Soon after my birth my parents brought me to Zhitomir, in northwest central Ukraine, about 140 kilometers west of Kiev, Ukraine's ancient capital. Zhitomir, where as I said my paternal grandfather owned a small gristmill, was then a prosperous city of about twenty-five thousand people, with good shops and transportation. Strong influences from Poland and Russia mixed with the Ukrainian core in the life of the town, and all three languages were common there. In our home we spoke Yiddish.

I had important early experiences in all these languages, but until the time of my bar mitzvah my most important language was Hebrew. I first learned to read and write in Hebrew, and I even tried to write poetry in Hebrew. (In truth, to this day I cannot write even a single poetic verse in any language!) Although later I read the Yiddish-language novels of Sholem Aleichem and Mendel Moikher Sforim, I never liked Yiddish very much. I spoke Ukrainian and Polish and later Russian with my friends, and to all outward appearances I was indistinguishable from them.

When I was five years old, my father, Lev, put me in the Heder, a Jewish religious school for young children. My father was not a religious Jew, and we did not strictly observe all the rules of our faith. Yet my father loved the Jewish culture and the Hebrew language. My mother did not know Hebrew. Father followed most of the Jewish ceremonies and regularly visited the synagogue, invariably bringing me along. He loved the singing there. To hear that singing was his passion, a lovely hobby, one might say. The cantors of Zhitomir and of our synagogue were my father's best friends.

There was a strong tradition of singing in the Jewish community in Zhitomir. In the 1920s, some Zhitomir cantors moved to the United States and became famous cantors there. A few became opera singers. I knew them, but I cannot now recall their names.

So I began my education in Hebrew. At age six I studied the Bible at Heder, including the story of Sodom and Gomorrah, which strongly impressed me. It seems to me that the story was not taught to us to stress the sinfulness of Sodom but rather as an example of the historical accidents and destructive experiences endured by the Jewish people. I started many conversations about this story with my father and my teacher, trying to understand why the Jews were so often attacked as a people. I remained at the Heder only a couple of years, until shortly after the October 1917 revolution brought the Bolsheviks to power in Russia, although I continued my Hebrew studies until my bar mitzvah in 1924.

In general I was a very inquisitive boy, eager to learn everything I could, and I read voraciously. No one directed my reading. Between the ages of eight and ten I read in Hebrew such internationally known books as *Spartacus,* by the Italian writer Raffaelo Giovagnoli, and *Quo Vadis,* by the Polish writer Henryk Sienkiewicz. I also read a textbook on zoology, because I collected butterflies and beetles.

The Pogroms

Spartacus greatly excited me and stirred my imagination. The Roman slaves' fight for freedom struck a chord with much that I had learned of Jewish history and with much that was happening in Ukraine in 1918 and 1919. Before the Soviets took firm control of the country, political power in Ukraine, and in Zhitomir itself, often changed from one day to another. The nationalistic army of Simon Petlyura, a former Ukrainian general, the Germans, and many different gangs all occupied the city in turn. One of the worst gangs was led by the Russian Nestor Makhno, a vicious man with political ambitions. During these years there were many pogroms and massacres, and people frequently went hungry because their food had been stolen by soldiers or by the members of gangs.

Jewish families often separated during the pogroms as a weak form of security. Many Jewish women gathered in one place with their youngest children. My mother stayed in such a house with my brother, Israel, who was five years younger than I, throughout a pogrom perpetrated by Simon Petlyura's army. Meanwhile, my father was sheltered in the house of a good Ukrainian friend.

I was able to move about freely during the pogrom because I did not look like a Jewish boy. I played on the streets with my friends and spoke Polish with them. At night I slept at their homes, or on a few occasions in my parents' empty apartment. I periodically went to see what was happening with my father and mother, our relatives, and the friends of our family. I served as a messenger for other Jewish families as well as my own, but of course I kept a special eye on the houses where my father and my mother were. The two houses were far from each other on different streets.

Sometimes the pogrom makers asked my friends and me to point out the Jewish houses. But the boys never did so. I learned of anti-Semitism from the gangs and the armies that came to Zhitomir, not from our neighbors, who did all they could to help and shelter us Jews.

The Ukrainian friend who protected my father was well known in Zhitomir, though I never knew what his business was. When Simon Petlyura's army occupied Zhitomir, many of his officers visited this man regularly in the evenings. They had crowded parties at his house with wine, music, and dancing. I saw how very many people came to visit my father's friend in the evenings, and I wondered how my father could escape detection in those circumstances. One day I visited this house when none of Petlyura's people were about. It was a big house with a huge entry hall lined with wardrobes and long coat racks. The housemaid and the hosts greeted visitors in the entry hall and helped them to hang their coats. When I came in that day and asked for my father, he climbed out of a large wardrobe like a bear leaving his lair. During parties, my father was concealed in that wardrobe by all the hanging coats of Petlyura's officers!

My mother, together with ten to fifteen other women of different ages, spent her time in a dark room during the pogrom. The shutters of the small house where they stayed were always closed. They sat and waited in fear for the pogrom makers to burst into the house to rape, maim, or kill them. Once after such an invasion, I came and saw that my mother's ears were bleeding; her shoulders were covered with blood. These robbers had noticed her earrings and torn them out. I must assume that God protected our family and our friends during that pogrom, however. As far as I know, not one of our relatives was killed or violated.

I vividly remember the terror of that pogrom.

Early in 1919, Soviet power became more stable in Ukraine. I do not recall any other pogroms happening after that time. Families were able to unite again, and my father employed a teacher to extend my learning of Hebrew and of Jewish history and literature. My teacher, Abram Slutsky, became a close friend of our family. He taught me until my bar mitzvah, visiting our house two or three times a week. In 1925, when I was fourteen years old, a year after my bar mitzvah, he moved, as he had said he would, to Jerusalem.

Apparently it was not then difficult to emigrate. At the same time, my father's brother, Shlomo Alpert, also moved to Palestine. Apart from my father, he was the closest male figure to me during my childhood. He was a member of the Jewish Party "Poialey Zion," which operated in Zhitomir at that time. In English the group's name roughly means "the labors of Zion." It seems to me that my deep belief in freedom and my other social ideas took shape under my uncle Shlomo's influence. After he was in Palestine for a year or two, Uncle Shlomo invited his younger brother, Shmaya, and his sister, Endel, to join him in Palestine. Aunt Endel Alpert settled in what was to become the state of Israel and remained there for the rest of her life. Uncle Shmaya Alpert, however, was not pleased with the land of Israel. He moved back to Russia years later and lived in Moscow, although I had no contact with him.

After the departure of Uncle Shlomo and my Hebrew teacher, I felt very much alone. These two men contributed greatly to my intellectual and moral growth. They took pleasure in my inquisitive nature, and they eagerly answered my endless questions or helped me to find answers for myself in books.

My parents were not by temperament and training able to take such an active role themselves. They loved me and encouraged me to follow my own interests. They seemed to recognize early on that I was an intellectual child, and they trusted that I would blaze my own best path in life. Events proved them right, but in the short term I was sad to lose the two men who most stimulated my boyhood love of learning and discovery.

A Letter from Israel, 1980

After 1925 I never heard from my Hebrew teacher again. But in 1980 a letter from Israel brought my childhood close to me. That year was a crucial time for me and also for other Jewish refusniks who had applied for exit visas and been denied them. We had few freedoms and we were under pressure from prosecutors and other officials, particularly from the KGB. Many people were arrested at that time, as I will recount later. I was especially anxious when, to compound matters, doctors found that my wife, Svetlana, who was then forty years old, had a congenital form of heart disease. Her life was at risk, and she had to have open-heart surgery as soon as possible. This diagnosis was made by two of the best heart specialists in Moscow. Based on their findings, they were actually astonished that she was still living.

Svetlana went into the hospital. On the very morning of her surgery, a letter arrived from Lea Alpert, Shlomo's wife, who was living in the kibbutz Afikim. I was very surprised to receive this letter because our letter exchanges with the West had largely been cut off, and I knew that we were receiving only about ten to twenty percent of the letters mailed to us from abroad. Nevertheless, this letter from Israel and some others from the West somehow got to me that crucial morning. Why the censor let them through is inexplicable. Curiously, about a year before, Herman Lebowitz, a cousin of the American physicist Joel Lebowitz, had been allowed to visit his relatives in Israel. I asked him to find my relatives, and he managed to speak with them by telephone, telling them about me and about our refusnik status.

From Lea's long letter (written in surprisingly good Russian) I learned that in 1935 Shlomo had gone to Latvia and to other Baltic countries to encourage Jews there to go to Israel to rebuild their Holy Land. At that time the Baltic countries were free and independent, but in Latvia, Russian influence had been widespread since the time of the czar. Lea and many other young women and men followed Shlomo. Shlomo and Lea were later married. He was one of the people who organized and built the famous kibbutz Afikim. He was a tractor operator there who rejected many offers for other positions, even for the leadership of Afikim, where he was highly respected. Lea related that on each Shabbat dozens of people came to them for the evening Shabbat ceremony and for a festive dinner. Their home had a specially built large room with a long table just for this purpose. Lea wrote that Shlomo had frequently spoken with her fondly of "Yanya," which was my childhood nickname. So he had remembered me all these years! Unfortunately, he died about two years before she wrote that letter. Later I received a letter from my aunt Endel, but my response did not reach her. The brutal authorities, who respected neither privacy nor family connections, cut off our letter exchange.

The Red Cavalry, the Budyonovtsy

Two more events from around the time of the pogroms have stayed with me strongly all through the years. They occurred in 1919 at Passover, the great Jewish festival of freedom and redemption that commemorates the sparing of the Jews' firstborn sons during the plagues in Egypt. Our large extended family had survived the pogroms and other upheavals of those years without suffering anything terrible, and we sat down to the Seder meal with a feeling of celebration.

Grandfather Moishe was sitting in his chair at the head of the long table in the hall on the second floor of his apartment. On his left sat his grandson Yanya, or Yakov — me. Following the Jewish tradition, I hunted for the Afikomen, a special piece of matzo wrapped in a napkin. If I found it, I could ask for a gift, as is the custom. Grandfather had hidden it somewhere close to him. My brother, Sulya (Israel), who was then three years old, was sitting on grandfather's right side, also looking for the Afikomen. Around the rest of Grandfather Moishe's table were his three daughters and four sons, a daughter-in-law, a son-in-law, a granddaughter, and several other relatives. Two old women who helped my grandmother serve the dinner sat at the end of the table. The door to the kitchen was behind them. The table was covered with a white tablecloth. Red cherry liquor, the nastoika made by my grandmother many months before, was taken from the cellar before the Seder meal of gefilte fish, minced eggs and liver, other cold dishes, and of course matzo and some biscuits baked with a fine matzo meal.

Suddenly, noisy footsteps clattered up the stairs connecting the kitchen with the front door of the house. Three or four armed men, with sabers at their sides and with large red stars on their peaked caps, appeared in the kitchen doorway. Grandfather calmly continued his ceremonial talk and the Passover prayers in Hebrew. He only nodded his head from time to time to acknowledge the soldiers. The rest of the family remained silent. The military men simply stood there, uttering not a word! They stayed there for several minutes, looking at us, and then one of them, the chief, nodded. The soldiers turned and left us. As we continued the Seder, we had to give special thanks that on that day of all days we had been passed over and left in peace.

The armed men were soldiers of the Mounted Army of Semyon Budyonny, Budyonovtsy in Russian. Their peaked caps with red stars and earflaps were called Budyonovki. The army came to Zhitomir on their march to Poland. "Dayosh Warshavu" (Take Warsaw) was emblazoned on their banners. Fortunately, they never reached Warsaw. They stayed in Zhitomir for many days, occupying the houses of residents. They cleaned out the cellars, where the people stored potatoes, meat, fruits, and homemade wine for the winter and for times of scarcity.

Soon after the Seder evening, two of the military men asked politely to have a bedroom in my grandfather's apartment. One of them was a senior officer. But they never broke into our cellar or stole from us. They even brought us bread and other food. I remember them playing with me a lot while they stayed there. When the Budyonny troops left Zhitomir, our boarders gave me presents: soldiers' underwear and overcoats. My mother altered them for my father and me. The troops also gave my father a small nickel-plated revolver, but he threw it into the well in our yard.

Recalling that unusual evening, I think that the Budyonovtsev soldiers' behavior and respect for us resulted from the elevated, noble atmosphere of the Seder. They could sense that holy and quiet atmosphere even though it was a stormy time of conflict outside.

One day, when the Mounted Army was still in Zhitomir and I was playing on the street, crowds of people began streaming toward Malyovanka, a large open area on the outskirts of the city, which was used for public games and soldiers' drills. Curious to learn what the excitement was all about, I joined them. On our way, I heard that Leon Trotsky, the famous revolutionary and one of the creators of the fledgling Soviet State, was going to address the Budyonny army there. At that time Trotsky was a Narodny—or People's—Commissar, the military minister of Soviet Russia. The people of Zhitomir said that Trotsky was of Zhitomir origin, and they were very proud of him. So I saw and listened to a Leon Trotsky speech, although I cannot remember what that famed orator said. When I returned home, my father spanked me soundly for being away too long and without permission. I had earned the slaps on my posterior that day, though I do not remember any other time when that was necessary. My Budyonny adventures were finished, and Zhitomir too entered a more stable time as Ukraine was absorbed into the USSR.

4

A Time of Transition

In 1919, at eight years of age, I began my official schooling when I entered a Soviet primary school, the Labor School for Primary Education. I attended that school until 1925 and then received three years of secondary schooling at Zhitomir's Industrial Technical College.

The courses in these schools were too easy for me. For the most part I educated myself about school subjects and also about other subjects that sparked my interest. Some of my teachers understood this and encouraged me in my efforts. When my class graduated from the primary school in 1925, our Russian language teacher presented me with the words, "Here you have a professor."

Becoming a Researcher, 1919–1928

From 1919 on, I began to read widely in both fiction and nonfiction, mostly in Russian but also in Ukrainian. Before that I usually read in Hebrew. As I said above, no one directed my reading; it was a spontaneous process. Often I read one or two books meant for adult readers each week. At first I read by candlelight or used a kerosene lamp in the evenings, because electric power was not then common or reliable in Zhitomir.

My curiosity about the world made me ask many common childhood questions about natural phenomena and other things. I still remember pondering, why is the sky blue? And when was the wheel invented? Around the age of eight or nine I began to write these questions down in a notebook in which from time to time I recorded ideas and discoveries and copied favorite passages from my reading. This notebook was one of the things that disappeared from my parents' apartment after their deaths.

The origin of the wheel and the blueness of the sky were two good lines of inquiry for a young boy. The blueness of the sky puzzled humankind for thousands of years, until it was famously explained by the Nobel Prize–winning English physicist John William Strutt, the third Lord Rayleigh, in his 1870 study "On the Light from the Sky: Its Polarization and Color." In 1967 a U.S. scientist, James Wait, mailed a copy of the original manuscript of this paper to me in Moscow from England. It was printed in an old style and looked as though it had been written on parchment. As usual, I was not allowed to take part in a symposium in Cambridge, where James Wait was hoping to see me.

At school I was, above all, interested in geometry and arithmetic. I found books outside the school program that contained arithmetic and geometry problems and tried to solve all the exercises in those books. One of them was a book of geometric problems by Salmon. Over the course of about a year I carefully worked through all the problems in the book. It seems to me now that if I were to try to solve those problems today, using only the knowledge I had at the time, I would not be able to do them. But as a young boy I was bursting with energy and creativity.

My mathematics teacher in the primary school was astonished at my having those books and at the level of my interest; he said that the books were specifically written for teachers. This teacher supported and encouraged my enthusiasm. He was a Russian (in Russian parlance, not a Jew), an obese but kind man with a large head of thick hair. He once told a few other students and me the following instructive but unlikely story.

At the beginning of the century an old Jewish shoemaker with a long gray beard went to the university in Odessa, the beautiful port city on the Black Sea. The shoemaker roamed the corridors of the university for a long time looking for someone who would talk to him. At last someone stopped to ask the shoemaker what he wanted and then took him to meet a professor of mathematics. During the ensuing conversation the professor was astonished to discover that the old shoemaker had independently arrived at the idea of differential and integral calculus. The shoemaker had never heard of Isaac Newton or Gottfried Leibnitz. After his visit to the university, he learned Latin and read Newton's *Principia Mathematica* in the original. Was this a true story or a fairy tale invented by a clever and good teacher to encourage his students? Either answer is possible, is it not?

Around 1923–24 I became enthusiastic about electricity. I began to find as many popular books about electrical engineering as I could. One of my two best friends, Tolya (Anatoly Grinberg), shared my interest in science. Together we designed and built various electrical sets: dynamos, engines, even a working telephone. We did not have step-by-step instructions and ready-made materials, as might be found today in a kit or model manufactured for children's use. Shops with such things did not even exist in Zhitomir then. Instead we tried to figure out from books what each piece of equipment required. Then we scrounged in the trash for screws, metal plates, electrical coils, and so on, or bought them at the flea market. For example, we read that a dynamo includes a rotor and wire, but we had to solve for ourselves the problem of just how the rotor and the wire should be used. When we decided to make a telephone, we had only a picture of a Bell telephone in a book, without any specific technical details. Telephone service in Zhitomir was then very rudimentary, and neither of us had a telephone in his house. For two or three years we enjoyed solving such problems together.

Tolya and I formed a wonderful friendship in primary school with Motya (Mark Zilberman). They became my closest friends for many years. Motya was an intelligent, gentle, and kind person. He was more interested in the humanities than in science. Tolya and I spent more time together because of our common hobby.

The mid-1920s were the years when amateur radio activity became popular all around the world. Zhitomir too soon had an amateur radio society. It seems that there Tolya and I met a young engineer named Senya (Semyon) Killion in 1925. Senya must have been about ten years older than we were, but he became our good friend. Senya was a ham radio operator. You might say I caught the radio bug from him. In 1926, I created my first valve radio receiver using a double-grid vacuum tube. The double-grid tube was nice for ham radio operators because it required smaller batteries than other tubes did. Except for the tube, which I bought, I designed and made all the parts of the radio: the variable condenser, the induction coils, the variable resistance, and the wooden housing. In 1929, when I was in Moscow, I officially became "Radio Nablyudatel-RK-1479," that is, a wireless observer.

During my primary school years I had other hobbies, as well. In 1921–23 I began to collect butterflies and, in particular, special beetles. It was easier and cheaper for me to maintain a good collection of beetles than butterflies, because butterflies should be saved in special frames with glass doors. I learned and still remember some of the Latin names of the beetle families in my collection, for example, *Kurqurlionidae, Carabeidae,* and *Coccionolidae.* I followed the instructions in textbooks on zoology and kept these collections as carefully as a museum would, covered in cotton wool and held in paper envelopes that I made myself. Alas, it is a pity that I lost them. I left my large collection of beetles behind in Zhitomir when I moved to Moscow in 1929. Although I always planned to get them at some point in the future, together with my other beloved things, I never did so.

I also participated in the school amateur theatrical group and the school choir. I had a good strong alto voice and was even a member of the children's city chorus. In one performance on the school stage, I played a "death-cup," a toadstool. I was on my knees during the entire performance and was covered with a large red cup with white spots. I talked with the other toadstools in the garden about how roughly people were treating us. Although I do not remember any of my lines in that role, I recall that the play was a bit philosophical and didactic and was recommended by our literature teacher. As for my singing in the city chorus, I once sang "O Sole Mio" on the stage of the city theater. I still remember some couplets of that song in Russian:

> Ya znayu solntse eshche svetlei
> I eto solntse svet tvoikh ochei
> Oni goryat vo t'me
> I svetyat yarche solnechnikh luchei.

I translate this verse as, "I know a brighter sun; and this sun is the light of your eyes. They glow in the darkness and shine brighter than the sunbeam."

Nowadays Svetlana and I frequently enjoy listening to a compact disc recording of "The Three Tenors," Luciano Pavarotti, Placido Domingo, and José Carreras, performing "O Sole Mio" at the Baths of Caracalla in Rome. Hearing these great artists brings back that moment, more than seventy years ago, when I stood alone on the stage and felt the energy and emotion of the music as a performer. In general I love music. It excites me and inspires me to attempt great deeds.

When I was fourteen or fifteen years old I became interested in both political and social issues. I followed the debate over the future development of the country that Leon Trotsky and Joseph Stalin carried out in the newspapers, each publishing polemics against the other's views. My understanding of the Soviet form of socialism and my attitude to the Communist leadership changed drastically many years later. At that time, however, I believed that the Soviet system was a good one for all humankind. Still, I did not become a "Pioneer" (the name of the children's Communist group), nor did I later become a member of Komsomol (a teenage Communist organization), and I never joined the Communist Party. Why was it so, even in my childhood? It is difficult to answer this question precisely, but I know absolutely that I did not want to join those organizations. Perhaps it was my deep passion for my "research" works with electrical and radio devices and insects that usurped other interests in my childhood and teenage years. I spent all my free time on those hobbies. Perhaps also it was because I needed and enjoyed my personal freedom, as I remember, even in the early years of my life. My parents gave me the gift of that freedom, and I did not want to hand myself over to the restrictive demands of the Communist organizations that everyone should be alike and march in step. It was against my character. Yet at that time and for many years, I did believe in "scientific socialism," which sought to bring to future generations of humanity a more perfect life.

Actually, owing largely to the influence of the books I read, I was raised and educated in the romanticism of the revolution and in the social-democratic ideals of the *"Decembrists"* and the *"Narodniks."* The Decembrists were the Russian noble revolutionaries who in 1825 rose against serfdom and the tsarist autocracy. The Narodniks spawned the Narodnichestvo movement (from the word *Narod,* "the People"), the secret Russian political movement of 1861–95 against the tsar's rule. The central goal of the Narodniks, who came from broad circles of the intelligentsia, was to achieve peasant democracy and a distinctively Russian form of socialism. They fought a repressive autocracy through agitation and terrorist acts.

I read and was impressed by the books and novels of the most distinguished Russian thinkers. Among them, Vissarion Belinsky, a famous literary critic, was one of the most noteworthy Russian revolutionary democrats of the nineteenth century. His books, *Homeland Records* and *Literary Reveries,* and his articles in the journal *Contemporary* (created by Alexander Pushkin), inspired many generations of Russian people. I recently found extracts of some of Belinsky's writings in my files. Alexander Hertsen, the Russian writer, philosopher, and revolutionary, championed social democratic ideals in Russian society through his book *Who Is Guilty?* and in his autobiographical novel, *My Past and Thoughts,* a masterpiece of Russian classical literature. I was surprised not to find the name of Hertsen in any American encyclopedia. He was a great person.

Many of my generation were also absorbed by the revolutionary democrat Nikolai Chernyshevsky's *Qu'est-ce que faire?* (What Is to Be Done?) and *Prologue,* and the literary critic Nikolai Dobrolyubov's essay "The Kingdom of Darkness." Chernyshevsky was arrested for his activities in 1862 and locked in the Petropavlovsky fortress prison in St. Petersburg. Two years later, in 1864, he was sent into exile in Siberia and spent nineteen years there.

One of the famous activists and leaders in the Narodniks' movement was the scientist and revolutionary Nikolai Morozov, who became an "Academician in Honor" of the Academy of Sciences of the USSR in 1932. He was arrested in 1880 and spent about twenty-five years in the prisons of St. Peterburg, the Shliselburg and Petropavlovsky fortresses. I learned a lot about the heroic, noble actions of the Narodniks from Morozov's very interesting and stirring *Tales of My Life*. I was excited to see Morozov at a resort for academicians in 1945. He was then ninety-one years old. I once watched him climb the stairs to the second floor of the resort with a load of books in his arms, but I was too shy to approach him. Morozov died the next year.

In connection with these thoughts of reform, revolution, and social justice, perhaps I should mention a childhood rebellion of my own. When I entered the Industrial Technical College in 1925, I eagerly looked forward to the course in physics. I had already begun reading physics textbooks and teaching myself as much as possible. Even then I had the feeling that I wanted to become a physicist and make discoveries.

To my dismay, the physics teacher taught very perfunctorily and frequently made mistakes. At first when I saw that he gave a formula or some other information that was wrong, I spoke up passionately. "Oh, that is not right!" I protested, and I gave the correction from my reading. But when the teacher continued to be negligent, I began to speak to the other students. I said that it was not right for us to have such a teacher and that therefore we should not have to attend his lectures. In short, at fourteen years of age, I organized a student strike. We boycotted the teacher's class and petitioned the school administration for a new teacher.

The teacher fought back by accusing me of being a troublemaker who continually interrupted him and disrupted the class. I did interrupt. I could not restrain myself when I saw how badly he taught, with contempt for the subject and for his students. But the school administration did not listen to my objections, and they threw me out of the college.

My parents were very upset that I had been expelled, but they did not blame me. When I told them about the teacher's mistakes, they said, "Yanya, if it is so, you are right." I did not get a bad reputation with my classmates' parents, either. They all wanted their children to have good teaching.

Luckily, the district Department of Public Education conducted an investigation into the matter. I cannot recall now if I wrote any letters to protest my being thrown out of the school. But I was summoned several times to talk to the district education officers. They also spoke with other students. And after a couple of weeks, the investigation was concluded and I was told to return to school. When I did so, I was happy to find a new physics teacher, who did not make mistakes!

As a matter of fact, I would not say that I led this uprising because of my political reading. Rather, my rebellion flowed from my scientific reading and my impulsive temperament.

Reading Fiction

My account of this stage of my life would not be complete without some mention of the books I read. Reading novels was for me a pressing need. I wanted to learn about the natural phenomena of human beings, just as much as I did the natural phenomena of insects and electricity. In general, after reading a novel, I think a lot about it. I like to discuss it with my friends. This does not mean that I remember very well the content of even my favorite books, but I do remember very well what the matter of my interest was and what impressed me most about the books I read. Some of the writers I read in my youth are still familiar names, but many are not very well known nowadays, especially in America.

I read with passion the books of Jack London, and especially his *Call of the Wild, White Fang,* and later *Martin Eden.* But I also read the little-known social novels of the Polish writer Eliza Orzeszkowa and the plays of the Belgian dramatist Maurice Maeterlinck, who won the Nobel Prize for literature of 1911. His play *The Blue Bird* was one of the hallmark productions of the famous Art Theater in Moscow. I saw it there in 1931.

In spite of my passion for electricity, radio, and science in general, I was not very enthusiastic about science fiction, as, for example, the writings of Jules Verne. I read them, but without much delight. I enjoyed historical novels more. I have already mentioned the impact on me as a young boy of *Spartacus* and *Quo Vadis.* I liked adventures of the Middle Ages, and in particular Henryk Sienkiewicz's *With Fire and Sword* (in three volumes). Only recently did I learn that he received the Nobel Prize for literature in 1905.

Among the novels and plays that made a deep impression in my memory and in my thinking was the profound drama *Before the Sunset,* by the German dramatist, poet, and novelist Gerhart Hauptmann. I remember also his fairy tale *The Sunken Bell.* Much later I saw an excellent performance of that play by the remarkable Vakhtang Theater in Moscow. Recently I learned that Hauptmann became a Nobelist in literature in 1912. Likewise I saw the witty comedies of the Irish writer and poet Oscar Wilde, *Lady Windermere's Fan* and *An Ideal Husband* in Moscow, but I read them as a teenager in the 1920s along with Wilde's philosophical novel *The Picture of Dorian Gray.*

I reread many times the especially interesting and deep novels of Lion Feuchtwanger: *Jew Suss, The Family Oppenheim, The Spanish Ballad, False Nero,* and a dozen of his other novels. Another of my favorite writers was Stefan Zweig (an Austrian), especially his *Amok* and *Confusion of the Senses* and his biographies of Balzac and Mary Stuart.

I have mentioned here a small number of the novels that I chose to read in my childhood and teenage years, in the 1920s and later in Moscow. The younger I was when I read a particular book, the less likely I was to appreciate it fully, of course, but my imagination was fired by good stories and interesting characters and my intuition carried me along even when I did not quite grasp all the subtleties. When I reread a book later in life I was struck not so much by what I missed as a child but by how accurate my first emotional and intuitive response was.

At that time I most enjoyed stories where love and intimate friendship dominated. This passion of mine continued and remained predominant when I moved to Moscow and for many years after. I always felt a necessity to have good friends; I liked to discuss any question with them openly. It was the idealistic and romantic side of human life that influenced me from the beginning and continued to do so for many decades. Largely for these reasons, my favorite author was the French writer Romain Rolland, especially his novels *Jean Christophe* and *Annette and Silvie*. One novel is about a genius musician and rebel, Jean, and about the lofty friendship between him and Oliver, a deep and sensitive man. The second novel is about the great friendship of two young women. I read almost all the novels of Rolland and his artistic biographies of Beethoven, Michelangelo, and Tolstoy. Rolland received the 1915 Nobel Prize for literature.

My favorite super-romantic novels about love were *Victoria,* by the Norwegian writer Knut Hamsun, *Kyra-Kyralina,* by the Romanian writer Panait Istrati, and *Joy's Wing,* by the Ukrainian writer Lesya Ukrainka. Another book similar to those novels was *Being Honest with Myself,* by the Ukrainian writer Vladimir Vinnichenko. To this day I have extracts from *Victoria* as well as other novels in my files. Recently I learned that Hamsun shared the 1920 Nobel Prize for literature. It troubled me to learn also, many decades after I had read *Victoria,* that Hamsun sympathized with Nazism and was condemned in 1946 for his collaboration with the fascists during World War II.

I did not just read about love. In school I made friends with a classmate named Nadia. She invited me to her home and there I met her sister Fira, who was one year younger, and her sister Zina, who was older. They were the daughters of a prosperous and important man in Zhitomir at that time, and they were all very beautiful. When I saw Fira, with her shining blonde hair, I lost my heart. We became friendly and we took long walks together and talked about our hopes and dreams. But then we quarreled over some trivial thing, as often happens with young people. When we met on the streetcars, we did not speak to each other. In America there is an expression, puppy love, is it not? That was my relationship with Fira.

The events of life are unpredictable, however. Fifteen years later, during World War II, when the German blockade of Leningrad was lifted, I took the second possible train from Moscow to Leningrad, to consult with members of Abram Fyodorovich Ioffe's institute. Walking on Nevsky Prospekt, the great street that runs from the railway station and ends close to the River Neva and is filled with shops and cafes, I met Fira again. We both were taken aback at the suddenness of that meeting. It was like a dream. For a while it seemed to me that it was my destiny to . . . But later, back in Moscow, that dream faded.

My attraction to girls and to being in love, which began when I was a schoolboy, had in general only to do with imagination. Imagination has been an inseparable part of my nature, in scientific research too. I have often thought about things that seem unrealizable. But who knows? I was enamored and imagined.

I also wanted to learn about sexual matters from books. The first such book I read when I was fourteen or fifteen years old; it was a novel, *Behind the Closed Door,* by Sergei Friedlander. About five years later I read a thick book called *The Sexual Question* by Auguste Forel, a famous Swiss psychiatrist and neuropathologist. I found the Russian translation of the book in the Lenin Library in Moscow soon after going there. Forel was also active in public affairs. I have kept many excerpts from that book in my files. But I don't want deeply to recount in this book stories of love and friendship. Those stories are full of imagination, dreams, mistakes, and disillusionment. I am incapable of describing such events and feelings.

I loved to collect books. My first library, which I left in my parents' apartment before I moved to Moscow, was not large; it contained only a few dozen novels. Among them, however, were the complete works of Hamsun, Maeterlinck, and Wilde. There were other special books that I bought from a bookseller in Zhitomir that have never been reprinted.

I left a large part of my second library of belles-lettres and social and historical texts, numbering three to four hundred volumes in all and including fifty volumes of the *Complete Soviet Encyclopedia,* at the home of my first wife, Irina. We separated, but we are good friends to this day. I am not sorry that a considerable part of my second library is with her.

My third library was partially assembled together with Svetlana. We had about two thousand volumes, including scientific books. In the USSR there are many more translated books, published in very cheap editions, than are available in other countries. Of our large collection the Soviet agencies allowed us to take only about three hundred volumes to the United States when we emigrated in 1987. We sold the remaining portion of our library, including unique collections and artistic albums, to bookstores, which were most pleased to buy them.

I left a large collection of scientific books in my fields of research at the department and laboratories that I had organized (and chaired) at the Academy of Sciences of the USSR, where I had worked for nearly fifty-five years.

A Turning Point

Now I come to the first great turning point in my life. In the years recounted here I learned much, read much, and did much. I became an independent and self-reliant fellow when I was thirteen or fourteen years old, and I educated myself in many areas. At the Industrial Technical College I was taught the trade of carpentry and cabinetmaking. I taught myself another skill in those years, that of technical drawing, because I loved to draw and did it well. I earned a fair amount of money executing and copying technical drawings for people in Zhitomir. Although throughout my life I have enjoyed working with my hands, I did not want to spend my life as a cabinetmaker or a draftsman. I wanted to continue learning, working, and advancing my education, and to become a researcher in physics.

The only institute accessible to me for higher education, however, was the new one that opened at that time in Zhitomir. My friend Tolya Grinberg had the chance to go to the big city of Kiev for his education. His parents, who were better off financially than mine, were able to send him to the Polytechnic Institute in Kiev, one of the best and most famous of Russian institutes. Vladimir Zvorykin, the inventor of the television picture tube, the famous mechanical scientist Stefan Timoshenko, and the chemist Nikolai Uspensky were students at that institute. They emigrated to the United States in the 1920s and became prominent researchers there.

I passed all my entrance examinations at the institute at Zhitomir with the highest grades, but I was not admitted. At that time the privilege of being admitted to an institute of higher learning was accorded only to the children of workers and peasants. My father was not a worker (*rabochii* in Russian); officially he was included in the category of office workers *(sluzhashchiy)*. The rule was strictly followed in Zhitomir. It seems that in Kiev this was not so, because Tolya's father was also an office worker.

Soon after being turned away from the institute in Zhitomir, I decided to go to Moscow to be closer to the great world of science, to find a job there, and to pursue more self-education in libraries. I saved money for the trip from my drafting work; I even sold my precious photographic camera. I put the books of my library, some files and notes, and my collection of beetles in my parents' attic. I did not know what awaited me in Moscow, but I was full of optimism and eager to try my luck. Let me now tell you what happened when I got there.

5

Moscow, 1929 and After

It was the beginning of 1929 when I set out for Moscow with the few rubles I had saved from my drafting work. It was the first time I traveled outside Zhitomir. Although I had no definite prospects, I did have a lifeline in Moscow, my aunt Lisa, my father's sister, and her husband, Nathan Meyerovich.

Aunt Lisa was a slender, delicate woman, innately aristocratic, who never spoke very much or very loudly. Her marriage was on one level a study in the attraction of opposites, for Uncle Nathan was a big, noisy, unkempt fellow. But they were both sensitive, kindhearted, and generous people. They met in Zhitomir, when Nathan went there on business for Tass, the Soviet news agency. He was not a journalist but an administrative employee. Lisa and Nathan fell in love and married, and they went to live in Moscow.

Aunt Lisa and Uncle Nathan opened their home to me. They lived modestly in two separate rooms in a large apartment that also housed three other families, with one kitchen and one bathroom among them all. Aunt Lisa and Uncle Nathan gave me a bed in the corner of one room, and Uncle Nathan made it his special project to help and encourage me. Nothing lit up this big-hearted man's broad, good-natured face so much as an idea for helping a relative, friend, or neighbor.

To find a job in Moscow at that time it was necessary to register at the *birzha truda,* or the labor exchange office. I presented myself there as an unskilled laborer. I cannot recall precisely why I said nothing about my carpentry and drafting or, more significant, my facility with electrical and radio equipment. It seems to me now that I was solely intent on learning physics in the library. I was ready to work hard, but I wanted free time to read. I was not sure that I could ever afford to become a full-time student.

In any event, the birzha sent me to one of the building sites of Mosstroy, the Moscow municipal construction authority, which was running major construction projects throughout the city. At the building site, I was hired to work on a building brigade, or crew, of unskilled workers. Of all the members of the crew, about ten to fifteen persons, I was the youngest.

Ten or twelve large buildings of several stories each were going up on this site. Several building brigades worked at the site, all responsible for hauling in building materials, carting away refuse and excess materials, and cleaning dirt and debris from the finished areas of the buildings. The brigades were all paid the same base wage, 1 ruble 47 kopecks per day for each man, but the more a brigade accomplished, the more kopecks its members received. Each brigade was responsible for recording its completed jobs on a list, which had to be submitted to the financial vice-manager of the site every two weeks.

As we worked outside in the Moscow winter, I gradually realized that my brigade only received the minimum wage, because no one on the team wrote well enough to keep track of the work we did. I started to write the jobs down carefully as we completed them. I gave the list to the crew leader, and our wages quickly rose to 3 rubles 47 kopecks a day. This was cause for celebration among the crew, and soon the news of our salary increase became the talk of the building site. The other members of the crew and the crew leader himself asked me to become the crew leader, but I did not want to displace anyone from his role.

With 3 rubles 47 kopecks a day, I could not only live in Moscow. A small loaf of good French bread then cost 5 kopecks. With 3 rubles 47 kopecks a day, I could save up to buy a ticket to the Moscow Art Theater, the theater of Konstantin Stanislavsky, the great originator and proponent of Method Acting.

From its founding by Stanislavsky in 1898, the Moscow Art Theater transformed world theater through the impact of its productions and the rapid spread of Stanislavsky's principles of acting. I read about the theater when I was a dreaming boy in Zhitomir, and I yearned to see a performance there. When I first went to that modest building on the corner of Gorky Street and Khudozhestvennyi Proezd (Art Passage), it was to see Maxim Gorky's own *The Lower Depths,* which I had read in Zhitomir. It is a cliché to say that I entered the Moscow Art Theater as if I were entering a new world. But that was indeed my experience, as I saw Gorky's classic story brought to life on the stage. It put my head in the clouds.

Then I walked out of the theater, and there on Gorky Street I saw a drunken woman. I had never seen a drunken woman before. I had not imagined that such women existed. It was for me an unexpected phenomenon.

So you see that I was very naive. But I was learning all the time. When I went to the Moscow Art Theater again, I saw *The Days of the Turbins,* the dramatization of Bulgakov's novel *The White Guard.* The novel and the play explored how the Russian revolution divided the country's officer corps and many families, just as the Civil War in the United States did. People who were once united suddenly found themselves on opposite banks of the river, as the Russian saying goes. One became a revolutionary, the other became an enemy of the revolution. As I recall, *Pravda* reported that Stalin saw and approved the production. But some years later the rest of Bulgakov's works, such as his satiric fantasy of the devil in Moscow, *Master and Margarita,* were banned by Stalin's regime.

The system deemed this one work of Bulgakov's to be politically correct. But that did not alter the truth of Bulgakov's vision of what happened to the Russian people and would happen to us again during my lifetime. More than once in times of crisis, we Russians have suddenly found ourselves on opposite banks of the river from our countrymen, our friends and colleagues, and even our families. I could not help but be aware that this process was to some extent going on even then.

Of course, I did not go to the theater every night. Most nights from 6 to 10 P.M. and most Sundays (the one day off at that time) I happily spent in the Lenin Library reading physics and mathematics. At this time I also read the classic writers: Lev Tolstoy, Honoré de Balzac, Lord Byron, Fyodor Dostoyevsky, Alexander Pushkin, William Shakespeare, Marie-Henri Stendhal, and my favorite poet, Mikhail Lermontov. Lermontov was Pushkin's near contemporary and died at an even younger age. It was a tragic feature of the tsarist court culture in which they lived that both writers died in duels, Pushkin at thirty-seven and Lermontov at only twenty-seven. Lermontov is still underappreciated in the West. I knew many of Lermontov's verses by heart, such as these lines from "Demon," which just now come to my mind. In Russian they are as musical as the most entrancing song.

> The exiled Demon winged his way
> Above the earth of sin and crime,
> And memories of days sublime
> Rose in his mind in bright array
> When in the realms of light and day
> He shone amidst God's seraphim;
> When comets in their courses fleeting
> Were happy to exchange a greeting

And smile with tenderness on him; . . .
The exiled Demon in his flight
Beheld the Caucasus below:
Kazbék with peaks of diamond light
Aglow in their eternal snow.

Years ago I learned that Lev Landau loved Lermontov. He said, "Lermontov was the greatest poet of all times," and he also felt that Lermontov's prose was better than Pushkin's.

So I established a rhythm of life for myself in Moscow. Most nights and Sundays I went to the library and read. From time to time I saw a play, visited a museum, or attended a public lecture. Soon after arriving in Moscow at the beginning of 1929, I joined the Moscow Radio Club, and I also went there frequently. Five or six older members and I designed and built a short-wave radio transmitter. We brought various items from home for this project, including aluminum pans and wires. At that time I also became a member of the Society of Friends of Radio of the USSR. Note that the word *friends (druz'ya)* — not *amateurs* — was used in the name of the society. We used the club's radio transmitter for communications with other ham radio operators. And early every morning from Monday to Saturday, without fail, I reported for work on the building site.

One day a tall, handsome man strode onto the construction site. Everyone else knew who he was and deferred to him. A co-worker explained that this was Constantin Nikolayevich Chernopyatov, the principal architect of the project, on a periodic visit to check its progress. On this day he was apparently also curious to meet the young worker who was being talked about all over the building site. He engaged me in conversation and I found myself saying that I could draw well. He immediately asked me to come to his office the next day. There I showed him my drawing ability and told him about my desire to become a physicist. He then offered me a position as a draftsman. From the very beginning he gave me challenging work that was not connected with Mosstroy's construction projects. Chernopyatov was taking part in many architectural competitions, and he asked me to prepare the drafts and detailed axonometric views of his designs. Sometimes he gave me only a rough sketch, and from that I extrapolated elaborate, detailed views. I also began to accompany Chernopyatov to building sites, carrying plans and maps and a logbook for recording the progress of different projects.

Chernopyatov was delighted with my work. He even began to suggest that I should become an architect. He urged me to enter the Moscow Institute of Architecture, and I am sure that he would have helped me to do so. But although I loved architecture, I was even more interested in physics. And to become a physicist, I would sooner or later have to leave Mosstroy.

"The Thinker": 1967, 1970

Working at Mosstroy was not my last involvement with architecture, however. At the end of 1967 or a little earlier, when I was working at the institute IZMIRAN, I asked Nikolai Pushkov, its director, to petition the Academy of Sciences to construct a new building for IZMIRAN's Space Plasma Physics Department, which I organized and headed. The main purpose of my request was to be in a location of low electromagnetic noise. This was necessary for our experiments, for clear and precise recordings in the laboratory of the radio waves received from satellite radio beacons.

Pushkov approved my proposal and made the appropriate application to the Development Department of the Presidium of the Academy of Sciences. This department oversaw building projects for the academy throughout the USSR. At that time it occupied a big three-story structure in Moscow. Its staff comprised hundreds of people, including many engineers and architects. Soon after our application was made I learned that the head of that department, the chief architect of the academy, was none other than Constantin Chernopyatov, my old boss at Mosstroy. He was even a member of the academy's presidium. It was satisfying for me to learn this and to see again how the paths of people cross and how our world is, in fact, small. I had not heard of Chernopyatov since the time when I was eighteen years old.

Months passed before a telephone call informed us that our application for new laboratories had been rejected. We were told that such a building was beyond the scope and budget of the Development Department's program and that we would soon be notified officially about the decision, when the academy's building agenda for the next two years was ratified. To my surprise, after several weeks another call informed me that the project had been approved and that I needed to collaborate with the design bureau, which would shortly begin to prepare the working drawings for the building.

What was even more surprising, as my caller told me, was how this came about. Approval of the academy's building program always took place at a session of its council presided over by the chief architect, that is, by Chernopyatov. During this session, the head of the facilities planning department announced that the structure for our new laboratories had been struck from the agenda. At that point, Chernopyatov interrupted, "This laboratory for Alpert must be built. The academy's prestige is based on scientists such as he." I was astonished but pleased to hear this. I did not know the source of Chernopyatov's information about me.

The new three-story building for my department was built in a birch grove and was located approximately a mile from the main institute building in the environs of Moscow, about twenty-five miles from the center of the city. I participated in the design of the building and worked there for a little more than two decades, until Svetlana and I moved to the United States in 1987 after having been refusniks for a dozen years. That building's laboratories were well suited to our work. The attractive two-story seminar hall, with floor-to-ceiling windows, was often used by IZMIRAN, especially for international meetings.

Two emblems were designed for our building. One was on the wall outside, above the entrance balcony; the second one was inside, by the entrance to the seminar hall. The outer emblem was a series of overlapping ellipses, appropriate for space research. The inner emblem I sketched from the drawing of my good friend, the well-known physicist-theoretician Lev Gor'kov. Gor'kov never told me what he had in mind when he made his drawing. When people asked me what it represented, I answered, "The Thinker contemplates the world, and Nature sticks a fork into the Thinker's rear." In other words, the laws of nature are vastly more rich and intricate than the human mind can imagine, and Nature astonishes and confounds the human researcher.

In preparing a sketch for the emblem, I asked the artists to make the fork red. When I told Lev Gor'kov and his wife, Lyalya, about this, Lyalya said that the color of the fork should be changed. Otherwise people would conclude that it was anti-Soviet propaganda, that the image of the Thinker with a red fork signified scientists working and the Communist Party preventing them. In the end the artists who made the emblem chose the colors, and without telling me they made the fork blue. A curious story is connected with that emblem.

As I have said earlier, I was never allowed to accept any invitations from the West to attend conferences, to become a visiting professor, and so on. Nikolai Pushkov made the request for a visa for me to go abroad many times without success. In 1970 he invited the Communist Party secretary for the large Moscow district that included our institute to see our new building. He wanted to demonstrate the success of my research work and especially my work on satellites. Pushkov hoped this would help me obtain permission to go to the West.

The party official arrived for his visit and came to my office for a talk about my department's research. He looked attentively at the walls of my office. The only photo on display was a large picture of Albert Einstein, along with a poster of some of his words. The following is my translation of the Russian version displayed on my office wall.

> *I believe in intuition and inspiration.*
> Sometimes I feel that I am on the right path but cannot explain my confidence. When the Solar eclipse of 1919 confirmed my conjecture, I was not at all surprised. I would have been surprised if it had not happened.
> *Imagination is more important than knowledge,* for knowledge is limited,

whereas imagination involves all the world, stimulates progress, and promotes its evolution.

Strictly speaking, imagination is a real factor in scientific research.
— Albert Einstein

According to Soviet tradition offices would usually display at least a portrait of Vladimir Lenin, if not pictures of Lenin and the current party leadership; here there was none. Then we went to the laboratories and to the seminar hall. Here the party head saw portraits of the famous Russian scientists Lev Landau, Leonid Mandelshtam, Nikolai Papalexi, and Sergei Vavilov. There were no portraits of the leaders of the USSR. On leaving the seminar hall, the party head noticed the emblem with the Thinker. He stopped abruptly. He was confused and astonished. "What is that?" he asked. I explained its meaning as usual, "The Thinker is searching, and Nature sticks a fork into his rear." He immediately replied, "I know what it means," and quickly left the building. That Communist bureaucrat was clever enough to understand and give another meaning to the emblem, exactly as Lyalya Gor'kov predicted. On the stairs in the entrance hallway, he glanced sternly at the small, nonstandard image of Lenin hanging there, the only image of Lenin in our building. Nothing changed after his visit.

It is a pity that the fork in the emblem was never painted red. In 1990, when I was invited to Moscow for the celebration of the fiftieth anniversary of IZMIRAN, I was happy to see the emblem still hanging in its place.

It strikes me now that I never made any effort to contact Chernopyatov, and I wish that I had done so to thank him for building such a good facility for my research department. At the time I did not wish to presume on our old acquaintance. Nor did I wish to cast any doubt on why he had approved the building or to cause him trouble by association with me, a suspicious character, as seemed clear, in the eyes of the bureaucracy and many people.

A Second Turning Point

At the end of 1929, while I was working for Chernopyatov at Mosstroy, letter after letter arrived for me from my parents in Zhitomir and from friends. They all urged me to return to Zhitomir to enter the new technical college (*technikum* in Russian) that had recently opened there. They wrote that my secondary educational diploma from the Industrial Technical College of Zhitomir, where I had studied from 1925 to 1928, would help me to enter as a fourth-year student of the college. Within a year I could earn a diploma as a heating engineer, as Tolya Grinberg was doing. Tolya was one of those who wrote urging me to be practical. Why I followed their advice I cannot tell now.

It was perhaps because I was lonesome for the places of my childhood. In any case, at the beginning of 1930 I left Moscow for Zhitomir and became a student of its technical college.

At the technical college I chiefly studied thermodynamics. The work was easy for me. I passed various examinations, and at the end of the summer I prepared a graduate design for my diploma. My design was for a steam boiler project of the Grabe system for an electrical station. I finished all the calculations and drafts for the design some time in September. Unfortunately, I did not save any copies of the data from that project. In the fall of 1930 I was sent for three months of practical training in engineering. This work was in a temporary heating engineer's position and was part of the college's program. Depending on my successful work and on the quality of my graduate design, the council of the college would decide what level of graduate diploma I would receive.

My practical training took place in the small village of Terny in a sugar refinery not far from Bryansk, beginning in November 1930. In the basement of the building the refinery had three boilers, which regulated the refining process. Any interruption in the necessary volume of the steam would destroy this process, and it was my job to keep the volume constant.

One night, during a long, heavy rain, the boiler room flooded to the depth of about half a meter. It was a critical situation. The boilers began to fail, and the heavy rains continued without letup. We pumped out water, but the pumps were bad. We filled up all the chinks and windows, but we did not have much material for this task. We worked frantically to stabilize the power and temperature of the fire chambers. But there were only three boiler workers and me, an inexperienced nineteen-year-old, to do the job. More than once, the workers thought that the fight was lost and wanted to give up. But through the long, exhausting night we succeeded in keeping the boilers going. I was very proud that we stood this test.

My apprentice period ended at the beginning of 1931. The final step in becoming a heating engineer was to return to Zhitomir to defend my graduate design and get my diploma. My job reviews at the sugar factory were excellent, and the factory's director offered me a permanent position as an engineer after I received the diploma.

There was a battle in my mind. The heating engineer's diploma would guarantee me a position with a good income and would make my parents happy. Perhaps it would even offer a path to work in science, as my friend Tolya hoped it would for him. After completing his diploma as a heating engineer, Tolya would in fact find a job at the Academy of Science's Physical Technical Institute in Leningrad, organized and directed by Ioffe, where he worked for the rest of his life. But at the beginning of 1931 such a path seemed very uncertain and indirect. On the other hand, there was nothing certain for me in Moscow.

I chose to go straight from Terny to Moscow, again with nearly empty pockets. There I would resume my reading in the Lenin Library, and I would seek work that was in some way connected with my dream of becoming a physicist. It was the second turning point in my life.

6

My University, 1931–1934

In February 1931 I was back in Moscow looking for a job. But not just any job, as before. Thus I did not go to the labor exchange or to Mosstroy. I went instead to the Ministry of Communications and to the reception room of the head of the ministry, the Narodny — or People's — Commissar Alexey Ivanovich Rykov, where I asked to see one of the commissar's assistants. At that time the Soviet bureaucracy was not too rigid. The doors of the ministry were open to the public, and it was possible to walk directly into the reception room. An old Bolshevik revolutionary, Rykov was one of those who built Soviet Russia after the revolution.

Of course I was naive to take such a bold step, but I thought it was worth a try. The greatest luck in my life is perhaps simply that I was born with an optimistic temperament. From the time I was a young boy I had an inner faith that somehow or other I would be able to do what I wanted in life. So when the reception staff asked why I wanted to see one of Commissar Rykov's assistants, I told them straightforwardly that I had come to ask for a job as a radio technician. They listened to me seriously, without any smiles or condescension, and sent me to see Rykov's scientific adviser, a man named Shostakovich (he was not, I think, any relation to the composer). Imagine my meeting this high official! Here I was, just short of my twentieth birthday, coming in off the street without an appointment, without any relevant credentials or training, to say, "I am an amateur radio operator. I have come to ask for a job at the radio institute." And imagine Shostakovich talking to me in depth about my amateur radio activity and my dream of researching physical phenomena.

Shostaskovich was an unpretentious man with an intellectual face. He spoke to me as to an equal. He sensed my capabilities immediately, and he believed in my passion for science. At the end of our meeting, he made a telephone call. The next day I started at the Ministry of Communication's Experimental Radio Station as a laboratory assistant, which was a permanent position for a technically qualified person. It was the beginning of a dream coming true.

Self-Education and Research

My time at the Radio Experimental Station was a time of self-education, and I considered it to be my university. In quick order I became known for my ability to fix any equipment that was faulty or broken. Soon I was managing all such technical matters. And before long I was given the chance to take an active part in the station's research.

At that time the main project of the department where I worked was to test the clarity of radio waves on different frequencies in Moscow and other parts of Russia. Konstantin Ryabov, the department's chief engineer, needed this information for two international conferences in Geneva that allotted the frequencies of the radio band among different countries. If two radio stations in Moscow and Berlin broadcast on close frequencies, for example, they would interfere with each other.

To make these tests we needed an accurate field-strength meter. I designed a suitable meter, which was built according to my specifications in the station's workshop. Using the new field-strength meter and other sensitive devices, in 1931 I made my first investigations close to Moscow at a special observation point of our institute. It was a small house located several miles from the railway station of Polyany. I measured and studied the daily course of the amplitudes of the electric field of many long- and middle-wavelength radio stations at various distances from the observation site. Figures 3a–3c show some results of those measurements.

I performed similar measurements in 1932 at different locations not far from Moscow and also during a two-month expedition in western Russia. The first stop on the expedition was Odessa, on the Black Sea. From Odessa we went to Bryansk, Minsk, and other places in Belorussia (now Belarus), visiting mostly small towns or villages where radio noise was low or nonexistent. Not until 1964 did I publish examples of the records of those observations in one of my books.

On this expedition I was accompanied by an older man, a member of the

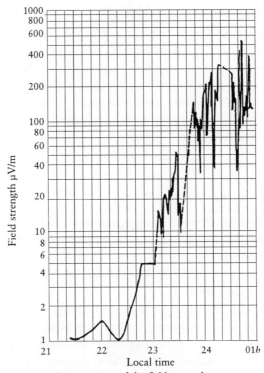

Measurements of the field strength at
λ = 435 m, at a distance of 1250 km from
the transmitter.

3. Daily time dependencies, recorded in Moscow, of the amplitudes of radio waves radiated by broadcasting stations

Communist Party who was authorized to carry a revolver. Conditions were not always safe then in regions such as the Polish border, where we might well be set upon by robbers. We could certainly be taken for easy marks, if not for downright suspicious characters ourselves, when we arrived at a remote country railway station, loaded down with boxes of mysterious equipment, and asked for directions to the local *sberkassa* (a kind of bank). There we drew money to hire a horse-drawn carriage to transport our boxes and to rent a place to stay, preferably at some distance from the railway, because the railway electrical lines would produce radio noise. The local people were always clearly curious about us, looking on as if to ask: Where do these people come from and what are they doing here? What is in their boxes? But they never asked us.

In one small, out-of-the-way village in Belorussia we rented a room in a poor house for a few days. We slept on the floor, there being no beds. In the

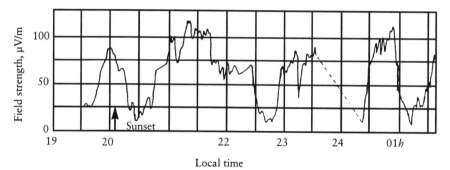

Measurements of the field strength at λ = 1724 m, at
a distance of 2470 km from the transmitter.

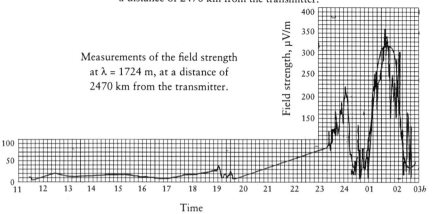

Measurements of the field strength
at λ = 1724 m, at a distance of
2470 km from the transmitter.

middle of one night I was awakened by the sound of someone walking stealth-ily along the exterior wall of the house, which was surrounded by a fenced yard. My pistol-packing colleague was fast asleep. I took the revolver from under his pillow, and with my other hand took a powerful electric lantern with a large reflector. I slowly opened the outside door and looked out into the dark night. I heard the creak of the yard gate, then I moved my hand forward with the revolver and switched on the lantern. I saw two people blinded by the light. They had not seen me — only the revolver in my hand. They immediately ran off, and we were not disturbed further in that village.

While I was carrying out these tests near Bryansk I had pleasant and unex-pected meetings with two good friends from my teenage years in Zhitomir. The world is small, and our paths crossed. Both Tolya Grinberg and Senya Killion were working at a place close to Bryansk, which was a large and important industrial town in a region of dense forests. During World War II a strong partisan army operated in these same forests and fought well against Fascist troops.

Tolya had arrived from Kiev to work at a factory for his prediploma internship. I learned that Senya was married, and I spent an evening at his home near Bryansk with him, his wife, and their young daughter. I also had many meetings with Tolya. During the week I was in Bryansk, Tolya came by train to see me every day.

One twilit evening Tolya and I sat on the steep shore of the River Desna and spoke about the social and political life of our country and about the fate and character of the Soviet people. I reminded Tolya of the biblical story of how Moses led the Jews out of slavery in Egypt to the border of the Promised Land. But the people refused to go there and fight to win a new home for themselves. Their slavery in Egypt had made them passive and fearful. In punishment God decreed that the Jews would have to remain in the wilderness for forty years. During that time, their children would become free people and would be able to inhabit the land. Thus in 1932 I understood that the Soviet brand of communism, which was totalitarianism, produced a generation of thoroughly dependent and depressed people. Many people in my country did not even know what it meant to have free choice. It was obvious that my homeland was in deep decay. I understood that the state was rotting and that it would collapse just as the Roman Empire once did.

In the 1950s I also spoke with friends in Moscow about this fear. My concern did not mean that I did not believe in the ideals of socialism, ideals that were the dream of many people throughout the world. Yet I felt that humankind in general and the Russian people in particular were not ready to build such a system. A deep chasm still exists between the consciousness and the achievements of human beings and the ideals of socialism. Heroic, distinguished people sincerely and selflessly tried to build socialism in the USSR. Only much later did I learn who many of the builders of that system really were. The failure of their efforts is a tragedy of world history and of Great Mother Russia.

To Be Young in Moscow

Not long after I went to work at the Experimental Radio Station, I was assigned housing of my own, a small room in a two-story wooden apartment house owned by the station. There was only one bathroom in the building, directly beneath my room. I heard the water running day and night, but I never paid it any mind. I counted my blessings to have a place of my own, a job doing radio science, and free time to study. Once again I began to frequent the Lenin Library every evening and Sunday.

The Lenin Library is one of the great libraries in the world, in the same rank as the Bibliothèque Nationale, the British Library, and the Library of Congress. Today it includes more than 28 million volumes in 283 languages. Even in the 1930s it required a complex of buildings to house its vast holdings in every area of human interest and endeavor. The main reading room and public areas of the library, however, occupied a beautiful three-story mansion built in 1782 in an ornate French style by the great Russian architect Vasily Bazhenov. By the early nineteenth century the house passed into the hands of Count Rumyantsev, who served as the Russian ambassador to Sweden and Prussia, held various high government posts, and was a member of the Academy of Sciences. In 1862 the house was turned into a museum to display the count's art collection. The Rumyantsev Museum later became the Rumyantsev Library, which was renamed for Lenin in 1925.

The main reading room, with long wooden tables for a hundred or more readers, was on the second floor of the library. On the third floor was a small cafe where one could buy tea and cakes. As I read physics and mathematics night after night, I became familiar with the library staff and, at least by sight, with the other regular library users. One of the other readers who was always there was a pretty young woman who dressed very simply. She was as intent on her reading as I was on mine. Sometimes we sat at the same table, and I saw that she was reading mathematics.

After several weeks, during which we began to smile and nod greetings to each other, I spoke to her in the library tea room. I learned that this quiet young woman was very clever and possessed a good sense of humor. Bella Slutskaya, for that was her name, was a year or so younger than I. She was the daughter of a Jewish couple from Kiev. Before the pogroms they were prosperous people; Bella's father owned a factory. But when Simon Petlyura's army took over Kiev, Bella's father was rounded up with other Jews to be shot. At the last moment, he escaped. But the family lost nearly everything it owned. They managed to get to Moscow, where they lived in a small room in a poor suburb and scraped along as best they could.

When the library closed at 10 P.M. every night, Bella and I would walk together the two or three miles to her home. Sometimes the young Israel Gelfand, whom we also met in the library, joined us. Gelfand came to Moscow from a small village and became one of the most famous mathematicians of our time. While walking, we often discussed different aspects of life and science and the books we read.

Step by step, Bella and I fell in love. In 1933 she moved into my simple, small room, and we lived there together until the beginning of World War II. We were very happy. We did not have much money, but we never thought about riches. We were young and enthusiastic about our studies. We had enough money to live. We saved up to go to the theater now and then, and once even to a modest resort. Every day we discussed our books and ideas. We dreamed about our future, when she would be a mathematician and I would be a physicist. We wanted above all to read and learn more.

We had wonderful friends who often came to see us in our tiny room, where there was space for not more than five or six people to stand or sit on our bed. In the late 1930s, Semyon Belenky, Boris Geilekman, and Vitaly Ginzburg became my best friends, and they visited us many times. We spent good evenings with them in that nest chatting, eating, and drinking wine, and it was a happy time indeed.

For a while Bella and I thought we might be married. But during World War II, when we were in Kazan', we separated on good terms. Bella was working at the Kurchatov Institute, and she eventually married a physicist who worked there. I can only be grateful for the experiences we shared and for our amicable parting.

Report to People's Commissar Rykov

In 1932 a new engineer, an expert in transmitters, began to work at the Experimental Radio Station: Professor Alexander Kazantsev of the Moscow Electrical Institute. I suggested to him that it would be interesting to follow up the experiments of the Americans George Breit and Merle Tuve, the creators of the pulse-sounder method for research of the ionosphere. In 1925 Breit and Tuve were the first to establish directly the existence of the ionosphere from the reflection of radio impulses from the conducting layer of that near-earth plasma. I was fourteen years old when that happened.

To conduct similar experiments we needed both a transmitter and a good receiving device with an oscilloscope for observing and recording the reflected radio signals. Kazantsev made the pulse transmitter, and I made the rest of the apparatus. Our simple device was imperfect, but it was one of the first impulse radio sound ionosphere stations in the USSR. Despite its imperfections, we recorded clear reflections from all the layers of the ionosphere. Many of our colleagues, who visited during those observations, were delighted and surprised to see the reflected radio signals on the screen of the oscilloscope. The receiving devices were installed at the house of the vice-director of the station, about five kilometers from our offices, where the transmitter was. Later we learned that Professor Bonch-Bruyevich did the same work simultaneously in Leningrad. About ten years afterward I extended this line of research by creating, together with my collaborators at PhIAN, a unique configuration of devices that allowed us to take perfect films of each reflected pulse from the ionosphere every 1/50 of a second.

In 1931–33 I studied many professional papers on the propagation of radio waves and on the ionosphere, many of which were published in German and English. I thought that a network of collaborating institutes and laboratories should be established to study such scientific and technological problems further. It was clear to me that direct investigations of the ionosphere and of the propagation of radio waves should be accompanied by laboratory experiments for simulating the observed phenomena. I wrote a thirty-one-page proposal for such a network with the aim of sending it to Commissar Rykov. Today when I read what I wrote, its earnest enthusiasm seems a bit naive, but I do not find any scientific mistakes in it.

For some reason I did not tell anyone at the Experimental Radio Station about my report. Perhaps I thought that they would not appreciate it or that they would think me impertinent. Remember that at that time I was only self-educated in radio and physics. But I did want a professional in the field to see it before it went to Rykov. The most distinguished radio engineer I knew of then was the academician Mikhail Shuleikin. He was a professor at the High Technical College of Moscow and also the scientific leader of radio investigations in special military radio laboratories. As I wrote in Chapter 2, much later I learned that Shuleikin found the F-layer of the ionosphere three years earlier than Edward Appleton, who received the Nobel Prize principally for that discovery.

I decided to show Shuleikin my report. Then I learned that he was not only a distinguished professional but also a kind-hearted gentleman. I found his home telephone number and asked him for an appointment. He suggested that I leave the report at his home and then call again. When I telephoned a few days after dropping off my report, he invited me to come to see him.

Shuleikin was forty-eight when I saw him, seven years before his death. He had the appearance of a man with a delicate constitution. He spoke very slowly and quietly, as if he had no energy to spare. But he was very gracious, and we spent a pleasant evening together over tea and cakes. He talked about interesting optical phenomena, such as the oblique reflection of light from rough surfaces. At the end of the evening, Shuleikin said, "Nothing in your report needs to be changed. Everything is correct as it is written. You must submit it to Alexey Rykov." I was very happy to hear this. Shuleikin's approval helped me to be confident about my ideas. I soon brought the report to Rykov's office. Figure 4 shows the first and last pages of that handwritten report, translated below.

Memorandum to the People's Commissar, Comrade Rykov

Faraday, who discovered the laws of electromagnetc induction, Maxwell, the creator of the theory of the electromagnetic nature of light, Hertz, who discovered electric rays, experimentally confirming the Faraday-Maxwell ideas, and Popov, who for the first time tried to transmit rays to distances, are the fathers of contemporary radio techniques! Actually they are pillars of the most interesting and deepest fields of human knowledge, those which lead us to the final goal, the knowledge of substance.

The nature of electromagnetic oscillations in all the frequency band, starting with the long low frequency waves of wireless telegraphy, was confirmed.

There are ringing and steadfast words of Hertz in his report of September 1889: "The light is an electrical phenomenon, the light itself, the light of the Sun, the light of a candle, the light of the firefly. . . ."

. . . A brief review of the contemporary knowledge of the ionosphere and propagation of radio waves, the method of their investigation, and some conclusions are given on pages 2, 3, [and] 30 of this manuscript. One of the most important conclusions is the necessity for a laboratory simulation of the process in the ionosphere (i.e., in a magnetoplasma) at a special institute.

I see how such an institute can promote fast progress of science. And as Dr. P. Meny wrote in his book: "Undoubtedly that day is not far away, when such a scientific radio station will appear, where physicists will be able to devote themselves to abstract scientific investigations." I am sure this day is now coming for us, it is the tomorrow day. Let us imagine that such a scientific radio station exists; it is abstract in its investigations, but it does not forget that such an abstraction, a distraction, is only the way, the method and not its essence.

Ya. Alpert

January 9, 1933

Not long afterward I was asked to see Shostakovich. He was most polite and spoke positively of our first meeting. But whereas during that meeting he had been expansive and jovial, now he was a man of another style. He seemed both anxious and stern, as if he were trying to keep troubling thoughts in check. He said, "Yours is a good idea, but now is not the right time to promote it." Much later, remembering that meeting and Shostakovich's mood, I imagined that in 1933 he already feared that the sword of Damocles hung over him. For it is sad to relate here that Shostakovich and Rykov both became victims of Stalin's terror. Rykov was condemned to death in March 1938. He was shot two days after his sentence was passed. I do not know exactly when Shostakovich was arrested and executed, but I do know that was his fate.

Soon after seeing Shostakovich I decided to enter the physics department of Moscow State University. I was very much aware of the gaps in my education. Since first arriving in Moscow I had made it a habit to go every week or two to the university physics department to read the bulletin boards. I began to learn who was who in the world of physics and came to know figures such as Mandelshtam by sight. And whenever I read on the bulletin board that there would be a public lecture, I tried hard to attend. In this way I attended lectures

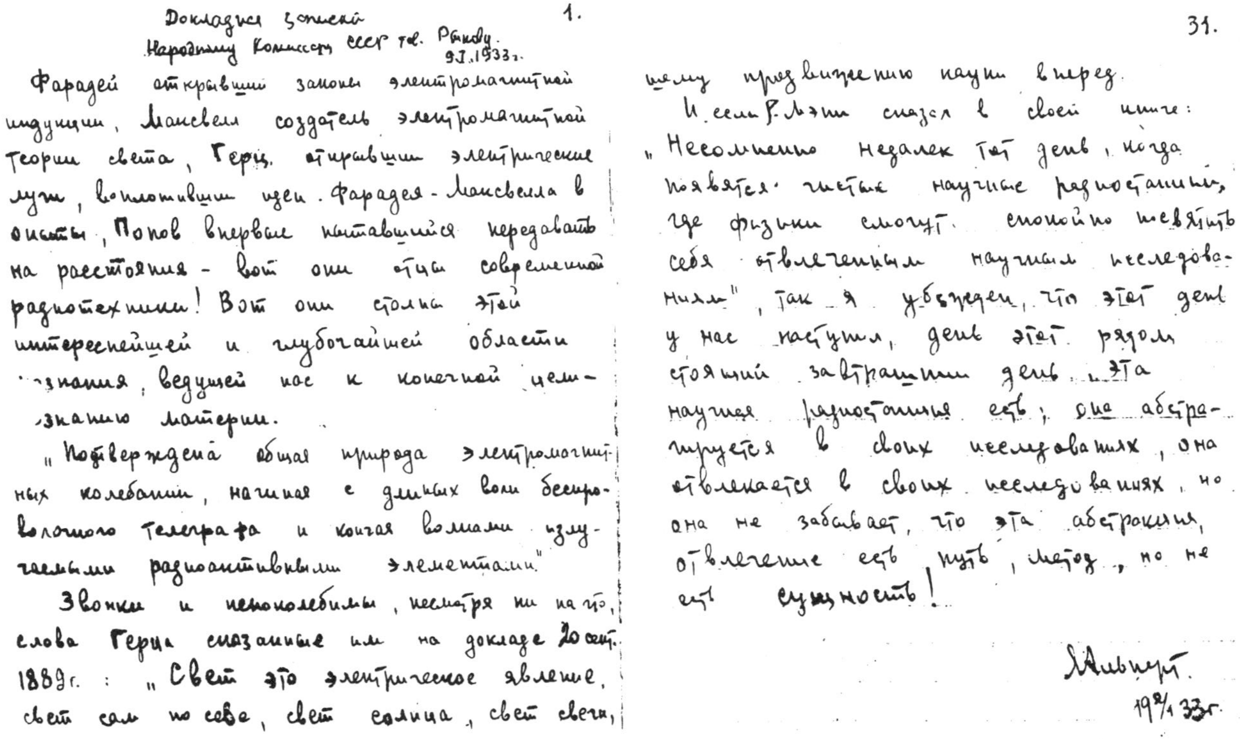

1.

Докладная записка
Народному Комиссару СССР тов. Рыкову.
9.I.1933 г.

Фарадей открывший законы электромагнитной индукции, Максвелл создатель электромагнитной теории света, Герц открывший электрические лучи, воплотивший идеи Фарадея-Максвелла в опыты, Попов впервые пытавшийся передавать на расстояния – вот они отцы современной радиотехники! Вот они столпы этой интереснейшей и глубочайшей области познания, ведущей нас к конечной цели – познанию материи.

„Подтверждена общая природа электромагнитных колебаний, начиная с длинных волн беспроволочного телеграфа и кончая волнами излучаемыми радиоактивными элементами"

Звонки и непоколебимы, несмотря ни на что, слова Герца сказанные им на докладе 20 сент. 1889 г.: „Свет это электрическое явление, свет сам по себе, свет солнца, свет свечи,

31.

всему продвижению науки вперед.

И если Р. Лэпп сказал в своей книге: „Несомненно недалек тот день, когда появятся чистые научные радиостанции, где физики смогут спокойно посвятить себя отвлеченным научным исследованиям", так я убежден, что этот день у нас наступил, день этот рядом стоящий завтрашний день и эта научная радиостанция есть; она абстрагируется в своих исследованиях, она отвлекается в своих исследованиях, но она не забывает, что эта абстракция, отвлечение есть путь, метод, но не есть сущность!

19/I 33 г.

4. The first and last pages of the thirty-one-page memorandum submitted to Commissar Rykov on 9 January 1933

by Mandelshtam, Alexander Witt, and even the great Danish physicist Niels Bohr, among others. That lecture hall was for me a sanctum sanctorum. It represented the world of physicists I wanted to join, and I dreamed about entering it as a bona fide student of the university.

It would certainly have been nice to be able to become a full-time student. But I needed to earn my living. So I enrolled in the university as an external student, carrying a full course load but submitting some of my work by correspondence, and continued to work at the Experimental Radio Station. At the end of 1934 I learned from the newspapers that the Academy of Sciences was moving both its headquarters and the Physical Institute of the Academy of Sciences, PhIAN, from Leningrad to Moscow. If the Experimental Radio Station of the Ministry of Communications was my university, the Physical Institute was my academy of higher learning. But that tale requires a chapter of its own.

7

My Academy

Having read in the newspaper that the Academy of Sciences' Physical Institute (PhIAN), the academy's preeminent physics institute, was moving from Leningrad to Moscow, I went to its new location and found an almost empty building. I approached one of the few people in the building and explained that I was a radio technician and that I was looking for a job. This man pointed to another man and told me, "There is Nikolai Papalexi. Go talk to him." It was my good fortune that Nikolai Papalexi, the head of PhIAN's oscillation laboratory, was there that day.

My job interview with Papalexi was very short. I described my work at the Experimental Radio Station. In response, Papalexi immediately offered me a job as a laboratory assistant in the oscillation laboratory. The job paid only about half as much as my job at the radio station. But I felt lucky to begin to work among distinguished physicists. In due course, PhIAN became my academy of higher learning.

When I first reported for work, however, there was no one to assist. The scientist under whom I was supposed to work, Vladimir Migulin, was still working in Leningrad, along with three other of Papalexi's collaborators: Agasi Charakhchyan, Ashot Melikyan, and Evsey Pumper. Four other members of the oscillation laboratory, Maxim Divilkovsky, Semyon Khaikin, Mikhail Philipov, and Sergei Rytov—all past students of Leonid Mandelshtam at

Moscow State University and now themselves faculty members there — divided their time between the university and the institute.

At that time I learned from Sergei Rytov that Divilkovsky had transcribed an entire course of Mandelshtam's lectures, "The Theory of Oscillations," given over two terms in 1930–31 and 1931–32, and that students sometimes borrowed his transcription. At Rytov's suggestion, I asked to borrow it. For my first couple of months at PhIAN I diligently studied the transcription and wrote it down in a notebook word for word, and diagram for diagram, so that I would have my own copy, 161 pages written in a very small script (figure 5). I still have that thick notebook today. For many years, Divilkovsky's transcription passed from hand to hand among physics students as a treasurehouse of insights into physics. Eventually Mikhail Leontovich edited the transcribed lectures and published them as volume 4 of *The Complete Works of Leonid Mandelshtam.*[1]

Mandelshtam was an excellent teacher and a great scientist, the most distinguished of the physicists who saw deeply the oscillatory nature of various kinds of physical phenomena. His maxim was, "Optics, Mechanics, Acoustics all speak their national languages. Their international language is the language of the theory of oscillations." As I said at the beginning of this book, Mandelshtam was the guru of one of the most noted groups of physicists in the Soviet Union. His scientific prestige in both the USSR and the West was enormous. When he was elected to the Academy of Sciences he was endorsed by dozens of Soviet institutes. As for his standing in the West, let me give you some examples.

The German physicist and future Nobel laureate Max Born resigned from the Nobel Prize committee because Mandelshtam and Grigory Landsberg never received the prize, as Chandrasekhara Raman did in 1930, for discovering the combination scattering of light. With K. S. Krishnan, Raman published a short paper on the discovery in the English journal *Nature* in 1928. Raman brought his paper to *Nature* just after visiting Mandelshtam in Moscow. At that meeting Mandelshtam told Raman of experiments Landsberg and he had done to establish the existence of this phenomenon in crystals. Mandelshtam and Landsberg had in fact already tried to publish their results in 1926. They had not been able to do so because of Russian secrecy regulations. Mandelshtam added that he was also preparing the quantum theory of the effect. Raman made no mention of Mandelshtam's and Landsberg's work in his paper in *Nature*. They published their paper on combination scattering of

1. L. I. Mandelshtam, *Complete Works* (Moscow: Publishing House of the Academy of Sciences of the USSR, 1948–55).

можно определить значение u в любой точке внутри объема v, если заданы значения u на поверхности объема.

Найденное решение при этом единственное; это следует из того, что если $u - u' = 0$ на границе, то оно равно нулю и во всех точках внутри объема [доказательство геометрическое простое: сила — вектор потенциальный, и замкнутых линий нет; если источников нет, то и поля нет].

Спрашивается: существует ли потенциал внутри объема v при всяком, произвольном распределении его на поверхности?

Составим ур-ие: $u(p) = \int_S v(p') \frac{\partial}{\partial u}\left(\frac{1}{r}\right) dS$, где p — точка внутри объема, p' — точка на поверхности. $u(p)$ и $v(p)$ — вспомогательные функции; $v(p)$ удовлетворяет ур-ию Лапласа всюду, и всюду непрерывна. $u(p)$ имеет скачок на поверхности. Если потенциал есть $u_i = f(p)$, то всюду внутри объема: $u_i = u - 2\pi v(p)$, откуда:

$$\int \dot{v}(p') \frac{\partial}{\partial u}\left(\frac{1}{r}\right) dS - 2\pi v(p) = f(p), \text{ или: } v(p) = \frac{1}{2\pi}\int v(p') \frac{\partial}{\partial u}\left(\frac{1}{r}\right) dS - \frac{1}{2\pi} f(p)$$

Это — неоднородное интегральное ур-ие с ядром $\frac{\partial}{\partial u}\left(\frac{1}{r}\right)$. Наш вопрос теперь звучит так: имеет ли это ур-ие всегда решение, при значении $\lambda = \frac{1}{2\pi}$, и произвольной функции $f(p)$? Но однородное ур-ие заведомо не имеет решения при этом значении λ, ибо если $f(p) = 0$, то потенциал всюду нуль. Так как наша теорема об альтернативе верна и при несимметричном ядре, то значит неоднородное ур-ие всегда имеет решение при любом виде $f(p)$

light in 1928, but it appeared four months after Raman's.[2] I think that Mandelshtam anticipated the phenomenon even earlier through his deep intuition into the oscillating nature of physical phenomena.

I mentioned in the previous chapter that in 1934 I attended a lecture at Moscow State University by Niels Bohr, the 1922 Nobel laureate in physics. (The 1926 Nobel laureate in physics, Jean Baptiste Perrin, also spoke that day.) During the question period following his lecture, Bohr quickly answered every question put to him except one. On this particular subject Bohr said that he must defer to Mandelshtam, who understood it much better than he did. The auditorium fell silent, and Mandelshtam, a very modest man, grew disconcerted and began to fidget.

A postcard mailed to Mandelshtam by Albert Einstein in July 1913 also illustrates the great respect Mandelshtam enjoyed in the world community of physicists. The card read, "Dear Mr. Mandelshtam! Just now, at a symposium, I presented your beautiful work on surface fluctuations. Ernfest had told me about it earlier. I regret that you are not here. With all best greetings, A. Einstein." On that card are the signatures of the participants of the symposium.

Unfortunately, many scientists in the United States do not know who Mandelshtam was. Yet the translation of the five volumes of his complete works into English would be an exceptional contribution to the scientific literature and would constitute a solid basis for the teaching of physics to both professionals and students.

Papalexi's achievement may not have been quite as wide-ranging as Mandelshtam's, but he too was a superior scientist, one of the most distinguished radio physicists of his time. He played a dominant role in the development of radio technique and radio physics in Russia. In general he was a pioneering scientist. For example, as early as 1928 he discussed with Mandelshtam a way to observe radio signals reflected back by the moon. On the basis of the development of radar, Papalexi concluded in 1944 that such an experiment was realizable and that it should be possible to estimate the distance between the earth and the moon with a margin of error of only twenty to thirty kilometers. Because of the war, however, Papalexi did not try to carry out the experiment, which would have been far ahead of its time.

Mandelshtam and Papalexi collaborated on research into oscillatory phenomena for dozens of years before PhIAN moved from Leningrad to Moscow. During this period Mandelshtam lived in Moscow, but in addition to teaching

2. L. I. Mandelshtam and G. S. Landsberg, "Scattering of Waves in Crystals," *Zeitschrift für Physik* 50 (1928) 169.

and conducting research at Moscow State University he was a consultant to different institutes in Leningrad. Papalexi moved to Moscow with PhIAN and continued his collaboration with Mandelshtam there. Mandelshtam seldom came to PhIAN, however. He preferred to work in his apartment, which was in the same building as his laboratory in the university physics department. But if he was not often at the oscillation laboratory in the flesh, if you will, the spirit of his ideas was always present.

Whereas I saw Papalexi every work day for many years, I only met Mandelshtam infrequently. The indelible impression Mandelshtam left on me was his extraordinary flexibility of mind. Wherever one's ideas pointed, Mandelshtam immediately followed and understood the essence. I dearly wish that I could discuss with Mandelshtam the work I have been doing over the last few years. I believe that he would at once grasp and like my thinking and that he would have fruitful suggestions to make.

My First Research at PhIAN

Although I went to PhIAN with many ideas for ionospheric research, I did not expect to set my own research agenda as a laboratory assistant. And in any case I wanted to try to contribute to the research program of Mandelshtam and Papalexi and become part of their team. I had no degree, and I knew that I had much to learn.

After studying Mandelshtam's lectures and reading journal articles on nonlinear radio investigations, I decided to attempt an experimental and theoretical study of nonlinear oscillating phenomena in a radio system. The experiment required a radio set that I designed and built myself, using parts left over from my days as a ham radio operator. At that time the Institute of Physics did not yet have a large and well-organized workshop.

No one knew about my research. I worked completely independently, both theoretically and experimentally, and often spent ten hours a day or more in the laboratory designated for Vladimir Migulin. I hesitated to talk about the project, because I was self-educated and I was unsure that I would be able to accomplish the task I had set for myself. Not even Papalexi knew anything about it.

I finished my study in the last few months of 1935. I wrote up the results in my first scientific paper, "On Nonlinear Autoparametric Resonances in a System Under the Influence of Two Sources of Oscillations," and gave it to Papalexi for approval. Meanwhile Migulin appeared, and I gave him a copy of my paper as well. Although he returned it to me without any comment, he had added his name to it as an author, so that the paper read, "V. Migulin and Ya.

Alpert." Naturally I was shocked. Since childhood science had been for me a sacred thing, a "clean" pursuit, something without falsification.

I went to Papalexi. He was astonished that I had done that research, and he understood why I had wanted to present it to him as a surprise. He approved the paper as it was, with a few oral remarks. Then I showed him the other copy, the one to which Migulin had added his name, and asked, "How is this possible?" Papalexi became thoughtful, and then he looked at me and said slowly, "Yakov Lvovich, let it be so. Do not argue over this. You will achieve your own aspiration in your life." That was in 1935, two years before the time of Stalin's terror. Papalexi knew what was what and who was who, as they say. But it was not until many years later that I understood his reaction.

As time went on it emerged that Migulin was indeed a favorite of the system. At the end of World War II he was given charge of an institute at Sukhumi, where captured German scientists were brought and put to work on secret projects. Migulin was also one of the few Soviet scientists who regularly enjoyed the opportunity to travel to the West.

Of course it is not just in the Soviet Union that established scientists unfairly put their names on the work of younger ones. The important thing is that Papalexi would never have done so. And that when he read my paper, Papalexi approved it and quickly asked the director of PhIAN to promote me from laboratory assistant to scientific worker, despite my having no university degree. This was not an aberration. Relations in general were very democratic at PhIAN, and ideas were judged on their own merits. Two other assistants without diplomas, in different departments, received similar promotions around this time.

Mandelshtam, Papalexi, and the Radio Interferometer

The main thrust of the research program conceived and directed by Mandelshtam and Papalexi from 1936 to 1941 was to investigate the velocity of the propagation of radio waves along the surface of the earth. At that time a wide range of values for the velocity of radio waves were published, including even that it was equal to 0.7–0.8 of the velocity of light. Establishing the correct value was a fundamental scientific problem at that time. Finding it would open up a new research field, that of the still-classical problem of the propagation of radio waves along the surface of the earth. The research was also important for various radio navigation purposes and for geodesy, and thus for civil and naval marine research.

To carry out their research program Mandelshtam and Papalexi created the radio interferometer. This instrument allowed the phase structure of the field and velocity of radio waves to be studied deeply for the first time. With it one could measure precisely the average value of the phase velocity of radio waves between two remote points, even ones hundreds of kilometers apart, and estimate the distance between two points if the velocity across the appropriate region were known. The radio interferometer was similar in many ways to the optical interferometer that Michelson and Morley used to test whether space was a vacuum or was filled with a substance known as the ether. It was designed and adjusted in Leningrad, principally by Eugene Shchyogolev, Ivan Borushko, and Klara Viller. It was later adapted for practical navigational use by the Central Research Institute of Geodesy and by the Hydrographic Department of the Northern Management (*Glavsevmorput'* in Russian) by Gruzinov, Meshcheryakov, Mindlin, Smirnitsky, and many others.

The radio interferometer consists of two separate radio sets, or two stations. One of them is the *setting station;* the second is the *reflecting station.* The setting station is moved from one point to another at various distances from the reflecting station. In some of my experiments, the setting station was set up and carried in a truck, and we made continuous measurements of the phase difference of the radio waves emitted from both stations.

The principle of these methods was schematically as follows. A radio wave of a frequency, f_1, radiated by the transmitter from the setting station (station 1) was received by the receiver of the remote reflecting station (station 2). These electromagnetic oscillations were coherently transformed by station 2 into electromagnetic oscillations of a frequency, f_2, which was precisely equal to $3/2$ f_1. The f_2 oscillations were amplified and radiated by the transmitter at station 2 and received by the receiver at station 1. Then frequency f_1 was slowly increased at station 1 to a value much smaller than f_1. Simultaneously, frequency f_2 of the transmitter of station 2 was also coherently increased. During this operation, the measured difference between the phases of the radiated radio waves at station 1 and of the radio waves reflected by station 2 was estimated. If the distance between the two stations was known, the value of the average phase velocity of those waves was calculated by a simple formula.

We Deploy the Interferometer on Land and Sea

To test the velocity of radio waves propagating along the surface of the earth in varied conditions, Papalexi organized a series of expeditions. The first of these was scheduled to take advantage of a full solar eclipse in the region of the Black Sea in 1936. Papalexi was in the seaport of Novorossiysk with five to seven collaborators. The setting station of the radio interferometer, station 1, was established at Ozereika, a place close to Novorossiysk. With one or two assistants, I established the reflecting station, station 2, at Falshivyi Gelendzhik, at the seashore, and later at Novolazarevskaya, close to Sochi, also at the seashore, thirty and two hundred kilometers respectively from Novorossiysk. At each site we set up a small expedition camp of two tents about five to ten meters from the edge of the sea.

Because the lines of sight between Falshivyi Gelendzhik and Novolazarevskaya, on one hand, and Ozereika, on the other, were under the free sea water, we were able to measure the velocity of the radio waves propagating through a not-very-thick, so-called skin layer of sea water. Sea water is a good electrical conductor. In addition, a calm sea is smooth; it has no deep undulations — roughness or other large obstacles — to reflect and scatter radio waves and thus complicate the routes of their propagation.

The expedition coincided with the solar eclipse so that we could perform a special series of observations specifically to learn the behavior of the phase of the radio waves (including their phase velocity) reflected by the ionosphere during the solar eclipse. Such observations had never before been made by phase methods. For that purpose so-called earth rays, the radio waves that propagate along the surface of the earth, were eliminated at the reflecting point, station 2. I performed the investigations there, using an antenna of a special type that was most sensitive to "sky rays," the radio waves reflected from the ionosphere. Mandelshtam conceived of this antenna and devised the scheme for it. Papalexi visited us at Falshivyi Gelendzhik many times. Once, he came with Mandelshtam to the second observation point in Novolazarevskaya, close to Sochi.

Later in 1936, together with one technician, I made many measurements of the velocity of radio waves in the northern part of the Crimea, on the steppes close to the city of Dzhankoy. The electrical conductivity of solid ground is many thousand times lower than the conductivity of sea water. It was therefore of special interest to measure the velocity of radio waves under such conditions. We spent several weeks at that location. Mandelshtam and Papalexi also visited us there. The reflecting station of the radio interferometer was installed in the cabin of a truck. We traveled by truck to measure the phase velocity at various distances from the setting station.

A large expedition to the Arctic was organized in 1937. This expedition began in Murmansk and used a small hydrographic ship, the *Papanin*. The reflecting station was installed on the ship; the setting station, which I operated with one technician, was on a deserted island, Vol'ostrov. We stayed there for several weeks in late summer, in a camp with three tents and an antenna about fifteen meters high.

Our first day on that island was disturbed by a mystery. When we awoke we found that the pans we used to cook kasha (groats), which were in one tent, had been gotten at by some animals and licked clean. There was also considerable disorder in the tent that served as our storeroom. Groats were our main staple. I decided to keep watch to learn what had eaten our food, and that night I saw a reindeer calmly stroll into our camp and go straight for our kasha. My assistant took a photograph of me with that reindeer, which was so tame that I could pet its face. Unfortunately, the photograph was of very poor quality. We later learned that in the summer people came to the other end of the island to fish. They lived there for weeks and domesticated some of the reindeer, the only permanent inhabitants of the island, which thereby lost their fear of human beings.

It was a nice, romantic life on that small island only a few miles in diameter, watching storms and looking at the waves break on the low-lying shore, among other pleasant activities. It was even quite warm sometimes during the day, although we regularly also had freezing nights. In the morning we awakened to freezing air and washed ourselves with very cold water. All in all, it was an interesting expedition. Our ship had to go to Dickson Island, too. On the way we passed through the small channel that separated the two parts of Novaya Zemlya (New Earth). We clambered on the rocky shore of that long, narrow island and saw the graves of lost pilots who had come to investigate the Arctic. We spent some days at the island settlement of Dickson while waiting for food and fuel. There we lived in a tent camp, instead of in the houses of Dickson. To vary our diet we shot wild ducks, which made for tasty food.

The following year, 1938, I again studied the velocity of radio waves in the steppe region close to Saratov, traveling there in a truck with a technician and a driver. These experiments were of interest because the region provided another type of solid ground. There, with Papalexi's approval, I began an independent study of the phase structure of the electrical field of radio waves in the close region of an antenna. I did this for my Ph.D. thesis and performed the theoretical calculations later, in Moscow. During that expedition we did not live in tents but in a rented apartment in a solitary house on the steppe. We brought a truck from Moscow and set the reflecting station of the radio interferometer in its cabin.

The development of the radio interferometer and the experiments with it constituted a new and outstanding event in radio science. On 28 April 1938 Mandelshtam summarized this work in a talk, "Interference Methods of Investigation of the Propagation of Electromagnetic Waves," at a special general meeting of the Presidium of the Academy of Sciences. This classic lecture was a memorable event for everyone who heard it. In one of his papers the physicist and historian Gennady Gorelik quoted from the diary of the academician Vladimir Vernadsky, the distinguished geochemist and natural philosopher. Vernadsky wrote about Mandelshtam's lecture: "It was a brilliant report. Seldom have I listened to a lecturer as I listened to Mandelshtam. For some reason, it recalled a lecture by [Heinrich] Hertz on his fundamental discovery, which I had heard in my youth in Munich."[3] At the end of the nineteenth century Hertz's experimental discovery of electromagnetic waves confirmed James Maxwell's theoretical prediction of the existence of such waves, which are one of the most fundamental properties of nature.

Mandelshtam and Papalexi presented a full account of the radio interferometer experiments (including their earliest stage at the Leningrad Industrial Institute in 1933) in *The Newest Investigations of the Propagation of Radio Waves,* a collection of papers which they edited and to which they contributed two of the most basic papers. The book was prepared for publication in 1941, but because of the war it was not published until 1945. It is unfortunate that the book was not translated into English. I wrote two papers for that book. Among other results, the book reported the first correct measurements of the velocity of radio waves, which we found to be only 1, 2, or 3 percent less than the velocity of light, depending on the dispersion of the waves in different media. This result was a milestone in modern radio physics.

Recalling the experiments of 1937 and 1938, I am reminded of those terrible years that were the worst stage of Stalin's terror. Like many others I did not understand fully what Stalin was doing to Russia. Only much later did we comprehend it all. Nevertheless, I did see and was greatly disappointed by the contradictory behavior of our leaders, by the general Soviet policies, and particularly by Stalin's friendship with Fascist German leaders and the fact that the Soviet government did not officially protest the brutal anti-Semitic pogroms in Germany. In those years I spoke out publicly about those events, writing letters to *Pravda.* Not one of my letters was published, however, nor was there any response from *Pravda*'s editor. No doubt the KGB watchers at *Pravda* noted these letters, however. Perhaps the letters were the KGB's first signal that I would have to be watched carefully and eventually dealt with in some way. In one letter (figure 6) I wrote the following:

> Dear Editorial Staff,
>   For several years all of progressive mankind and the Soviet people have been filled with indignation by the so-called "politics" of the brutal and thoroughly rotten gang of the Fascist "Leaders" and their dregs of society.

3. G. Gorelik, "Philosophical Grounds of the Soviet Atom Project," *Priroda* 7 (1994): 68.

<u>Уважаемая Редакция!</u>

В течении последних лет, все прогрессивное человечество и весь советский народ много раз возмущались так наз. „полицией" своры озверевших и прогнивших насквозь фашистских „руководителей" и их „подсобников".

Последние дни, озверевший фашизм убедительно показывает всему миру какого его знамя. Еврейские погромы в Германии вызывают сильное возмущение в самых широких недрах советского народа. Всему миру ясна бандитская идея ~~фашизма~~!

Самые широкие круги советского народа уверены в том, что советское правительство не может обойти молчанием эти „внутренние дела" Германии. Тем более интересно знать какие шаги принимает наше правительство в знак протеста против этих диких проявлений фашизма.

Буду очень благодарен, если вы найдете возможным ответить мне по указанному ниже адресу. С тов. приветом Шильберг
19.38.

6. The author's letter to *Pravda*, 20 October 1938

In the last days the fascists have demonstrated their brutality to the whole world. The Jewish pogroms in Germany arouse the strong indignation of the Soviet people. The gangsterish nature of fascism is clear for the whole world! Wide circles of the Soviet people are sure that the Soviet government cannot ignore those "internal affairs" of Germany. It is important for us to know about the protest and actions of our government against those wild manifestations of fascism.

I shall be very grateful for your answer to the address below.

With comradely regards,

Ya. Alpert

20 October 1938

At this time I passed a personal milestone. I completed four final examinations at Moscow State University together with regular students of the university and was graduated with honors in 1939 as a radio physicist. A story acclaiming my performance was published in the university newspaper, as I was the first person to pass the exams with the highest possible grades. My paper on nonlinear oscillations was accepted as my thesis.

. . . and in the Air

At the end of 1939 and the beginning of 1940 I made several flights in a balloon to study how the phase structure and velocity of radio waves change as the waves propagate up and away from a ground-based source. The point of the flights was to ascertain at what altitude the radio waves ceased to be influenced by the earth. For these experiments and some earlier ones I designed a new variant of the radio interferometer, a radio dispersion interferometer, for measuring the phase difference between two coherent radio waves radiated from a single point. The new instrument was built at PhIAN.

The regular radio interferometer, consisting of a transmitter and a receiver, could only send and receive waves on one frequency at a time. The dispersion interferometer had two transmitters, whose frequencies could be adjusted separately, and two receivers with recording devices. The receivers measured the differences in phase of the two frequencies.

The twin transmitters broadcast their signals from PhIAN's laboratory in Moscow. I monitored the receivers and recorders in the gondola of the balloon twenty to thirty kilometers outside Moscow at altitudes up to several kilometers. Sometimes I flew alone with the pilot; sometimes we were accompanied by Peter Ryazin, a colleague from PhIAN. For the flights we wore specially insulated flying suits and parachutes. We flew where the wind took us, but we only went up for an hour or two in fine weather. A truck followed us on the ground and collected us, the balloon, and the other equipment when we landed.

The balloon flights were exciting and fun. I wanted to parachute from the gondola to see what that would be like, but I was not allowed to do so. Because a free-flying balloon's descent cannot be precisely modulated, there were occasional moments of tension when we landed, especially on windy days. The landing procedure was first to release gas from the balloon and then, on nearing the ground, to throw out a long, heavy cable as a drag. One day, as we descended in an area of summer and weekend dachas, we threw out the drag cable just as a gust of wind spun the gondola around like a top. The combined impact of the wind gust and the drag cable hitting the ground tipped the gondola and spilled us over the side. Luckily we were only a couple of feet from the ground when this happened and we hurt only our pride. But then as we were picking ourselves up we found ourselves surrounded by armed soldiers. Unbeknownst to us we had landed at the dacha of the USSR's defense minister, Klimentiy Voroshilov. Once we explained what we were doing and showed the soldiers our flight permit, all was well. Nevertheless we were shocked by that event.

The Stalin Prize, 1939–1941

After the balloon flights I summarized my Ph.D. dissertation and completed theoretical calculations that were connected with that study. I also wrote some papers. Close to that time the Soviet government announced that beginning in 1940 the best works in the various branches of art, literature, science, theater performance, and so on would be honored each year by what would be known as the Stalin Prizes. Committees composed of distinguished artists, scientists, writers, and others were organized to select the recipients. The prize was of high monetary value compared with the highest annual income of the average Soviet citizen. The inaugural prizes were to be awarded at the end of 1940.

As I related in the first chapter, I was astonished and pleased to learn that the scientific council of PhIAN had submitted my name, along with those of Vladimir Migulin and Peter Ryazin, for the inaugural Stalin Prize in physics. Apparently, as I also noted above, the council wanted to make a point of honoring and encouraging younger scientists. The work cited by PhIAN was the series of investigations described above from 1936 to 1940 on the propagation of radio waves. The submission was accepted by the presidium of the Academy of Sciences. The academy's recognition of our achievement, and particularly of my contributions, was indeed an honor. My contributions to that work were the experiments described above, which I conducted. An important theoretical part of our research had been done by Ryazin. I also did some theoretical calculations. Migulin's part was the least—at that time, he was formally my boss at PhIAN. Remember that not much earlier I had been graduated from Moscow University and had not yet defended my candidate of science (Ph.D.) thesis. I did so only in 1941, before the beginning of World War II. Although I remember well how excited the members of the Physical Institute and my friends were about my being nominated for the prize, my spirits did not soar. I was glad, but I took it in stride.

Months passed. One day the academician Abram Ioffe, the chair of the award committee for physics, told a colleague—who in turn told me; it was not a secret—that our work had been chosen for the first-level prize in physics. The second-level prize was to be awarded to Flyorov and Petrjak from Ioffe's physical institute in Leningrad. All twenty-one members of the committee affirmed the selection. Soon I was called by the presidium of the Academy of Sciences. I was informed that in a few days they would ask me to come to the presidium in the morning to talk briefly about the work that my colleagues and I were doing. They said that on the morning of that day *Pravda* would officially announce the Soviet government's decision about the prizes and that representatives of all the scientific works of the academy that received prizes would convene and be congratulated. I was also invited to meet with the broadcasting committee to speak about the prize, so that my speech could be recorded for later broadcasting. I still have a copy of that hurriedly written speech.

On the day of the meeting at the presidium, there was nothing in the newspapers about the Stalin Prizes. Early in the morning a call from the academy informed me that the prizes had been canceled. Only later did the following story become known. On the night before the prizes were to be announced, Prime Minister Vyacheslav Molotov showed Joseph Stalin the text that had been prepared for the newspaper. It was well known that Stalin often had such meetings late at night. Stalin looked at the paper and said that that issue of *Pravda* had to be canceled. He declared that the committee's decision was wrong, that it had to be revised because the front-rank workers who had broken various records in mining, textile production, and so on, such as the exemplary miner Stakhanov, had not been recognized. Those typeset newspaper pages were destroyed and other information substituted.

In 1942 the committee for the Stalin Prizes decided to honor well-established scientists, taking into account their lifelong achievements. Mandelshtam and Papalexi were awarded the prize, and they were cited in particular for their work on radio wave propagation. I was indeed happy about that decision. Curiously, however, my speech about receiving the Stalin Prize was

Дорогой Яков Львович,

Мы рады отметить, что работы, за которые была присуждена Сталинская премия, были выполнены, благодаря дружному и умелому сотрудничеству всего коллектива, в котором Вы принимали существенное участие.

Примите наши самые искренние приветы и наилучшие пожелания.

Л. Мандельштам

Н. Папалекси

7. "Dear Yakov Lvovich,/ We are pleased to point out that the works which were nominated for the Stalin Prize were performed due to the concerted efforts and skillful collaboration of all the team and your considerable participation in it. We send you our very sincere regards and very best wishes,/ L. Mandelshtam, N. Papalexi."

broadcast after all. By chance my home receiver was turned on, and Bella and I heard the taped speech. Later Papalexi gave me a short note signed by both him and Mandelshtam (figure 7) and an envelope with a substantial part of their monetary award. They thanked me for my considerable contribution to the work cited by the prize committee.

The question of who receives credit for what is a common one in the scientific community. It arose for me many times. For example, in 1945, Stalin decreed that there should be special celebrations to mark the 220th year of the Academy of Sciences. In connection with this Sergei Vavilov published a seventy-one-page pamphlet, the cover of which (figure 8) read as follows:

> Academy of Sciences of the U.S.S.R.
> Lebedev Physical Institute
> Academician S. N. Vavilov
> Physical Cabinet
> Physical Laboratory
> Physical Institute

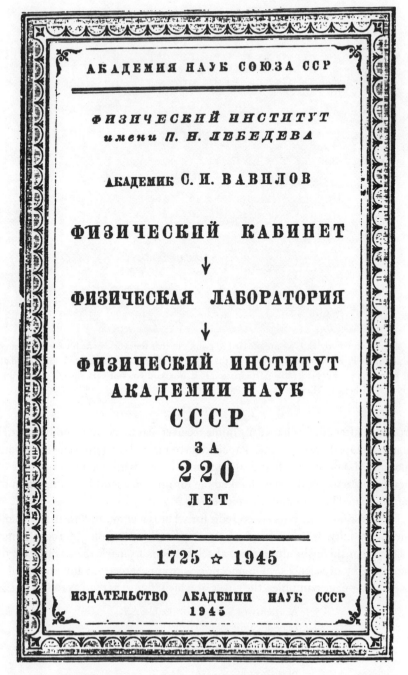

 АКАДЕМИЯ НАУК СОЮЗА ССР

ФИЗИЧЕСКИЙ ИНСТИТУТ
имени П. Н. ЛЕБЕДЕВА

АКАДЕМИК С. И. ВАВИЛОВ

ФИЗИЧЕСКИЙ КАБИНЕТ

↓

ФИЗИЧЕСКАЯ ЛАБОРАТОРИЯ

↓

ФИЗИЧЕСКИЙ ИНСТИТУТ
АКАДЕМИИ НАУК
СССР
З А
220
ЛЕТ

1725 ☆ 1945

ИЗДАТЕЛЬСТВО АКАДЕМИИ НАУК СССР
1945

8. The cover of the PhIAN volume celebrating the 220th year of the Academy of Sciences

The Academy of Sciences of the U.S.S.R.
over
220 Years
1725–1945
Publishing House of the Academy of Sciences

This account of PhIAN's storied history included a list of the recent studies, "which at least seem to be the most considerable in importance." The first two studies in that list are

1. "The interferometer method of investigation of propagation of radio waves," L. I. Mandelshtam and N. D. Papalexi
2. "Propagation of radio waves above the Earth's surface," L. I. Mandelshtam, N. D. Papalexi, P. R. Ryazin, E. L. Feinberg, V. V. Migulin

From a purely scientific point of view, item 1 deserves its preeminence. But, as I have stated, the radio interferometer method was conceived not at PhIAN but at the Central Radio Laboratory in Leningrad by Mandelshtam, Papalexi, and many of their young colleagues. Its use was brought to fruition at PhIAN, however, and that is what item 2 commemorates. This achievement is the same one for which PhIAN's scientific council nominated me, together with Migulin and Ryazin, for the Stalin Prize in 1940. Yet my name is absent from the list given here and from the pamphlet as a whole. Of those who are listed, only Mandelshtam and Papalexi were principal participants in the work. Ryazin contributed significant theoretical calculations used in that work. Feinberg conducted some peripheral theoretical studies of radio wave propagation, but they were not connected with the radio interferometer investigations that were nominated for the Stalin Prize. His results were never used by us in the treatment of our experimental data, and he was not nominated by PhIAN for that prize. Migulin took part in only a few of the experiments described above. I conducted most of these experiments, and I also made some theoretical calculations connected with them.

I do not mention this story as it concerns me, although I had made the main experimental contribution to this work. Certainly it was very strange, but also funny, to find myself left out of an official history of PhIAN's accomplishments. (Ironically, I was the scientific secretary for PhIAN's part in the academy-wide commemorations ordered by Stalin.) Far more important to me was that Mandelshtam and Papalexi recognized my contributions by writing to me so graciously and so generously sharing with me a part of the money that went with the Stalin Prize. My point here is only to show how the truth was insulted even at an institute such as PhIAN, which boasted many people of integrity in its ranks, beginning with Mandelshtam and Papalexi and including, not least, Mikhail Leontovich, Sergei Vavilov, and many others.

From my experience of Sergei Vavilov, I cannot believe that he was responsible for the obscene omission of my name from the list of those who did the radio wave propagation work. I suspect that the deed was done by one of the people who prepared data for that pamphlet. Perhaps because he was very busy, Vavilov trusted them and did not check the proofs carefully. After the fact it was wise to let sleeping dogs lie.

Wartime, 1942–1944

After Hitler's sneak attack on Russia, the Great Patriotic War with Germany began on 22 June 1941. The next day, as part of a series of steps to mobilize Russian science in the war effort, the presidium of the Academy of Sciences temporarily transferred me from PhIAN to the Geophysical Institute of the academy to accelerate testing of a radio-phase navigation system for the air force. This system was developed by the engineer Boris Konoplyov of that institute. (See Chapter 10 for a discussion of this inventive and energetic engineer, whose life was lost during a calamitous space rocket launching.) I worked with Konoplyov's team until October 1941, when the Academy of Sciences and many of its institutes, including PhIAN, moved from Leningrad and Moscow to Kazan', a city on the Volga River about 850 kilometers almost due east of Moscow.

It should be remembered that in the fall of 1941 German troops reached the outskirts of Moscow. Certainly, we were striving to help the Soviet military. Mandelshtam and many other older, distinguished scientists were moved by the academy to the eastern part of Russia, to a beautiful place close to the forest known as Borovoye, about fourteen hundred kilometers from Kazan'. Papalexi moved with us to Kazan' and often visited Mandelshtam in Borovoye. There they wrote their papers for the book that I mentioned earlier.

At the beginning of 1942, Sergei Rytov and I began to develop a radio system that could diminish the noise induced in the radio receiver by varying local sources of electrical oscillations. The main idea, influenced by Papalexi in particular, was the following. Radio noise induced in the receiver can be compensated for by an artificial signal, a subsidiary source of electromagnetic oscillations inserted into the input of the receiver, if its spectrum is similar to the spectrum of the noise. If the source of the noise were a harmonic oscillation, then the oscillations could in some cases be completely compensated for by oscillations of the opposite phase. Fully compensating for, and thus silencing, noise of a complicated shape is impossible. Nevertheless, our laboratory tests showed that this method sometimes worked well, and we began to develop a radio noise compensator. In 1942, together with Rytov and two or three technicians, I performed experimental tests on this system under actual conditions in the neighborhood of Kazan'. The theory of the method and some results of our laboratory tests would be published in 1944. In the meantime we thought that such a system might be especially effective on ships. I communicated with the navy, which decided to test the laboratory model of our radio noise compensator on military ships based not far from Murmansk at the Polyarnoye naval base. At the beginning of 1943, I left with two technicians to carry out that test. We had to obtain special permission from naval headquarters in Moscow to work with navy personnel and to travel by train from Moscow to Murmansk.

On the way we spent one night in Moscow. My assistants slept at their parents' homes, but I had a curious night. At that time the small apartment house in Moscow where I had been living with Bella was not fit for habitation. There was neither heat nor water. I therefore decided to go to the Hotel Metropol at Theater Square for the night. It was early evening, about 6 P.M., and the next day, very early in the morning, I would be traveling with my assistants to Murmansk by train. All the rooms at the Metropol were occupied, however. I showed the manager of the hotel my travel authorization, which said that I was from the Academy of Sciences and was traveling from Kazan' to Murmansk on naval business. He informed me that another physicist had arrived from Kazan' the day before and that he also was traveling on naval business. That man was Igor Kurchatov—the physicist who later became the Russian counterpart of J. Robert Oppenheimer, the director of the Manhattan Project. Unfortunately, he was not in his room at the time. To my surprise, the manager, who seemed to have thought the matter over, said, "Go to Kurchatov's room and wait for him." Then he gave me the key to the room. When I entered the room I found that there was only a single large bed. I was so tired that I lay down on one side of the bed and fell asleep right away. In my sleep I heard someone say, "Do not worry. Sleep. Sleep." It was Kurchatov.

Later I learned that Kurchatov had been in Moscow to visit the same office of naval administration as I had. He was also going to Polyarnoye, where he would test his and Anatoly Alexandrov's invention against marine mines. Both were members of Ioffe's Physical Technical Institute of Physics, which moved to Kazan' from Leningrad because of the war. Although Kurchatov and I knew each other, we never had any long meetings and discussions together. The following day at dawn I left the room while Kurchatov was fast asleep. When I met Kurchatov in 1950 and 1958 (see Chapter 2), I did not remind him of how we slept in one bed in Moscow one night at the beginning of 1942. It was the war, people behaved differently. In hindsight, I think he might well have enjoyed the reminiscence.

The Polyarnoye Naval Base

My trip to Murmansk and Polarnoye was the only time when my life directly touched the military conditions of the war. By 1943 the German troops that once knocked at Moscow's door had been pushed back and the Germans were on the defensive. But from a point about a hundred kilometers outside Moscow the Moscow-Murmansk train route was regularly bombed by German aircraft. The threat from the air meant that trains had to try to race along the dangerous track. Our train was stopped when there was any sign of risk, and there were many. It seems that the engine driver was in radio communication with a special security service. We were luckier than many other trains, which were bombed on their way to Murmansk, and we made the run without any losses. But much of Murmansk was smashed to rubble by the almost continual German air raids. We spent two nights there, staying on the second floor of a hotel whose third and fourth floors and roof had been destroyed by bombs and fire.

The technicians and I were then taken to Polyarnoye by ship. There was no fighting or bombing, but there was great tension in the air. Soviet and Allied ships and submarines were continuously coming and going on military duty. People were nervously waiting for ships and crews to return safely. We felt this strained atmosphere everywhere in Polarnoye.

All the while there were dancing parties, good movies, shows by performing artists, and meetings with writers and poets at different clubs. The American and British ships often screened U.S. and English films. I especially remember enjoying two movies starring Vivien Leigh and Laurence Olivier, *Waterloo Bridge* and *That Hamilton Woman*. Both movies were relevant to our wartime experiences. *Waterloo Bridge* was about the bombing of that bridge in London, and *That Hamilton Woman* concerned the travails, mainly romantic to be sure, of England's greatest naval hero, Lord Nelson. At that time it was very seldom possible to see a movie from the West in Moscow.

Many people were involved in efforts to help military personnel handle the stresses of the war. On the train to Murmansk, I rode in a private compartment and the technicians rode in another. In my compartment there was space enough for all our boxes of technical devices. There was also another passenger, the Soviet writer Vladimir Stavsky, who had been decorated after the revolution for his service in 1918–20. We had an enjoyable conversation about literature, science, morality, government, and many other things. Stavsky was traveling to Murmansk to read to military personnel from his novels. Shortly after that he lost his life in some accident of the war. Many years later his biographers came to see me to ask about our conversation. In his speeches in Murmansk and in some of his papers he had mentioned me. It seems he was much impressed by the range of my interests and reading, particularly my knowledge of the Russian poets.

We began our experiment in Polyarnoye on submarines. From the stories of submariners I learned about the hard conditions they endured during the war. They were in a more terrible situation than those in other military branches. When flying, pilots could freely see the sky and the earth. Submariners were in a dark world, often in a stuffy, hot atmosphere for many hours at a time and even for days. A crew had to keep everything sealed inside or risk being bombed. The discharge of air and water was forbidden while a submarine was submerged, because the submarine could be located by aircraft if bubbles appeared on the surface of the ocean. All excretions, secretions, and other traces of human activity in a submarine had to be undetectable.

After some trials of our equipment on a submarine, we transferred to a destroyer and made extensive tests in the harbor of Murmansk. Air raids frequently happened there. We saw aircraft shot down and pilots escaping by parachute. Often I helped to bring projectiles to the anti-aircraft guns. Ships surrounding us were hit, but we were somehow unscathed.

On 1 May, a favorite festival of the Soviet people to celebrate workers, the captain of the destroyer arranged a wonderful party for us. There was plenty of vodka, real caviar, and other good food. A brief air raid by the Germans also accompanied that party but did not shatter its mood. After our feast I played chess with the captain of another destroyer. Then I examined all the decks of the destroyer up to its apex. The captain told me that there was severe rocking at the apex of the destroyer. It was really so, and I was very shaken there. The captain had made many toasts in our honor, and I had drunk a lot of vodka. But I demonstrated that I was no weaker than the sailors were in the matter of drink. As a result of that swing, on my way down from the apex I retched, which in Russia we describe by saying, "He went to Riga." I do not know the origin of that saying, but such was the case with me at the end of the May festival at the Polyarnoye naval base in 1943.

Our journey back to Moscow was quiet and pleasant. The train did not stop. There were no bombardments. We were not in a special compartment but in a regular one, mostly full of pilots. Many of them were going on short leaves. They were in a good mood, and they told us many frank stories. I often heard that during the war Russian military personnel traveling by train were more frank than they were supposed to be.

Here is one story a captain and a colonel told us on that train trip to Moscow, although it scarcely involved a secret matter. Perhaps it was a legend of war rather than an actual event. In any case they told us that on a quiet day an enemy airplane appeared above Murmansk. A pennant was thrown to the earth. There was a challenge on the pennant: "Russians: Come out and fight!" The Soviet aircraft commander immediately contacted Moscow. Moscow accepted the challenge. One Soviet airplane rose in the air, and a long dogfight ensued. The Fascist airplane was shot down, but the pilot, a young Swede, escaped by parachute. The Soviet pilots declared that Swedish pilots were the best pilots of German aircraft. That pilot was soon after sent to Moscow and made to train Soviet pilots.

Soon after my trip to Murmansk, I returned to Moscow. I no longer went to Kazan', and I began to work again in my laboratory at PhIAN. Once again I did not have to stay in my former room in the small wooden house in Moscow. Instead, Papalexi offered me his large, comfortable apartment, which I occupied alone.

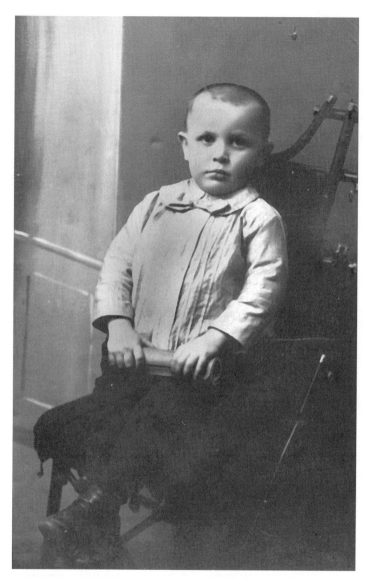

The author at age four, Zhitomir, Ukraine, 1915.

The author's parents, Gittle and Lev Alpert, Crimea, 1928.

The Labor School for Primary Education, Zhitomir, 1925. Ya = Yakov Alpert; 1 = Russian language teacher.

The Moscow Radio Club constructing a short-wave radio transmitter, 1929. Ya = Yakov Alpert.

QSL card received by the author in 1930.

Mosstroy building brigade, Moscow, 1929. Ch = Chernopyatov, principal architect; Ya = Yakov Alpert.

The author with Bella, Moscow, 1932.

Radio equipment devised by the author and used in experiments near Bryansk, 1932.

Leonid Isaakovich Mandelshtam

Nikolai Dmitrievich Papalexi (1), Ivan Borushko (2), Evgeny Shegolev (3), and Klara Viller (4), during PhIAN's experiments at Ozereika on the Black Sea, 1936.

Sergei Ivanovich Vavilov

Mikhail Alexandrovich Leontovich

The author aboard a destroyer, Polyarnoye, Barents Sea, 1943.

The author (2) with Alina Ainberg (1) and other members of his research team at PhIAN, Moscow, 1944.

The members of the 1947 solar eclipse expedition to Brazil aboard the *Griboyedov*. Seated (left to right): the expedition's bookkeeper, the author, Captain Gintsburg, Ushakov, Shishkin, Lebedinsky, and Khaikin. Behind them: Gnevishev (1), Ginzburg (2), Kalinyak (3), Chikhachov (4), Baluyev (5), and Shklovsky (6), Liepaya-Libava, Lithuania.

The author, Alina Ainberg, and Vitaly Ginzburg at the solar eclipse observation booth in Arasha Bareira, Brazil, 1947.

Brazilian visitors at the observation booth.

The senior staff of the solar eclipse expedition with the Brazilian official Benedito Quintino dos Santos. Seated: Mikhailov (left) and Quintino dos Santos (right). Standing (left to right): Lebedinsky, the author, Dukat (a Brazilian interpreter), Ginzburg, Pariisky, Vashanidze, Kalinyak, and Chevishev.

The Indissoluble Four, 1950. Clockwise from top left: Boris Geilekman, Vitaly Ginzburg, the author, and Semyon Belenky.

Irina Chernysheva, near Moscow, 1954.

The author with Vera Krayushkina (1), Vera Morozova (2), Dora Fliegel (3), and other
members of his laboratory at IZMIRAN outside the institute's main building, Vatutenky,
near Moscow, 1961.

The new building for the author's department at IZMIRAN.

Lev Gor'kov's drawing, entitled by the author "The Thinker," an emblem for the author's department at IZMIRAN.

June 15, 1963

Трудно было мне пережить тяжелое период войну. Меня не один раз арестовали, в 1945 январе приговорили на смерть. В слава советской армии я жив. Я живу, работаю и мечтаю о

August 5, 1963

Я создал Венгрия во время фашистского террора "Общество друзей СССР". Не раз сидел в тюрьме, чуть меня не расстреляли. Когда мы стретимся много тебе расскажу.

Geza Penzesh and extracts from his letters (see Chapter 12).

Peter Kapitsa hosts a roundtable discussion in 1973. Left to right: Isaak Khalatnikov, Ilya Lifshitz, Paul Dirac, Kapitsa, Andrei Borovik-Romanov, and Eugene Lifshitz.

Kapitsa's roundtable. Left to right: Nikolai Zavaritsky, Daniel Danin, the author, Yakov Smorodinsky, Isaak Khalatnikov, Ilya Lifshitz, and Paul Dirac.

The refusnik seminar at the apartment of Mark Azbel, 1977, including Irina Brailovsky (1), Mark Azbel (2), Mario Grossi (3), James Langer (4), and Benjamin Levich (5).

The refusnik seminar at Mark Azbel's apartment, 1977, including Andrei Sakharov (6), the author (7), Valdimir Yakir (8), and Benjamin Fain (9).

"40 Years of Research on VLF Propagation: A Tribute to Professor Ya. L. Alpert,"
a special session at URSI's international congress in Helsinki in 1978, including Owen
Storey (1), Dr. Likhter of IZMIRAN (2), and Robert Helliwell (3).

Arno Penzias with the author and Svetlana Alpert.

The refusnik seminar at the apartment of Victor and Irina Brailovsky, 1978, including Joel Lebowitz (1), Victor Brailovsky (2), Jens Larsen (3), Alex Ioffe (4), Ives Quéré (5), and the author (6).

Yuri Orlov in internal exile, 1984.

Andrei Sakharov after his hunger strike
in Gorky, the photograph Elena Bonner
gave the author in 1985 in secret because
"[The authorities] don't know I have it."

The refusnik seminar in honor of Maimonides and Niels Bohr, including Alex Gribanov (1), Edward Nadgorny (2), Leonid Ozernoy (3), Alex Ioffe (4), Alex Roitburt (5), and Leonid Dickey (6). At left hangs an English newspaper with a photograph of Natan Sharansky crossing the border from East Germany to West Germany, 1986.

The refusnik seminar in honor of Maimonides and Niels Bohr, including Mark Freidlin (7), Alexander Lerner (8), Yuri Rodin (9), Solomon Alber (10), and the author (11).

The refusnik seminar in honor of Maimonides and Niels Bohr, including Klots (1), Gribanov (2), Buzytsky (3), Dickey (4), Irlin (5), and Rozenzweig (6), shown with the model boat that was the symbol of the author's Moscow apartment.

The author and Svetlana Alpert with Kevin and Eliza Klose and their children, Moscow, 1981.

Reports from the Moscow Refusnik Seminar, volume 491 of the Annals of the New York Academy of Sciences, 1987.

Joseph Begun's son during a demonstration on the Arbat for Begun's release from prison, Moscow, 1987.

The press conference in Andrei Sakharov's apartment on 24 December 1986, following his release from internal exile.

Mustafa Jamilev and his wife, following his release from exile in Siberia, Moscow, 1986.

With Henry Kissinger at the U.S. Embassy in Moscow, February 1987.

Left to right: Misher Mershion, Elie Wiesel, Herman Kogan, the author, Vladimir Slepak, Inna Begun, and Masha Slepak, in Moscow, October 1986.

With Norman, Charlotte, and Stasya Zabusky, Moscow, 1986.

A farewell meeting at the author's home with Eugene and Marina Chudnovsky, Moscow, 1987.

Members of the French Academy of Sciences visit the refusnik seminar at the author's apartment, 27 June 1987. Standing (left to right): Leonid Brailovsky, Svetlana Alpert, and Victor Brailovsky. Seated (left to right): André Guinier (foreign secretary of the French Academy), the author, Laurant Schwartz, Henri Cartan, Nicole Cartan, and Solomon Alber.

A farewell meeting with Andrei Sakharov and Elena Bonner in their kitchen in Moscow, 1987.

A farewell meeting with Lev and Lyuba Pitaevsky, Moscow, 1987.

With Lev and Lyalya Gor'kov, Moscow, 1987.

With Vitaly Ginzburg, Moscow, 1987.

BLESSED ARE
THE
PEACEMAKERS

*Дорогому Якову Львовичу
и дорогой Светлане
на добрую память*

25/XI-88 А. Сахаров

1989

Andrei Sakharov

The calendar that Andrei Sakharov gave the Alperts on their last meeting.

Françoise, Françoise, Jr., and Owen Storey, Washington, D.C., 1989.

Physics Research Students, May 1907.

N.Papalexi.   H.F.Dawes.   D.F.Comstock   J.Kunz.   F.Zaviska.   W.Burton.

W.A.D.Rudge.   H.F.Biggs.   G.Brodsky.   T.H.Laby.   G.W.C.Kaye.   P.D.Innes.   J.Satterley.   J.W.Bispham.

C.Chittock.   F.Horton.   Miss Saltmarsh.   Prof.J.J.Thomson.   A.A.Robb.   N.R.Campbell.   A.Wood.

C.A.B.Garrett.   W.H.Logeman.   R.D.Kleeman.   J.A.Crowther.

Nikolai Papalexi (first on left in last row) and other physics research students at Cavendish in 1907.

At the Cavendish Laboratories in Cambridge, England (left to right): Gordon Squires, Abram Ioffe, David Shoenberg, John Deakin, Archibald Horvic, Nevill Mott, the author, Antony Hewish, Pam Hicks, Robert Willstrop, Svetlana Alpert, Shirley Fieldhouse, Kenneth Budden, Martin Rees, Antony Pippard, and David Tabor, 1988.

Ives Quéré, Frank Laloe, and Susan Laloe play for the author, Paris, 1990.

With Joseph Birman (left) and Joel Lebowitz at the author's eighty-fifth birthday party.

With Pierre Hohenberg at the author's eighty-fifth birthday party, New York, 1996.

Marina and Eugene Chudnovsky, Miriam Sarachik, and Yuri Orlov, at the author's eighty-fifth birthday party.

Becoming citizens of the United States, Boston, 1993.

With Svetlana at Lake Louise, Canada, March 1996.

8

New Beginnings and New Research, 1944–1951

I consider the years I have described in the previous chapter and the time of the war to have been my "academy." I learned much in that period and I worked much. In my research during those years I mainly followed the scientific program of Mandelshtam and Papalexi. From the very beginning of my work at PhIAN, however, I had my own ideas for research of the ionosphere. I began to realize those ideas at the end of 1943 and the beginning of 1944, a decade after I wrote to Commissar Rykov.

Study of the ionosphere was a new field of research at PhIAN. Nikolai Papalexi supported my aspirations and plans, and he arranged for me to have my own laboratory. He was not only a distinguished scientist; he was a person of high moral standards and good will. I talked earlier about the first seven years of my research at PhIAN. Here I talk about another industrious period at PhIAN, also of seven years' duration and one that was only ended by General Malyshev of the KGB. But first I want to tell you briefly about how I was living at this time.

As I have already said, when I finished my tests of the radio noise compensator in Murmansk and Polarnoye, I did not return to Kazan' to rejoin the other members of PhIAN but went instead to Moscow. The apartment house I lived in before the war was uninhabitable, and Papalexi generously gave me the key to his apartment in one of the most exclusive neighborhoods of Moscow. For several months I lived alone in Papalexi's vast apartment, going to work every day in PhIAN's nearly empty laboratories and taking my meals in the Academy of Sciences' dining hall.

One day as I left PhIAN and began to walk down the street I heard behind me, "Yanya, is that you?" I turned around to see a friend from before the war, Irina Chernysheva. It happened that she was teaching German in the building next door to PhIAN. She had walked out into the street just after me, and she had recognized me from behind.

Irina and I first met in 1933 because of my own efforts to learn German. I wanted to become proficient in the language in order to keep up with the work of German scientists. In the 1930s there was a cultural center in Gorky Park where people could study many different subjects free of charge. When I went there to take a course in German, I was immediately struck by this vivacious young lady with fluent German. We became friends and we took long walks together, speaking German. Irina was very patient with my mistakes, and I must say that our conversations greatly improved my German. But we were both busy with our separate lives and we could not often meet. Then the war came and we lost track of each other.

It was wonderful to see Ira again. In the interim she had married a Russian officer and had a child, a boy about two years old. Irina and the officer had already separated, however, and she was living with her mother and her son, Leonid, in two rooms in a large communal apartment. Not long after our chance meeting, Irina and I realized that we wanted to be together. In 1944 we married, and I moved in with her and her mother and son. We all got along very well together. Irina's mother was a good-humored, clever lady about seventy years old. Leonid eventually became a physicist, and he now works in an institute of the Academy of Sciences.

Later I will speak a little more about Irina and our good life together. What comes to my mind now is the general feeling of optimism we shared at the end of the war. Everyone in Russia had reason to be proud of the mammoth, well-organized war effort. When Fascist Germany surrendered on 7 May 1945, the streets of Moscow were crowded all through the night with happy people looking forward to brighter days. Irina and I were among them.

A Statistically Inhomogeneous Structure of the Ionosphere

The new investigations of the ionosphere plasma that I began at the end of 1943 were mainly labor-intensive experimental work, starting with a modification of the commonly used radio pulse method. But they also involved theoretical calculations. The story of the project well illustrates the obstacles and the opportunities that Soviet scientists faced.

The primary purpose of my new research was to learn in detail the structure and physical nature of the ionosphere. For that purpose I modified the radio pulse method as follows. Our experimental devices permitted the recording of all the radio impulses (50 per second) emitted by the transmitter and reflected by the ionosphere at various fixed frequencies. Such radio pulses are normally emitted every 1/50 or 1/60 second, that is, at a frequency of 50 or 60 cycles a second of the electricity supply. I wanted to learn how the amplitudes of all the sequences of pulses changed over time. The pulses come in doublets of the separated signals of the extraordinary and ordinary packets of waves. The anisotropic nature of the ionosphere, a medium of free electrons and ions in a magnetic field, has a double refracting property that produces the doublets of pulses, the extraordinary and ordinary packets of waves, and oppositely polarizes them.

Soon I learned that it was enough to record these signals every 1/5 to 1/10 second in order to investigate the variations in amplitude of the packets of waves. That result was in itself an important new characteristic of the ionosphere. I estimated the relaxation time, the variability of the conditions of the reflecting zone. Sample records of this are shown in figure 9. On one set of reflections of the doublets of pulses there were quiet conditions. The ionosphere was not disturbed, that is, not obscured by large ionized clouds. Another record showed reflections when the ionosphere was very disturbed; large ionized clouds covered it. Large clouds were those that were many times larger than, or were commensurate with, the so-called reflecting Fresnel zone, named for the French physicist Augustin Jean Fresnel (1788–1827). The incident waves reflected, or let us say scattered, by those clouds produce complicated groups of pulses. Under such conditions, single pulses are not isolated. Yet our main focus was to learn how the amplitudes of individual pulses changed over time under periods that could be considered "quiet."

At those times the amplitude of the pulses changed continually from sequence to sequence, which was an unknown effect. It meant that the reflected undiffused single pulses did not represent individual unique packets of waves. Instead, each was the sum of chaotic interfering reflected radio waves. This brought us to a most important new understanding of the structure of the local reflecting region of the ionospheric medium. It was not a homogeneous medium, even when I saw single reflected pulses, that is, when there were no large ionized clouds in the local reflecting region. This meant that the Fresnel zone of the magnetoplasma that formed the single reflected pulse under quiet conditions consisted of many moving scattering centers, ionized clouds much smaller than the scale of the Fresnel zone, which under different conditions is equal to about twenty to thirty kilometers. The radio waves scattered by such cloud formations produce every single reflected packet of waves.

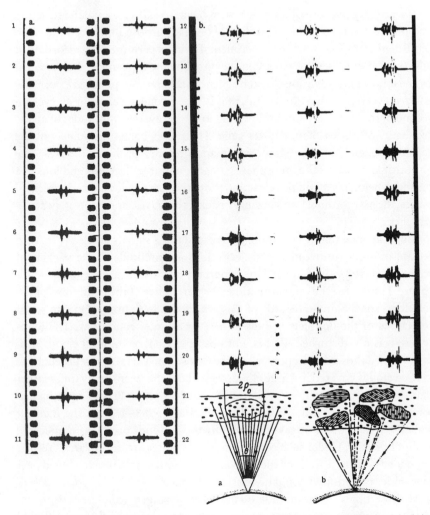

9. Records of doublets of pulses reflected from the ionosphere in quiet (a) and disturbed (b) conditions, filmed with the Zeit Lupe camera

These results led to a new theoretical description of the electric field of reflected packets of waves and of the distribution function of their amplitudes. As a result, I was able to estimate the spectra of velocities of moving scattering centers. Without going into the scientific details of these results here, I can say that the size of these small scattering ionized clouds must be about a hundred meters or less. In a sense, the discovered phenomenon is similar to the Brownian movement of particles in any liquid or to the thermal movement of molecules and atoms in any gas. Those small clouds are scattering centers moving chaotically in the magnetoplasma.

The main conclusion of that research was that the ionosphere is *a statistically inhomogeneous medium*. When I presented these results to the council of PhIAN in a large auditorium, I showed a film of the process I was describing. It was exciting to see the "life" of the ionosphere, the "breathing" of that rapid physical phenomena. The film, as its viewers later told me, was perhaps the first such demonstration of rapid physical processes. I was extremely pleased that Sergei Vavilov, who as director of PhIAN and president of the academy had helped me in organizing the experiments, gave me many words of praise when I finished my presentation.

In that same period I also learned how the trajectories of extraordinary and ordinary waves change in the ionosphere. I measured the direction of the arrival of the doublets of signals, that is, how the energy flux of the signals, the so-called Poynting vector, transfers to the observation point. I calculated the trajectories of the propagation of those packets of waves in the ionosphere theoretically. I also found by my calculations that the direction of the group velocity of those signals is collinear, that is, in parallel, with the Poynting vector. This was a new theorem of electrodynamics, which made such calculations much easier. When I told Eugene Lifshitz about the theory, he included it in an upcoming edition of the prestigious Landau-Lifshitz volumes. He wanted to footnote the fact that I found this theorem. But I told him it was too trifling to note.

One of the research problems I wished to investigate at this time was the process of ionization of the atmosphere at different altitudes above the surface of the earth. As a corollary of that I wanted to estimate the value of the ultraviolet flux of emissions of the sun, which is chiefly responsible for the formation of the ionosphere of the earth. For this purpose it would be useful to make observations during a solar eclipse, when for short periods the moon screens the sun's ultraviolet emissions.

A Solar Eclipse in Moscow, 1945

A solar eclipse took place in Moscow in July 1945. For a week before and a week after the solar eclipse I continuously observed conditions in the ionosphere. Each day I began those observations five to six hours before and up to two hours after the time of the forthcoming solar eclipse.

Nothing unusual occurred until the day of the eclipse, when disturbances in the ionosphere were observed about four hours before the optical eclipse. The fact that the disturbances preceded the optical eclipse indicated that they were connected with the eclipse of the solar wind, the stream of corpuscular particles of protons emitted by the sun. The eclipse of the solar wind occurs before the regular optical eclipse. The stream of these particles stretches out behind the sun like a train. My observation of the ionospheric disturbance gave me the difference in time between the eclipse of the solar wind and the optical eclipse, and this made it possible to calculate the velocity of the solar wind as equal to about 400–500 km/second. It was a new and important characteristic in the knowledge of the physics of the sun. At that time a value of 1,600 km/second had been predicted theoretically by astrophysicists. About ten years later my calculation of 400–500 km/second was confirmed by direct measurements on U.S. satellites. Appleton thought that ascertaining the solar wind's velocity with observations during a solar eclipse would require tests only about two hours before the optical eclipse, because he believed the theoretical value of 1,600 km/sec estimated by the English astronomer Milne. But Milne's value was mistaken. In science, as in the rest of life, we have to believe but also to check. We also need to be lucky. My observations helped not only to establish the true value of the velocity of the solar wind. They were also crucial in showing directly the action of the solar wind on the ionosphere.

I published the results of my observations in *Nature* and in two journals of the Academy of Sciences of the USSR in 1945 and 1946.[1] Nevertheless, when I talked about these experimental results at a conference of the American Geophysical Union in Baltimore in 1988, I learned that American researchers were not familiar with my articles. I was surprised to hear remarks and questions such as "It is impossible!" and "How did you do that?" The audience did not want to accept that I had estimated the true velocity of the solar wind in fine experiments many years before it was done in the West with observations and satellites. American and English scientists did not generally make an effort to follow Russian science closely until after the launch of the first Sputnik, but I thought my *Nature* article might have been noticed.

In 1945 I also found, by treatment of the experimental data on the ionosphere published by U.S. researchers, that the value of the flux of the ultraviolet emissions of the sun was about 1–2 ergs/cm^2, ten to twenty times larger than the value of about 0.1 erg/cm^2 then used by astronomers. In that study it took me a couple of days, with my assistant Alina Ainberg, to solve numerically a nonlinear differential equation "with our fingers" — without the use of a computer. The astrophysicist Joseph Shklovsky wrote about the result in his book *The Solar Corona* and told me that it was a revolutionary element of the knowledge of the sun. Twelve to fifteen years later U.S. researchers confirmed

1. R. L. Smith Rose, "The Solar Eclipse in 1945 and Radio Wave Propagation," *Nature* no. 3976 (January 1946); Yakov L. Alpert, "The Solar Eclipse in 1945 and Radio Wave Propagation," *Doklady* 49, no. 4 (1945); Yakov L. Alpert and B. N. Gorozhankin, "The Solar Eclipse in 1945 and Radio Wave Propagation," *Bulletin of the Academy of Sciences of the U.S.S.R.* 10, no. 3 (1946): 245.

the estimated value of the ultraviolet emissions of the sun by direct measurements on satellites.

This sketch of my work shows that my last years at PhIAN were fruitful. I had worthwhile ideas, and I knew how to develop them. But I was stopped by General Malyshev, as I noted above.

How I Realized My Experiments

Despite the highly schematic description of the experiments, it is evident that to fulfill them I had to have a series of rather complex instruments. One was a camera for the high-speed filming of reflected radio signals. Such movie cameras were not made in the USSR. Thus, in the period during and soon after the war my dilemma was how to assemble such equipment quickly without any additional funding.

It occurred to me that military organizations had to have radio transmitters, radio receivers, and also radio direction finders, equipment that could be adapted for use in my experiments, which took place under mobile conditions. I therefore asked Sergei Vavilov to ask the Military Radio Communications Department for help. He wrote to the military and I followed with a telephone call to schedule a meeting at which I could explain the research project. The military personnel were most responsive, and in a short time they found such equipment as we required. The types of transmitters, receivers, and so on that were necessary for our research were no longer used by the military, who had gone on to more advanced equipment. Among other things they sent us a military mobile radio direction finder, a booth containing a complex of antennas conveniently adapted for my work. All the necessary equipment was given to us, including a good truck, and we paid nothing for any of it. I had only to adapt everything to suit my experiments and to assemble some other necessary parts of the sets in my laboratory.

At that time I learned from reading the literature that the first-ever camera (as I remember) for filming rapid processes similar to those I sought to observe had been produced in Germany. It was called a Zeit Lupe. To buy that camera, however, I needed foreign currency, or "golden rubles." I do not remember the cost of the Zeit Lupe, but it was expensive. It was a rather complicated and heavy piece of equipment, made specifically for laboratory use and commercial films. It was 1944, wartime. There was no foreign currency in PhIAN's budget. Again Sergei Vavilov helped. He asked the presidium of the Academy of Sciences for the necessary funds, and the academy found the money. We bought the Zeit Lupe and began to test all my equipment.

The transmitter and other subsidiary equipment were located in the laboratory. The radio receiver and oscillograph were put in the booth of the radio direction finder. I used the Zeit Lupe only for observation in the laboratory to film the pulses reflected by the ionosphere. Nikolai Papalexi took a great interest in my experiments and supported them enthusiastically, which helped greatly in realizing the project. He visited us many times when the observation point was close to Moscow, about thirty kilometers from PhIAN.

Our van, where the transmitter was set, our campus with its tents, and my young collaborators are seen in the photograph captioned "The author with Alina Ainberg and other members of his research team." Most of my colleagues worked with me throughout the period of the observations. The team included a permanent assistant, junior research assistant Alina Ainberg, senior scientist Boris Gorozhankin and a radio engineer who worked with him, a graduate student, an undergraduate student, two or three technicians, and a driver. The van moved at various fixed distances from the observation point in a range of five to fifty kilometers from the receiver's point. Gorozhankin always operated the transmitter. The observation point was in the extensive grounds of the Institute of the Earth's Magnetism, Ionosphere, and the Propagation of Radio Waves of the Academy of Sciences (IZMIRAN), where I later worked for nearly thirty-five years, from 1952 to 1987.

At the end of 1947 I described the full results of my experiments and theoretical calculations from 1943 to 1947 in a series of articles.[2] I included the results in more detail in my thesis for my scientific degree of doctor of physical and mathematical sciences. I defended the thesis in 1948, and thereafter continued to pursue these and similar lines of inquiry. When my sixteen years of active and fruitful research at PhIAN were terminated by General Malyshev of the KGB in 1951, I left behind all the records of that research: the unique complex of settings, the films, the Zeit Lupe, and my own file records. To this day I do not know what happened to them. The experiments were not continued at PhIAN, and similar research was not conducted in the West. I am sure that if I had been in communication with foreign colleagues, such experiments would have been pursued in the West.

Despite my frustration and outrage at the end of this scientific work, I recall that time with satisfaction: I had done well! And that, after all, is the main duty for which we exist.

What I have not yet told you is that before Malyshev suddenly ended my research at PhIAN, I had to interrupt it for more than a year in 1946 and 1947, because of an extraordinary project conceived by Nikolai Papalexi.

2. For example, Yakov L. Alpert, "On the Structure of the Atmosphere and the Processes in the f-layer of the Ionosphere," *Journal of Experimental and Theoretical Physics* 118, no. 11 (1948): 995.

9

A Unique Solar Eclipse, 1947

In 1946 Nikolai Papalexi proposed to Sergei Vavilov, the director of PhIAN and the new president of the Academy of Sciences, that the academy mount an expedition to observe a solar eclipse that would occur in Brazil the next year. What made this particular eclipse worth studying was its duration. The duration of a total eclipse is typically only about one to one and one-half minutes. The duration of the total eclipse over Brazil would be three minutes and thirty-six seconds. The partial solar eclipse would also be long — two hours, thirty-two minutes, and twenty-nine seconds. The Brazilian eclipse would thus be an unusually rich source of data.

Papalexi further proposed that in addition to performing optical observations, a Soviet expedition should also observe the radio emissions of the sun. This was a pioneering idea. Radio astronomy was then still in its infancy. Papalexi was not an astronomer, but this idea typified his innovative thinking.

Vavilov embraced Papalexi's proposal and sought a meeting with Joseph Stalin to win his approval for it. Above I spoke a bit about what one might call the delicate relations that existed between Sergei Vavilov and Joseph Stalin. Vavilov approached Stalin on matters that other scientists avoided. For example, during one meeting with Stalin, Vavilov said that whereas under the tsar scientific workers could save some money in the bank, now they had to look for a second job just to cover their living expenses, and that in consequence their work was much less productive. Stalin was well informed about the situation, which had begun after the revolution and had continued for many years. When I entered PhIAN as a laboratory assistant, my salary was half what I had earned at the Experimental Radio Station. Soon after Vavilov's conversation with Stalin, the salary of scientific workers doubled or tripled.

If it was bold of Vavilov to suggest that some things were better under the tsar than under Marxism-Leninism, it was also risky to propose in 1946 that the Soviet Union mount an elaborate, purely scientific expedition to the other side of the world. Stalin might well become angry at the suggestion that resources should be devoted to such a project when the country was still recovering from the devastating effects of World War II. But that did not happen. Instead Stalin gave the order to organize the expedition, which meant that all the officials of the USSR had to help to realize the project. Perhaps Stalin thought the expedition would have good propaganda value; perhaps it was merely his caprice.

In any case a special government decision regarding the expedition was soon announced, and organizational work started at PhIAN. The academy named Papalexi to head the expedition, with me as his deputy at Vavilov's and his request.

On 3 February 1947, however, about three months before the solar eclipse, Papalexi died of a heart attack. We at PhIAN's oscillation laboratory lost both our chief and our friend. We also lost the initiator and head of the expedition, an exceptional scientist and a person of high morals. Three years earlier Leonid Mandelshtam, his best friend and colleague of dozens of years, had also died. Many people thought that Mandelshtam's death hastened Papalexi's. In memory of Mandelshtam and Papalexi two special volumes of the *Bulletin of the Academy of Sciences of the USSR* were published.[1]

Thus, the expedition to Brazil was to take place without Papalexi. The full weight of organizing the expedition now fell on me. The academy named Alexander Mikhailov, the director of the Pulkovo Astronomic Observatory in Leningrad and a corresponding member of the academy, to succeed Papalexi as head of the expedition. But soon after being chosen, Mikhailov left for Brazil with two other astronomers, Nikolai Pariisky and Alexander Vashakidze, to choose the site for our camp and await our arrival there. Mikhailov named Pariisky as his deputy. Later the academy also chose a third deputy head of the expedition, the famous polar explorer Georgy Ushakov. At that time Ushakov was a congenial, sun-bronzed man of forty-six, a veteran of many expeditions

---

1. The *Bulletin of the Academy of Sciences* was published in Russian and French. The volumes dedicated to Mandelshtam and Papalexi are *Bulletin de L'Académie des Sciences de L'U.R.S.S., Série Physique 9*, nos. 1 and 2 (1945) and 12, no. 1 (1948).

to the Arctic. He was also a member of the Communist Party, and it was evident that he had been appointed to be our political deputy. It was a given that at least one member of the Communist Party had to be part of the expedition's leadership.

At any time, and in any country, scientific expeditions are romantic events for the participants. For Soviet researchers, who were isolated from the outside world, that event in 1947 was extremely exciting. Remember that the doors to conferences and visiting professorships abroad were almost completely closed to all of us. Dozens of Soviet scientists, even very famous ones, called me to ask to be included in the expedition. One corresponding member of the academy, later a full academician, pleaded, "Yakov Lvovich, I shall clean the ship. I shall help you do anything. Include me in the list." Fielding all these calls was a delicate matter. Fortunately, I could honestly say that the final decision was not mine but Sergei Vavilov's. It was he who had to approve the personnel for the expedition. Then the list had to be officially sanctioned, which of course meant that the KGB oversaw our plans. Such were the rules of the Soviet land. As it happened, a couple of very good scientists did come along, more as helpers than as investigators in their own right.

Organizing such an expedition would be complicated under any circumstances. It was especially so in my country after the war. It was not simple to obtain foreign currency; it was difficult to find much of the technical equipment we needed; and it was hard even to obtain special packing material for all the instruments, which had to be kept dry and protected from being shaken. But Joseph Stalin had given us his *dobro,* which is Russian for "Okay!" and thus the doors of every institute and ministry were open to us. To secure a suitable ship to carry the expedition to Brazil, for example, I met the Minister of the Merchant Marine, Peter Shirshov, who personally recommended the cargo ship *Griboyedov.* After our talk I went to the small Baltic seaport of Vindava in Lithuania to inspect the ship, and found it to be just what we needed. It is worth noting that Shirshov spoke not just as a high official but from personal experience of an expedition's needs. He was one of four explorers who were stranded in the Arctic on a drifting ice floe over the winter of 1937–38, surviving on supplies dropped from the air until three ice breakers reached them. It was a sensational exploit in its day, covered by all the world's press.[2]

2. The other three explorers were Evgeny Fyodorov, Ernst Krenkel, and Dmitri Papanin, the expedition's leader. The hydrographic ship that PhIAN used on its expedition to test radio wave propagation in the Arctic in the late summer of 1937, during which the reindeer ate our kasha, was named for Dmitri Papanin, whose previous explorations had already made him famous. The rescue was organized by the polar explorer and mathematician Otto Ulavich Schmidt, who later became vice president of the Academy of Sciences.

With nearly all our difficulties overcome, on 17 March 1947 the members of the expedition began to arrive in Liepaya-Libava, the Baltic seaport where the *Griboyedov* was moored under the command of Captain Victor Gintsburg. On 26 March we were on board ready to leave for Brazil. As explained, three other members of the expedition staff had preceded us to Brazil. The expedition included a physician, Nikolai Baluyev, and even an accountant to track our finances.

Of course, we also had a KGB agent with us. That person arrived and was presented as a scientific representative of the presidium of the Academy of Sciences, although we all knew who the man really was. He was in his early thirties, very polite, modest, and intelligent. He was always eager to lend a hand with any task such as moving and setting up equipment. He never made a nuisance of himself or tried to influence anyone's behavior either on board ship or ashore in any foreign country.

The physician, Baluyev, was the last one to come to Liepaya-Libava because he had a great deal of trouble getting the medicine he needed for the expedition. From Moscow he brought many boxes with various medicines. At that time I had read in some books about Brazil that most of the terrible diseases known to humanity existed there. The risk of catching leprosy or yellow fever was said to be especially high. We were vaccinated in Liepaya-Libava against typhoid fever and cholera, but we had to wait until the ship docked in Southampton for a day to be vaccinated against yellow fever. Baluyev had to secure this vaccine, which had to be used within a week of its being prepared, through the Ministry of Foreign Affairs, and Sergei Vavilov himself took special care to see that the vaccine was obtained, personally cabling me aboard the *Griboyedov* to confirm that it would be waiting for us in Southampton. Many of us suffered greatly from those vaccinations, especially from the one for yellow fever. Some of our people had temperatures of 102°–105° F. We were also warned to be especially careful about drinking water in Brazil. It turned out that the dangers were exaggerated. The Brazilians laughed when we told them about the warnings we had received. Still, the fear of disease somewhat dampened the elevated mood of some members of the expedition.

The staff of the expedition included two groups of physicists from PhIAN, three groups of astronomers from Leningrad, Moscow, and Georgia, and a group of four botanists from Leningrad. The physics and astronomy program called for experiments in five major categories, which are listed here with the senior scientist in each experimental group.

Einstein's effect: the deviation in the gravitational field of sunlight (Alexander Mikhailov)

Radio emissions of the sun (Semyon Khaikin)

The ionosphere (Yakov Alpert)

The various properties of the outer part of the solar corona (Alexander Lebedinsky, Aram Vashakidze, and Sergei Kalinyak)

The chromosphere and the inner part of the solar corona (Mstislav Gnevyshev)

I included the theoretical physicist Vitaly Ginzburg in the ionosphere group, and Pariisky included the theoretical astrophysicist Joseph Shklovsky in the group on the investigation of the polarization of the solar corona. Very often, however, each accepted different responsibilities willingly and with a sense of humor.

When the botanists of the academy learned about our expedition, they appealed to the Soviet government to include them. Brazil is one of the richest countries in tropical flora. The botanists wanted to bring fresh flora to Leningrad to restore the hothouse of what had been the largest botanical garden in Russia. During the war it was destroyed by German bombs. The four botanists who joined us were Boris Shishkin, corresponding member of the academy and the director of the Komarov Botanical Institute; Sergei Yuzepchuk, a member of that institute; and Leonid Pravdin and senior scientist Leonid Rodin, both members of the Forest Institute of the Academy.[3] For his part the physician Baluyev planned to study the lepers in Brazilian hospitals.

Thus, the expedition had a large and varied program. On coming aboard the *Griboyedov,* many of us began to work with our instruments. A daily seminar was organized where we presented talks about our forthcoming experiments and other matters. For example, Ushakov told us interesting stories of his adventures in the Arctic, Baluyev discussed tropical diseases, and Ginzburg talked about the physics of the atom bomb. On our arrival in Liepaya-Libava , Semyon Khaikin and Boris Chikhachov, with the essential help of the crew of the ship, began to assemble and mount the large mobile antenna for the radio astronomic experiment.

Our departure, which had been coordinated with Minister Shirshov, was scheduled for 25 March. On that day, however, the port of Liepaya-Libava remained enclosed by a field of pack ice extending about three to four miles from the harbor. The old sailors of Liepaya-Libava had never seen such a situation; by that date the sea was normally free of ice. Each day we sat and waited for the ice belt to disappear or become thin. Unfortunately, the heavy

3. Rodin published a nice book about the expedition, *Five Weeks in South America: Impressions of a Naturalist* (Moscow: State Publishing House of Geographical Literature, 1949).

blocks of ice were unwavering. We had not left port and already we were becoming anxious about reaching Brazil in time. Ushakov and I were in daily communication with Shirshov and Sergei Vavilov by cable and telephone.

After a week, on 2 April, we were informed that the icebreaker *Sibiryakov* would leave its port of Riga, Latvia, and come to our aid. On 7 April it at last reached the pier of Liepaya-Libava, forcing its way through the heavy ice. The next day our ship left to anchor in the outer roadstead of the seaport of Liepaya-Libava, with the *Sibiryakov* close by. We had advanced only a short distance and were still blocked by ice. Minister Shirshov informed us that the longer we were held up in the Baltic the more he was considering moving the staff of the expedition to the *Sibiryakov,* because of the potential danger of mines remaining from the war. We rejected that idea and instead proposed that we continue to wait. Meanwhile, we were also informed that once we were able to proceed the *Griboyedov* would carry us from Liepaya-Libava to the small Swedish seaport of Karlsham for demagnetization, which would lessen the danger from mines. Finally, on Monday, 13 April, after a week of nervous anticipation, the ministry decided to try to take us out of the blocks of ice that surrounded us. The *Griboyedov* was towed, and we began to move.

There is a great superstition in Russia: no serious deed should begin on the thirteenth of any month, especially when it falls on a Monday. Yet we began our trip precisely on such a day, and no one so much as mentioned the superstition. We were all too relieved that the expedition, which we feared might be canceled, was finally under way. After about fifty minutes we were in free water. The ice was not strong, and the *Griboyedov* headed for Karlsham under its own power. The sea was as calm as though we were on a large lake. We cabled Shirshov, Vavilov, and the Soviet embassies in Stockholm, London, and Rio de Janeiro. Early on the morning of 14 April we were in the beautiful, cozy city of Karlsham. After a day there we headed for Southampton, reaching it early in the morning of 21 April. All those days our ship sailed slowly in a deep, unchanging fog. Two representatives of the Soviet embassy arrived from London, bringing us yellow fever vaccine and the foreign currency, U.S. dollars, that we needed for our journey. Although they had prepared an excursion to London for us, we were anxious to be on our way that day because 20 May, the day of the eclipse, was fast approaching. But I was particularly distressed not to go to London for a personal reason.

In Chapter 2, I wrote about my correspondence with Edward Appleton in 1943. I received Appleton's answer only at the end of 1944. At that time it was a risky step for a Soviet citizen to try to collaborate with a foreigner. We never knew what the reaction of the KGB would be. Although I wrote Appleton other letters, I had no idea if they were received, and I did not know if he wrote me letters the Soviet authorities would not deliver. Thus I was greatly surprised, on the eve of the expedition, when the physicist Victor Goldansky of the Academy of Sciences' Institute of Physical Chemistry told me that he had heard on BBC radio from London that the new Nobel prize laureate in physics, Edward Appleton, had received a letter from the Soviet scientist Yakov Alpert. The BBC reported that Appleton took the letter as a sign of improved relations between England and the USSR.

Although at that time relations between England and the Soviet Union were indeed tense, why was my letter interpreted as it was? Why did the Soviet censors decide to deliver one of my letters to Appleton? The answer may lie in the KGB's files. I can only surmise that for some reason the KGB found it politically useful to let one of my letters reach Appleton. In any case, when the *Griboyedov* was scheduled to stay in England for several days, I asked that a meeting with Edward Appleton be arranged. It seems that the KGB approved the meeting, for in Southampton a representative of the Soviet embassy in London was waiting to take me to meet Appleton. But because the Baltic ice kept us from leaving Liepaya-Libava for so long, the *Griboyedov* was now behind schedule. I had to stay on the ship or miss going to Brazil.

We Arrive in Brazil!

On 22 April the *Griboyedov* weighed anchor, and we headed for Brazil. But again we had bad luck. On leaving the English Channel, we found ourselves in a force-eight gale, and the storm became stronger and stronger. It even reached force eleven. The highest value on the scale of sea winds is a force-twelve gale. The ship began to lose speed and control, and we had to take refuge in the port of Plymouth. We cabled Vavilov in Moscow and Mikhailov in Brazil and wondered what fate had in store for us next.

On the morning of 24 April, however, we were able to set sail for Brazil without further mishap. We were delighted with the ocean, new kinds of birds, flying fish, and the clear view of the stars at night. It was especially exciting to see the Azores. Everyone came up on deck to watch the islands as we steamed by. For people who had never been outside Russia, the very word *Azores* was saturated with romance. We crossed the equator on 4 May and were duly sanctified before Neptune, the god of the sea. Following the age-old tradition, the sailors directed strong streams of water at us with the ship's hoses. Even some of our cabins became flooded with water. The sailors said that if the Neptune festival were not celebrated, the voyage would not be fortunate. It was a joyful experience indeed.

On 9 May we approached Rio de Janeiro. Much earlier, during the night, we had seen a point of light on the horizon that became increasingly stronger. Step by step that light took on a definite outline. We later learned that it was the famous large illuminated statue of Christ on a mountain high above Rio de Janeiro. On coming to Rio, we were informed that our ship had to go to the small seaport of Angra-dos-Reis, where we were to take a special train to the base camp chosen by Mikhailov for our expedition. The base camp was near a luxurious resort, the Grande Hotel de Araxa, close to the small city of Arasha Bareiro in the state of Minas Gerais at an altitude of about 980 meters above sea level.

We arrived at Angra-dos-Reis at night. On the morning of 10 May we awakened to find ourselves in a marvelous bay covered with tropical plants. The astronomer Nikolai Pariisky and Soviet consul Fyodor Rezov met us on the pier. The special train was waiting to take us to our base camp. At 8 P.M. we completed loading our large cargo onto the train and moved to Arashá Bareiro.

The solar eclipse was a popular event in Brazil, and much was written about it in the newspapers. The Observation Commission of the Solar Eclipse of 20 May 1947 was organized by the state of Minas Gerais, where the eclipse was to occur. Its president was an engineer, Benedito Quintino dos Santos, who welcomed and assisted our expedition along with others that had come from Canada, Czechoslovakia, France, Germany, Sweden, and the United States. The arrival of the Soviet expedition aroused special interest and received the lion's share of press coverage. Walking in Rio one day, I noticed a postcard with a photograph of myself for sale at a newsstand. The photograph showed me drinking strong coffee after dinner in Arasha. We had become as popular as film stars.

At that time it would have been highly unusual to see a group of Soviet citizens traveling anywhere in the West. Perhaps curiosity about us was especially great in Brazil because the first diplomatic relations between the USSR and Brazil were established only months before our expedition. The Soviet ambassador, Fyodor Surits, arrived not long before we did. The people from our embassy told us that the Brazilians thought all Russians had long beards and walked around the Kremlin with poleaxes, and many other such foolish things. Just as we believed, before our journey to Brazil, that we might easily contract every disease known to man there.

Many people appeared as early as 6 or 7 A.M. on the pier at Angra-dos-Reis. They came to stare at us as we unloaded all our things, and they wanted to talk to us, too. But we had no time to socialize. On our way to Arasha Bareiro, trains coming from the opposite direction were delayed at the stations where our train had to stop so that passengers could have a look at us. When we stopped for about an hour and a half at the small city of Lavras, where we had lunch, many people on the street stared at us. One young man held in his raised hand a pack of Russian Belomorkanal cigarettes and a Russian box of matches. The train frequently stopped to satisfy local people's curiosity.

On 12 May we came to the town of Bareira and immediately transferred our elaborate and heavy equipment from the train to cars. We then drove to Arasha and began to set up our instruments. Within a day all the astronomical instruments were set up. The transmitter for radio observations of the ionosphere was installed in a rented house in Bareira on 14 May. On 17 May we began our observations of the ionosphere, completing them on 24 May. This observation cycle was necessary in order to compare the conditions of the ionosphere before and after the day of the solar eclipse. Thus on 20 May, all settings, including the radio instruments in Bahia, were prepared for our observations. Our expedition crew was ready to research all the interconnected phenomena that would accompany the solar eclipse.

Ill was fate! Clouds covered the sun at Arasha for a dozen minutes precisely during the time of the full solar eclipse. All the days before and after the eclipse were clear, with no clouds. People who believe in divine intervention or who are superstitious might say that Monday, 13 April, the day our ship began its voyage to Brazil, played its role. Certainly we were taken aback and were downhearted. We lost all optical astronomical observations. The radio astronomic experiment in Bahia conceived by Papalexi and performed by Khaikin and Chikhachov was successful, however. And my group was able to perform its observations of the ionosphere because clouds did not affect them. Our experiment depended on the fact that the ionization of the atmosphere decreases during an eclipse and becomes close to zero at the moment of full eclipse. We wanted to see to what extent that would diminish the reflection of radio waves. We also wanted to ascertain the relaxation time of the ionization, that is, how long it would be after the eclipse before the ionization returned to its previous level.

During our stay in Arasha, many people visited our base camp. We also met with them at the hotel. Even nuns came to our camp. There were many Brazilian Jews, Russians, and other European émigrés among the visitors. I often spoke with our visitors, and below I talk about some of my impressions of those encounters.

Each evening we had a chance to watch films at the hotel. At that time Western films were seldom shown in Russia, and we were eager for them. None of the movies left a lasting impression on me, except for the quality of the color film, which was better than what was available in Russia. One evening, a young people's brass band played a concert at the hotel in Arasha in honor of our expedition. We also took part in an election of a "Miss Eclipse," in which one voted by buying a ticket. It seemed to me that the lady who became Miss Eclipse won the title simply because her father bought a great many tickets.

On 27 May we loaded our equipment on a train in Bareiro. The train carried it to Angra-dos-Reis, where the *Griboyedov* was moored. The staff of the expedition, however, traveled from Arasha to Rio by special airplane. That evening a meeting for observers of the solar eclipse took place at the Brazilian Academy of Sciences. Representatives of the various expeditions presented talks about their programs and results. Scientists from the United States explained that their observations of the ionosphere were made by routine methods and that their optical observations to research the Einstein effect had been successful. A French military group — civilian French astronomers had lacked the funds for an expedition to Brazil — also reported on its observations of the ionosphere. Alexander Mikhailov talked about his program for the observation of the Einstein effect, but he did not mention any of our expedition's other experiments. On the next day a crowded reception was held at the U.S. embassy. Two days later we went to Belo-Horizonte for a scientific meeting organized by Quintino and for a meeting with the governor of Minas Gerais. The members of all the solar eclipse expeditions gathered there. At that meeting Mikhailov repeated his earlier talk. Quintino asked me to present a talk about radio investigations, and I took the opportunity to discuss the Soviet expedition as a whole.

After a few days we were again in the magnificent city of Rio. The view from the plane was a beautiful prismatic mixture of wonderful architecture and glorious nature. Like many great cities, Rio also has its large slums. At the invitation of two beautiful Brazilian sisters and their parents, whom we met at the hotel in Arasha Bareira, Vitaly Ginzburg and I visited the restaurant Pao de Assucar at the famous mountain Sugar Loaf in Rio. We went there by means of a gondola lift above the bay of Batafogo. It was impressive traveling about a mile up the mountain amid gigantic trees to arrive at the Christ statue.

The long and wide beach of Copacabana in the heart of Rio, with its lovely tall apartment houses along the seafront, was impressive and had a surprisingly beautiful view. I first learned about that beach when I read that Stefan Zweig and his wife had poisoned themselves in one of those seafront apartment houses soon after their flight from the Nazis in 1934.

The Russian embassy in Rio organized a party for our expedition. Only the Soviets and the Swedish astronomer Öhman and his wife were at that party. We enjoyed the party with its good food, wine, and a lot of caviar. It was curious to see how much Mrs. Öhman, on the whole a restrained lady, relished caviar. Noticing that gave me an idea. We had a huge barrel of caviar on board the *Griboyedov*. The following day, when we were back on the ship, I asked the captain to deliver a large box of caviar (about a kilogram) to Mrs. Öhman at her hotel. The captain complied, and we were happy to imagine how excited Mrs. Öhman would be to receive that package.

On the day after the party at the Soviet embassy the last of our sightseeing in Brazil took place. We then traveled to Angra-dos-Reis, where the entire staff of the expedition gathered. The ship was destined for business in Argentina and Uruguay and then for Holland and East Germany. We were lucky: our voyage back to Leningrad would give us the privilege of seeing a large part of the world that was closed to other Soviet citizens.

Our Way Back

On 7 June we left Rio for Leningrad. Because the *Griboyedov* was a cargo ship, carrying sugar among other goods, we made many stops along the way. The first was on 12 June at Rosario, after Buenos Aires the second most important city in Argentina. The route to that port was along the large and wide Parana River. We became furious and protested when the customs check at Rosario took two days. They checked our documents, took our fingerprints, and so on. We learned that they had known beforehand that we were coming. Before the *Griboyedov* the last Russian ship to visit Rosario had been the sailing vessel *Tovarishch* (Comrade) on its way around the world in 1929. For two days, while we were undergoing the customs check, many cutters regularly surrounded our ship. They stayed at the side of the ship, and the people aboard spoke loudly to us in English, Russian, and Ukrainian. In the crowd were many Argentine Indians and Argentine brokers and dealers, as well as people who had left Russia and Ukraine at the time of, or shortly after, the October revolution. The latter included representatives of the Rosario Russian Committee. Later, before leaving Rosario, the ship was opened to those visitors, and the decks became a madhouse as dozens boarded.

When we were finally granted permission to leave the ship, we went for three days to Buenos Aires. The embassy of the USSR lodged us in a beautiful hotel. Now that I have visited many European countries, I understand why Buenos Aires is called the Paris of South America. The style of its city life, its people, shops, and streets I recollected when I was recently in Paris and Brussels. We had meetings at the Ministry of Foreign Affairs, the Institute of Relations with the USSR, and the Slavic Committee in Buenos Aires. One day we went by train to La Plata, Argentina's university city, and visited the Astronomical Observatory and the Department of Physics.

Our host at the university was a German physicist, Gans. I spoke with him in German. When he introduced himself he explained that he had arrived in La Plata only thirteen days earlier, and that before that he had been chair of the Theoretical Physics Department of the University of Munich. For many years the chair of that department was the distinguished physicist Arnold Sommerfeld. What a chance opportunity it was for me to meet Gans. I had read his paper "Fortpflanzung des Lichtes durch ein inhomogenes Medium" (Propagation of light through an inhomogeneous medium), published in *Annalen der Physik* in 1915, and cited it in my first book in 1947. Gans was surprised to hear that I knew about his work. I remember well that after that his mood changed and he spoke to me with restraint. Although I could not imagine then why that was, now, when I recall that event in reading over my notes, I realize that he must have thought that I had been given information about him and that our meeting was a Soviet trick.

Who knows what sort of person Gans really was or how he had come to emigrate to Argentina only thirteen days before our meeting? Many Germans escaped to Argentina at the end of World War II. Fascist Germany organized and prepared many settlements and colonies for their people there and kept a lot of money in the Argentine banks. We know that many fascistic activists settled there after the war. To my great regret such unpleasant and indeed sad thoughts come to my mind. The contradictory and complicated social and political order of our world is what brought them.

We returned to Rosario and to our ship on 19 June. After two days we tied up at Montevideo, the capital of Uruguay. Uruguayan scientists and representatives of the Soviet embassy met us at the port. The director of the Astronomical Observatory of Montevideo, Carlos Etchecopar, was among them. He had been in Brazil during the eclipse, and we had first met him there. In Montevideo the staff of the expedition was permitted to leave the ship without any delay. We went by bus to the Soviet embassy, where we spent a lovely evening. Our route from the port to the city of Montevideo, which was about twenty kilometers distant, was along a beautiful seashore. Impressive two- and three-story houses with lovely gardens punctuated the ocean beach, and we were told that such houses dotted the beach for two hundred to three hundred more kilometers.

We were under way again on 22 June and crossed the equator on 1 July 1947. We began to consider the results of our observations. In the evenings we saw many Russian movies, which we had already seen more than once on the outgoing leg of our journey. Among them were a version of Jack London's *White Fang,* a biographical film about Thomas Edison, and Sergei Eisenstein's *Ivan the Terrible.* We tried to entertain ourselves, for life on board was often wearisome. I grew a little philosophical at one point and wrote in my notebook, "What is the meaning of life? Love, science, nature, and music, the things which induce the best emotions, the best wishes, and the best dreams."

Finally, on 15 July, we tied up at the seaport of Rotterdam, Holland. Customs officials permitted us to leave the ship without delay. The Soviet ambassador, Vitaly Volkov, met us at the ship and took us to see Holland by bus. That small country is an exclusive phenomenon in human history, a singularity, one might say, to borrow a term from mathematics and physics. The canals of the Dutch are an expressive example of ingenuity, diligence, and vitality. Their distinguished painting, philosophical books, and works of jurisprudence constitute an astonishing achievement in world culture, and, as is well known, Dutch scientists have contributed greatly to our knowledge of the universe.

We went to the Hague, Delft, and Amsterdam. It was delightful to travel through the pristine countryside, small towns, and large cities on clean, beautiful roads. There were diversely colored fields, luxurious green groves, and many windmills. We saw a working sixteenth-century windmill in Rotterdam. In the Hague we visited the house of Baruch Spinoza. Spinoza was one of the philosophers I read closely and often; the mathematical precision of his thought greatly impressed me. We also visited the church where all the kings and queens of Holland are buried. Seeing tombs inside a church, common as that is in Europe, was a new and surprising experience for me. In Amsterdam many members of our expedition and the ship's crew visited art museums. But I wanted to see the architecture of that great city, so I walked along the streets for a few hours.

The most remarkable event in Holland, however, for both me and Vitaly Ginzburg, was our visit to Leiden the next day, where we spent a full day of our two days' stay in Holland. Physicists of my day all aspired to visit Leiden, the city founded in the twelfth century, and its university, founded in 1572. The great physicist Hendrik Antoon Lorentz founded the Theoretical Physics Department at Leiden University. For dozens of years that institute and the Kamerlingh-Onnes Laboratory were meccas for the world community of physicists. Lorentz was one of the creators of the contemporary classical science of physics. He won the Nobel Prize in 1902 for his work on the Zeeman effect. It was the second Nobel Prize ever awarded. In 1901 the German scientist Wilhelm Conrad Roentgen was awarded the first Nobel Prize in physics for the discovery of X rays. Heike Kamerlingh-Onnes founded his laboratory in 1904 and was its chair for thirty years. In 1913 he won the Nobel in physics for his research on the properties of matter at low temperatures and for the discovery of one of the most interesting and important physical properties of matter: superconductivity.

Lorentz bequeathed his office and the position of chair to Paul Ernfest.

Ernfest was a close friend of Albert Einstein. They corresponded regularly for about twenty years, until the tragic death of Ernfest in 1933, when he shot himself while in a deep depression. The cause of his depression was the incurable mental illness of his son. Ernfest did much research on the physics of particles, statistical mechanics, and so on. Through scientific discussions with physicists, Ernfest often played a leading role in the initial stages of the development of the quantum theory.

At that time Hendrik Antoni Kramers held the chair of the Theoretical Physics Department at Leiden University and occupied Lorentz's old office. Kramers's work on quantum theory and on quantum mechanics was well known. It was a tradition for physicists to sign their names on Lorentz's blackboard. Being in the office where Lorentz and Ernfest had worked and seeing the signatures of famous physicists from every part of the world on the back of his blackboard, I had a special feeling. The signatures of Einstein, Niels Bohr, Werner Heisenberg, Erwin Schrödinger, and many others were there. I was glad also to find the signatures of the Russian physicists Abram Ioffe, Peter Kapitsa, Lev Landau, and Igor Tamm there.

Before our visit to that office, the scientists of the university officially received us in a special hall. The vice-rector of the university said in his greeting that our visit was the first sign of the beginning of cooperation and exchange with Russian scientists after the war. Ernfest's widow, Tat'yana Alexeevna Afanas'eva-Ernfest, greeted us in Russian. She was a professor of thermodynamics at the University of Leiden. Her papers with Ernfest on thermodynamics and statistical mechanics had been published in *Handbuch der Physik* and were well known.

The head of the Kamerlingh-Onnes Laboratory was then Wangen Joannes de Haas, who took that position in 1924. De Haas's achievements were memorialized in the so-called Einstein–de Haas effect, the de Haas–Einstein method, and the de Haas–van Alphen and de Haas–Shubnikov effects. During dinner I sat beside de Haas, who spoke to me in English and French. In general, the Dutch did not like to speak German. In that way they demonstrated against the German occupation of Holland. During our conversation de Haas talked chiefly about his meetings and discussions with Einstein, Ernfest, Ioffe, Kapitsa, and Lorentz. It was difficult to understand him because of his mixture of English and French and even sometimes German words; he might start a sentence in English and finish it in French, and so on.

Afanas'eva-Ernfest approached me after dinner and asked me about the Russian theoretical physicist Semyon Shubin. I did not know Shubin, but I answered, as I thought was true, that he was working in Sverdlovsk. Today I know that Shubin, Matvey Bronstein from Leningrad, and Alexander Witt from Moscow were all killed in prison in their early thirties. They were victims of Stalin's terror in 1936–38. Igor Tamm wrote about Shubin, "He was one of the most distinguished of Soviet theoretical physicists." Landau collaborated with him in Leningrad and treated him as an equal. His works on the quantum theory of solid bodies were famous. Bronstein's particular contribution was on relativistic quantum theory and on the theory of gravitation. He also collaborated with Landau, who said that Bronstein knew much more than he knew. Alexander Witt was an excellent physicist, one of the creators of the theory of nonlinear physics.

Now, when I recall my conversation with Afanas'eva-Ernfest, I can only think that she knew the real answer to the question she posed, and I ask myself, was it possible that Western scientists learned about that evil one's deeds earlier than many of us did? I told Ginzburg about Afanas'eva's question, because he was in touch with many theoreticians. It seems that he also did not know the truth. Recently the Russian historian and physicist Gennady Gorelik told me that he believes that in asking me about Shubin Professor Afanas'eva-Ernfest meant Lev Shubnikov, who became a victim of Stalin's terror at the same time as Semyon Shubin. This is likely because Lev Shubnikov visited the Kamerlingh-Onnes Laboratory in 1930, which is when de Haas and he discovered the de Haas–Shubnikov effects. Shubnikov was an internationally known, distinguished physicist. I spoke with Afanas'eva-Ernfest when I did not know about either Shubin or Shubnikov, so perhaps I did not catch the name properly when Afanas'eva-Ernfest asked about her old acquaintance.

On the evening of 17 July we were again under steam navigation. After some hours a large and bright aurora borealis accompanied us. Two days later our ship was again demagnetized in the West German port of Kiel; then the ship traveled for business to the East German port of Rostock. We also stopped for a day in Warnemünde, a beautiful small health resort with a clean beach. We spent two days in Rostock, where we used the last of our U.S. dollars to rent a bus to travel to Berlin. We passed neglected dirty cities along the whole route, about 250 kilometers. After seven hours we were in a Berlin that had been destroyed by war. The view sharply contrasted with what we had seen crossing Holland. Of course we also saw all the famous sights of the destroyed Berlin and went to the beautifully green city of Potsdam. We visited the Astronomical Observatory and the well-known Einstein tower there. By chance, the German astronomer Grotrian was at the observatory and gave us all a tour. The trip to Berlin was over at 3 A.M. on 24 July. We left Rostock on the morning of 25 July. We passed the island Gottland, and the next day we passed Tallinn, the capital of Estonia. We saw far-off Helsinki, and on the evening of 27 July we came to

Kronstadt, Leningrad. We returned to Moscow on 28 July. Our extraordinarily interesting and striking voyage to Brazil had encompassed 134 days.

Several Remarks and a Deplorable Story

Here I would like to make a few short remarks about that expedition. First of all, it is difficult even to guess why Stalin gave his dobro to the expedition. Surely he enjoyed the idea of demonstrating to the world that the Soviet Union was powerful and resourceful enough to mount such an elaborate and expensive project so soon after World War II. But I also believe that what I earlier called the delicate relations between Stalin and Sergei Vavilov played a role. Remember that Sergei Vavilov's brother Nikolai had lost his life when Stalin gave Lysenko control of Soviet biological research. Now Stalin could demonstrate his solidarity with Sergei Vavilov, and with all of Soviet science, through his magnanimous support of the Academy of Sciences' expedition to Brazil. It is an example of the devilish play of Stalin's mind.

Whether my inference is correct or not, no other expedition received the support from its government or scientific establishment that the Soviet expedition received from the Soviet government and the Academy of Sciences. Nor were the other expeditions' research programs as broad or comprehensive as ours. The Soviet expedition was unique in its scope.

It was also, perhaps, unique in its security arrangements. I recounted earlier that a KGB person had been appointed to look after our ship. It was also very likely the case that some members of the expedition were instructed by the KGB.

Many times on the return from Brazil the captain of the *Griboyedov* and Mikhailov forbade us to leave the ship. In doing so, they were obviously following special instructions. But the KGB man, as I have said, never interfered openly in our affairs. In day-to-day matters he was a help rather than a hindrance.

At one South American port on the voyage home, although we never knew precisely where, some mysterious passengers boarded the ship. We did not see them until after the *Griboyedov* had left South America behind. One day, however, when our ship was approaching Europe, a strange lady approached us. She said that she was the sister of Arthur Edwards, a member of the German Communist Party who had been arrested in Brazil and imprisoned there for eight years. I never knew when the mysterious persons left the ship. But this event again showed that the KGB was permanently on board. Their people were everywhere in Soviet life in various capacities and roles. Their watchful eyes and their power were always over us.

I spoke with many people of different social groups in Brazil and in other countries along our route. Not only scientists but influential people were also among these. I was thirty-six years old, and I had had diverse experiences in Russia; I had collaborated with many people of distinct qualities, intellectual abilities, and cultures in our country. Yet after my meetings with Westerners, I was disconcerted. Never before had people spoken to me so much about money and business and so little about anything else. Among those people were also some immigrants from Russia. For me, it was a new and unknown experience. It was another world culture.

During the expedition I often spoke with young people about literature and writers. For example, I asked whether they had read the novels of Tolstoy, Dostoyevsky, Balzac, Stendhal, and others. Although their answers were often yes, after a few minutes of conversation I understood that they had read only synopses or abridged versions of the novels.

In Brazil for the first time in my life I saw enormous poverty. I saw many beggars in the different sections of Rio and other cities. Crossing Brazil by train, we saw habitations made of four walls with openings covered only by dirty rags. Although I never saw the inside of these houses, from the outside I saw windows without glass, entrances without doors, and black metal pipes sticking out of roofs instead of chimneys.

To these memories of an expedition that was, all things considered, a scientific success and a rewarding personal experience, I must add the following. In 1991 Joseph Shklovsky's *Five Billion Vodka Bottles to the Moon: Tales of a Soviet Scientist* appeared in English in the United States, with an introduction by the distinguished American astronomer Herbert Friedman.[4] One section of the book concerns the solar eclipse expedition to Brazil, and it is striking that nowhere does it mention Nikolai Papalexi and his initiating both the expedition as a whole and the pioneering experiment in radio astronomy. What is more curious is that Herbert Friedman's introduction states, "In 1947, for the eclipse expedition to Brazil, he [Shklovsky] brought along a radio telescope, the first ever to be used in studying an eclipse."

I was shocked when I read that statement. Friedman and I met thirty-five years ago at a Moscow meeting of the International Astronomic Conference, so I immediately called him to ask, "Where did you get this information?" Friedman answered, "It is exactly what Shklovsky told me."

"But it is a lie," I told Friedman.

Shklovsky is a very talented scientist, and long after the Brazil expedition

---

4. Joseph Shklovsky, *Five Billion Vodka Bottles to the Moon: Tales of a Soviet Scientist* (New York: W. W. Norton, 1991).

he did interesting work in radio astronomy. But in 1947 he had nothing to do with the inception, the design, or the implementation of the radio astronomic experiment on the Brazil expedition. The experiment was conceived by Papalexi. It was developed and carried out by Semyon Khaikin and Boris Chikhachov. Shklovsky, who was only included in the expedition at the request of his mentor, Nikolai Pariisky, had no investigative role whatsoever. When he arrived at PhIAN shortly before the expedition sailed, it was my first meeting with him. He cheerfully offered his help. I told him of the innovative experiment which Papalexi had initiated and which Khaikin and Chikhachov would perform, and I gave him some organizational tasks.

Actually, Shklovsky's statement to Friedman claiming responsibility for other scientists' work is not only a lie, it is an unforgivable sin. Once the famous mathematician Norbert Wiener wrote approximately the following: that an officer would be prosecuted in court for such a sin. But scientists often commit the same sins and still walk the streets with a clean conscience.

About two years after our conversation, Friedman met Vitaly Ginzburg in Washington, D.C., and told him about my call. Ginzburg confirmed the facts of the radio astronomic experiment during the solar eclipse in Brazil. In 1996 a book of reminiscences about Shklovsky appeared in Russia.[5] A younger colleague of Shklovsky's, V. Kurt, sent me the book in 1997. A translation of Friedman's introduction was included in the book, but the statement about the radio astronomic experiment during the Brazil expedition was silently omitted. I was again most disturbed to find this and called Friedman to ask him about the book. Friedman, however, knew nothing either about the book or about the translation of his introduction. He was as discouraged as I was to hear that the sentence in his paper about Shklovsky's statement was omitted without a footnote to mark the omission. Later I tried to speak with the colleagues of Shklovsky who had initiated the book of reminiscences, to ask how such an unpleasant thing could have happened. They simply avoided the point, preferring to move away from the truth. Such behavior speaks for itself.

After the expedition to Brazil I met Shklovsky many times at various scientific seminars, especially during the first years of the satellite era. I remember a very frank conversation I had with him sometime in 1959–60, while walking in a forest in the suburbs of Moscow. We spoke about the decaying nature of the Soviet regime, and I told him that the Soviet system would fall as the Roman Empire had but that the time of that crash could not be predicted. Shklovsky agreed. But he also was one of a few people who avoided meetings

5. N. S. Kardachev et al., *Joseph Shklovsky: Mind, Life, Universe* (Moscow: Yanus, 1996).

with me after my application for emigration in 1975. It happened during all the thirteen years of my and my wife's refusal time. When we did meet him — and once it was at a movie theater — he ran away. Such behavior also speaks for itself.

When I called Friedman in 1997 I told him that I had decided to write about Shklovsky's claim regarding the radio astronomic observations in Brazil. I was glad to hear that Friedman understood my desire to set the record straight on behalf of Semyon Khaikin, Boris Chikhachov, and especially Nikolai Papalexi. At the end of our short conversation he said that he is looking forward to reading this book.

Sputnik I, *1956–1958*

Links in Time

On 4 October 1957 I was stunned and excited to learn of the launch of *Sputnik I,* the first artificial earth satellite. It was one of the greatest achievements of the USSR, and almost as much of a surprise for me as it was for millions of people around the world. I say "almost" because for various reasons I knew that the space age was dawning and that the first glimmers of the new age might well appear in my own country. As a boy I dreamed of space travel. Now it was becoming a reality in my own lifetime.

In 1953–54, I saw that the scientific and technological conditions necessary to send objects and people into space were gradually falling into place. But even before that date I had some involvement, direct and indirect, with Russia's rocket program. In 1947–48, Sergei Vavilov asked me to draft ionosphere and radio wave propagation research proposals with relevance for radio communication. These proposals were to be forwarded to the General Staff of the Soviet army, and specifically to Marshal Alexander Vasilevsky. Nothing was said about the launching of rockets or satellites, although these ideas were in the air at that time. Shortly afterward, as I mentioned in Chapter 1, Sergei Korolyov, the leader and chief designer of many rocket and satellite efforts, asked me to collaborate on experiments for the first Soviet launch of the FAU (Freie Arbeiterinnen Union) rocket captured from the Germans.

The Differential Doppler Shift/Radio Phase Method

The experiments I outlined in the proposal for Marshal Vasilevsky were to employ a radio phase method that was similar to the one used for the first time by Leonid Mandelshtam and Nikolai Papalexi in creating their radio interferometer. But it would also differ in essential ways from the point of view of both physics and engineering. To put radio phase ideas to work on rockets and satellites would require new techniques and a new set of complicated instruments.

First of all, the results of radio satellite explorations of the ionosphere and magnetosphere depend on the anisotropic nature of that medium — the magnetoplasma. As I discussed in Chapter 8, radio waves propagating in such a medium split into two elliptical polarized waves, called ordinary and extraordinary waves. They are coherent waves, that is, of the same frequency at their source. But they propagate with different velocities and have different phases on arriving at the observation point, which they reach at different times.

Second, the satellite carrying a radio beacon is a fast-moving body. This means that there will be a Doppler shifting of the frequencies of the ordinary and extraordinary radio waves produced in the ionosphere. The velocity of the satellite carrying the radio beacon is about eight kilometers per second. Therefore, the Doppler-shifted frequency differences of the two coherent radio waves — that is, the ordinary and extraordinary waves — radiated by the source and recorded at the observation point will also be rather high. The exact differences will depend on the local characteristics of the plasma surrounding the satellite — specifically, on the electron density close to the radio beacon and on the integrated electron concentration along the trajectory of propagation of these radio waves to the observation point at the surface of the earth. The experiments must therefore exploit two physical properties, which can be called *differential and rotating Doppler effects*.

In preparing the ideas for this project, I had fruitful discussions with colleagues at PhIAN and with Mikhail Leontovich in particular. Leontovich had succeeded Nikolai Papalexi as the chief of the Oscillation Department, where I had a small team and a laboratory. Leontovich was the one who had to approve my proposal. Of course, he well understood all aspects of the project. But at that time people were influenced by the excellent radar that had been developed during the war in the United States and in England. The technical achievements that led to such devices were impressive indeed and unmatched in our country. Therefore, Leontovich thought that we should use that technique for in situ experiments in the ionosphere. In my discussions with him I emphasized the simplicity and clearness of the physics involved in the proposed Doppler-shifted radio phase method. The radar method would be much more complicated. In that case handling the experimental data — the pulses, packets of waves, their group velocities, and the amplitude of the packets of waves — would confront us with more complicated physical processes and mathematics and really with an unsolvable problem.

Soon after these discussions, Lenotovich reached an agreement with the Radio Ministry that this project for radio investigations of the ionosphere by rockets would be realized in one of the design offices and workshops of the ministry. The people who began to work with me were members of a department headed by Boris Konoplyov. As I related in Chapter 7, I came to know Konoplyov at the beginning of World War II, when the Academy of Sciences made me part of a team he led to develop a radio phase navigation system for the air force. At that time I learned that Konoplyov was a talented, ingenious radio engineer and a frank and honest man.

Konoplyov appointed an engineer to lead the team from his department and to coordinate the details of both the principal aspects of the development of the radio sets and their technical specifications with me. Konoplyov ordered that without my signature on the design drafts the laboratory of the design office could not produce any of the radio sets. His insistence on this puzzled me for some time. The engineer he appointed seemed a capable enough person. I had, in fact, recently reviewed and approved his defense of his Ph.D. thesis.

But Konoplyov must have well understood the character of the engineer, whom perhaps he appointed simply because there was no other suitably qualified person in the department. When the KGB general, Malyshev, fired me from PhIAN, this engineer became the manager of some of the rocket radio experiments I had conceived and, as I later learned, began to claim credit for my ideas. In May 1988 I attended my first international symposium in the West, a meeting of the American Geophysical Union in Baltimore. There I met some people from the USSR who told me that this person now claims that he was also the author of the radio beacon experiments on satellites, discussed below, which were realized at my laboratory at IZMIRAN in the 1960s. People behave in strange ways, do they not? At any rate, Konoplyov did what he could to document my role in the project.

One curious aspect of the whole affair was that the last design drafts were brought to me, and I signed them, on the morning of 1 March 1951, the very day when Malyshev told Leontovich of my exclusion from PhIAN. There is no question that Malyshev knew of my work on these designs: nothing of that importance could occur without KGB oversight. But I think it is only a coincidence that these things both happened on the same day. Malyshev's timing probably had less to do with waiting for me to sign the final design document than with wanting to remove me from PhIAN before Dmitri Skobeltsyn, the new director of the institute, a very honest and upright person, arrived from the United States. But who can say for sure?

It is sad to tell here that Boris Konoplyov was one of those who were killed in an explosion during the testing of a special rocket on 24 October 1960 at the Cosmodrom Baikonur in Kazakhstan. At that time he was the director of a highly confidential enterprise to design various systems for rockets. During the explosion dozens of civilian and military rocket professionals were lost, including a Hero of the Soviet Union, Senior Artillery Marshal Mitrophan Nedelin, who was then supreme commander-in-chief of the rocket forces of strategic operations of the USSR. The tragedy was later referred to in some publications as Nedelin's Catastrophe.

For years after being dismissed from PhIAN I had no contact with the confidential groups involved in Russia's rocket program, although I continued to pursue ionosphere research at IZMIRAN. But around the beginning of 1956 I was invited to the presidium of the Academy of Sciences by Gennady Skuridin and asked to consider how satellites might be used to investigate the ionosphere. Skuridin was the scientific secretary of a special committee that for many years governed space research programs like that of *Sputnik I*. From its inception in the 1950s until the 1970s, that committee was chaired by the academician Mstislav Keldysh, at that time the president of the Academy of Sciences. Keldysh was the chief administrator and scientific leader of Russia's satellite research programs, including the first flights into space with humans aboard. There was a saying about Keldysh, Sergei Korolyov, and Igor Kurchatov, the leader of the atom bomb project, that they were "the most powerful K's in the USSR."

Soon after my meeting with Skuridin in 1956 I prepared a brief program for experimental radio investigations of the ionosphere by satellite. The principal idea of the project was close to that I outlined above, in connection with the team from Boris Konoplyov's department at the Radio Ministry. Because of my dismissal from PhIAN, in 1956 I did not know that those experiments were in fact being carried out. Months went by, and in the beginning of 1957 I was invited to a large meeting, chaired by Keldysh, to discuss all of the proposed research programs for satellites. Dozens of people were there: academicians, engineers, and scientists from different fields, designers, bureaucrats, official representatives, and certainly people from the KGB.

In the course of the day the group from the special design bureau of the Ministry of Radio Engineering, which made the devices for the high-altitude rocket investigations that I proposed in the late 1940s, announced their project: to modify Langmuir probes for experiments on satellites. In general it was a good idea. What they were suggesting, however, was something that they had not thought through in terms of physics. They had not taken into account that the characteristics of the probes themselves would change if placed on fast-moving bodies such as satellites. New effects would certainly be produced owing to the interaction of the moving satellite with the magnetoplasma of the ionosphere.

When the presentation was over, I politely suggested, without criticizing the project itself, that measurements with Langmuir probes aboard satellites should be based on a new theoretical understanding of the phenomena involved with the probes. Otherwise, the treatment of experimental data would give spurious results. The theory of these phenomena, which is a complicated and delicate problem, was developed in the early 1960s. Those theoretical results appeared in *Space Physics with Artificial Satellites,* by myself, Alexander Gurevich, and Lev Pitaevsky, published in 1964 in Russian and translated into English in 1965.[1]

After my comments on the plan to use Langmuir probes, two engineers from the design bureau and their boss spoke rudely against me. They said nothing about the substance of my scientific remarks but only insisted that the new radio method for satellite investigations I had proposed was wrong. They even said that the underlying idea for such radio investigations by satellite was theirs. They claimed that they had created it for experiments on high-altitude rockets. Thus they lied. The high-altitude rocket project originated with me; I had conceived and designed those experiments. Moreover, they had not understood that the radio phase experiment with satellites that I was now proposing differed in some aspects from the one with rockets. Yet those people were still influenced by what the KGB had done to me in 1951. Neither Keldysh nor any of the other participants at that meeting objected to the attacks on me, although the story of how the KGB general had thrown me out of PhIAN was well known. When the discussion shifted to another topic, I rose and left the highly confidential meeting. At that meeting we learned that a *sputnik* would be launched soon, although we did not know when. After that incident, until the launch of *Sputnik I,* I broke off any connection with Keldysh's special committee.

Ten years later, in connection with the tenth anniversary celebration of the launching of *Sputnik I,* a special report in the newspaper *Pravda* (The Truth)

1. Yakov Alpert, Alexander Gurevich, and Lev Pitaevsky, *Space Physics with Artificial Satellites* (Moscow: Nauka, 1964; New York: Consultants Bureau, 1965).

published the results of the measurements made by the Langmuir probes. And as I had expected, they were wrong! On the evening of that anniversary day in 1967, there was a special celebration in Moscow in the large hall of the "Scientists' House" *(Dom Uchyonykh)* of the Academy of Sciences, a beautiful old mansion built by an uncle of the last tsar. In the lobby afterward I spoke with Sergei Korolyov about the incorrect results announced in *Pravda*. I told him the results could not be right. By their treatment of the experimental data the experimenters had not taken into account that the velocity of the ions in space was ten to twenty times faster than the velocity of the space probe. It was a very stupid, inexcusable mistake. Korolyov only shook his head, and I do not know whether he took any action in the matter.

Getting Science from Sputniks: The Radio Rise and Radio Set of Artificial Satellites

But what I have just related is putting things a little out of order. On 4 October 1957 the first artificial satellite went into orbit. The very next day I received a call from the vice-president of the Academy of Sciences, Vladimir Kotelnikov. He said, "You know that *Sputnik I* is in orbit, but we are getting no science from it. The president of the Academy, Mstislav Keldysh, asks that you think about this problem and tell us what science we can get from this satellite." In response, I asked for a couple of days to consider the problem.

When I put the telephone down, I had no idea what might be done. But within an hour it came to me. The next day I told Kotelnikov that even without special devices on the satellite we could get important scientific results from *Sputnik I,* namely, data about the structure of the ionosphere. To do that I had to get good ground station records of the signals emitted by the radio beacon aboard *Sputnik I.* I also asked to have access to a computer and to be assigned a collaborator to help with my calculations. Kotelnikov told me that many military radio receiving stations were tracking *Sputnik I* and recording its signals. All these data would be gathered by a military representative and would be given to me. The necessary calculations would be made on the computer at the Radio Technical Institute of the Academy of Sciences, which Kotelnikov directed. This project was carried out soon after our conversation.

At this point I want to give a general overview of the idea of that first scientific study by satellite. Any luminous body such as an artificial satellite, moving along a closed orbit around the earth, becomes optically visible at an observation point on the earth's surface when it rises above the horizon at that point. The rays of visible light propagate in the atmosphere and space on a nearly perfectly straight path. Therefore, the optical lines to the satellite as it

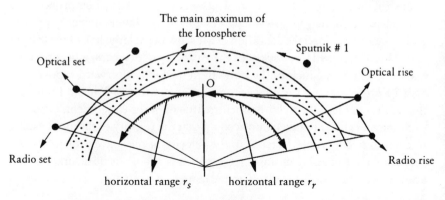

10. Radio rise and radio set data obtained from *Sputnik I,* 1957; O is observation point.

comes above the horizon are straight lines. The moving body optically disappears, at the same observation point, when the body falls below a straight line of the opposite horizon. Both these lines are tangents touching the point of observation. The lines of propagation of the radio waves emitted by satellites, however, are curved in the ionosphere, that is, in the ionized part of the atmosphere where free electrons and ions are produced. That happens because the frequencies of these radio waves are millions of times lower than the frequencies of the light.

This deformation of the radio waves' trajectory becomes appreciable at altitudes of 60–70 km above the surface of the earth; it is maximal at altitudes of about 250–350 km and becomes closer to straight lines at altitudes of about 1,000–1,500 km. Therefore, *the radio appearance* of a satellite precedes its optical visibility. Similarly, in disappearing from view, *the radio disappearance* of the satellite is late with respect to the disappearing optical view. This effect depends upon the ionization level of the ionosphere and, in particular, on the altitude distribution of the density of free electrons and ions, which are produced in the atmosphere under the action of ultraviolet solar radiation. Therefore, to determine the times of the rise and set of the radio signal, it is necessary to know the altitude dependence of the electron density of the ionosphere. On the other hand, if you know these times and the position of the body, and if you also have some initial data, that is, some characteristics of the ionosphere at that time, you can find the average, smoothed altitude dependence of the electron concentration. This, in general terms, was what was done in our study (see figure 10).

For that purpose, we used the radio signals of *Sputnik I* recorded at the military observation points. Most of them were very clear. Precise data on the

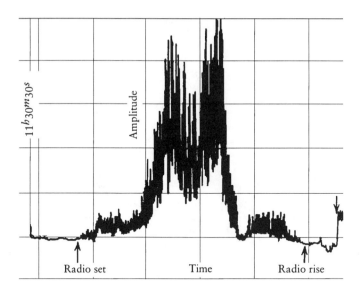

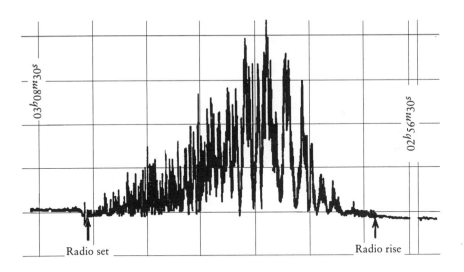

position of the satellite in all regions of its radio visibility near the point of observation, as well as the general characteristics of the ionosphere in an altitude range of about 80–300 km, were used in that study. These data were estimated by using the records of a so-called radio sound service, which regularly explored the ionosphere up to its main maximum at an altitude of about 300 km in many places over the USSR. Such services exist in the United States

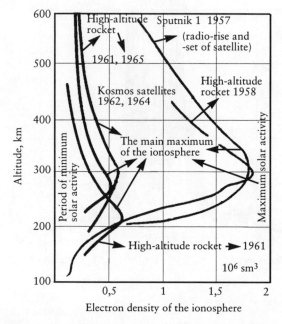

11. Altitude dependencies of the electron density of the ionosphere, estimated by satellite experiments

and in many other countries. They have various functions, including weather forecasting and establishing the clearest frequencies for radio broadcasts and communication. With the radio sound service data and the results of theoretical computer calculations of the horizontal ranges of *Sputnik I,* we found the average smoothed electron density dependence above the maximum of the ionosphere in the altitude range of 300–1,000 km (see figure 11). Before our work, the dependence at those altitudes was unknown.

What was the significance of these results? They were important not only because they were new. The data also contradicted ideas presented at the time in many treatises on the structure and formation of the ionosphere above the region of its maximal ionization at 250–350 km. Many researchers thought that the density of electrons would break up and immediately become very low above the main maximum (about 300 km) of the ionosphere. The *Sputnik I* data showed that the density did not fall off abruptly but instead declined very gradually. This result was confirmed by high-altitude rocket experiments as early as the end of 1958. But the data from these rocket experiments was confidential, and I only learned the results much later. Ironically, these rocket

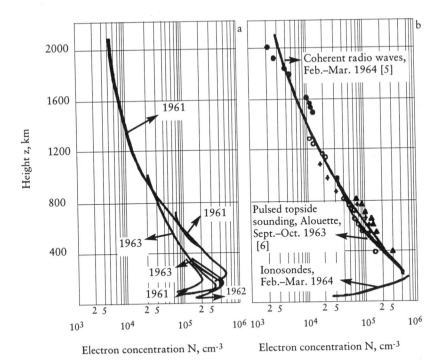

experiments had their origin in the experiments which I proposed to Marshal Vasilevsky and the design of which I directed until my dismissal from PhIAN in 1951.

When the results obtained by the high-altitude rocket experiments were published, the agreement with the data obtained from *Sputnik I* was rather good. In looking at such data, we must take into account the fact that the characteristics of the ionosphere change regularly over time. Sometimes these changes occur very rapidly during the course of a day. They also depend on the season of the year, on the geographic location of the observation point, and on the eleven-year cycle of solar emission activity. The results from experiments we did in 1962 and 1964 on the *Cosmos* satellites and the results from rocket launches in the United States and in the USSR in 1961, 1962, and 1965 also showed significant agreement.

It is also appropriate to describe here our other observations of radio waves with a frequency of 20 MHz radiated by the beacon of *Sputnik I* in October 1957. My young colleagues at Mirnyi in the Antarctic region performed them. The results of those observations were interesting and also new. For the first

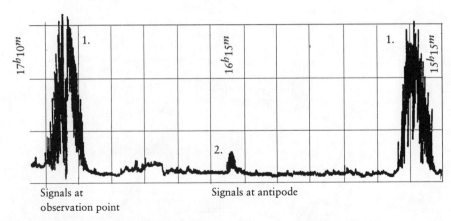

Signals at
observation point

Signals at antipode

12. The Antipode Effect, showing radio waves recorded at the South Pole when *Sputnik I* crossed the North Pole. 1 = radio waves from *Sputnik I;* 2 = radio waves from the Antipode (the North Pole)

time we found experimentally from the records of *Sputnik*'s radio signals the Antipode Effect, as it is known in the scientific literature. This phenomenon was theoretically predicted by the German physicist Wolf Schumann in 1952.[2] The nature of that effect is the following: the amplitude of the radio waves propagated above the earth increases very much at the antipode of the source of the emitted radio waves. These radio waves reach the antipode through the spherical wave guide formed between the surface of the earth and the bottom of the ionosphere. To elucidate, we could say that the amplification, the focusing, of these radio waves at the antipode is a result of their flowing together to the antipode from different directions. This large increase in the amplitude of the radio waves was seen in the records at the South Pole when the satellite crossed the ionosphere above the North Pole (see figure 12).

On Wednesday mornings Mstislav Keldysh crammed twenty to thirty people into his office to discuss space research. At one of these meetings I presented the results obtained from *Sputnik I.* There the people who performed the rocket experiments with Langmuir probes again tried to organize opposition against me. They said, "The things Alpert is talking about are not scientific results. They are only in his imagination." In contrast to his silence during the earlier discussion, Keldysh now cut them short, saying, "Well, then, bravo! If Alpert has discovered the correct method of dealing with this problem, he is a fine fellow [*Molodetz*]." My *Sputnik I* results were a matter of observation

2. Wolf Schumann, "Propagation of Electromagnetic Waves in the Earth-Ionosphere Wave Guide," *Zeitschrift für Naturforschung* 7a (1952): 149.

as well as imagination, but, if they had been produced by imagination alone, that would not have been too bad. After all, as I have already quoted Einstein: "Imagination is more important than knowledge."

When the results of the radio rise/radio set study on *Sputnik I* were announced, they created a sensation. They were the first scientific data obtained from the earth's first artificial satellite Many journalists called from abroad and asked about those results, and I was interviewed by TASS. By the end of 1957 I had written some articles about them, which were published in 1958. One of these was "The Electron Density of the Outer Ionosphere Estimated by Investigation of the Radio Signals of *Sputnik I.*"[3]

Mstislav Keldysh and the Wednesday Meetings, 1960–1970

Soon after the launch of *Sputnik I,* I was invited to come regularly to the Wednesday morning meetings in Keldysh's office at the Institute of Advanced Mathematics. Present were physicists, engineers, and specialists in celestial mechanics who calculated the trajectories of the space probes and satellites. Sometimes cosmonauts attended the meetings, although they were never introduced in that capacity. Their identity as cosmonauts was a state secret. But after a launch, when a cosmonaut's picture was published in *Pravda,* I sometimes thought, "Oh, yes, I saw him or her at Keldysh's seminar."

In general, there was a cooperative atmosphere at those meetings, which Keldysh always chaired personally. He was a powerfully built man of medium height, and he exuded a sense of toughness. A prominent mathematician and theoretician of mechanics, he had an active, intuitive mind and quickly grasped new ideas in engineering and physics. He spoke very slowly and deliberately, but also very decisively. He was a man who never said "Maybe." In this he was the very opposite of Mandelshtam, who often said "Maybe" and "Perhaps." Mandelshtam enjoyed thinking about and discussing what might be. Keldysh could not spare the time to do so.

Each Wednesday morning Keldysh opened the meeting by describing new projects for space research missions and announcing forthcoming launchings of new satellites and space probes. Then he asked for scientific research

3. Yakov Alpert, F. F. Dobryakova, E. F. Chudesenko, and B. S. Shapiro, "The Electron Density of the Outer Ionosphere Estimated by Investigation of the Radio Signals of *Sputnik I,*" *Uspekhi Physiki Nauk* 65 (1958) (in Russian) and *Doklady* 120 (1958) (in English). Dobryakova, a member of Kotelnikov's institute, calculated by computer the elliptical integrals that I gave her. Chudesenko, a military captain, compiled the military records of the radio beacon signals. Shapiro, my colleague at IZMIRAN, selected and prepared the ionosphere data from altitudes up to 250–300 km.

suggestions. He often interrupted the ensuing discussions, saying that our recommendations did not, in his opinion, represent an optimal approach. Then he would announce his decision about what to do. Sometimes his alternative decisions were not the best ones either. But, as I recall, they were never completely wrong. And they were never ambiguous.

Nevertheless, these scientific discussions were often unpleasant, because Keldysh followed the hierarchical tradition. If the directors of the institutes approved the projects proposed by members of their institutes — and as a rule these people were academicians — he did not argue with them. The difficulty with this was that the directors of the institutes were all too often driven simply by a desire to enhance their institutes' prestige by claiming a share of Russia's space program.

Once, we had a critical situation. I was sure that we should stop certain experiments that had been approved. I asked Keldysh for a private meeting, and after some days I spoke to him very frankly. In detail I told him my scientific assessment of the project and criticized the acceptance of some other wrong-minded projects. I said that, in general, the choices of the people and institutes having the responsibility and privilege of carrying out space experiments had not been good. Moreover, I added, "If Igor Kurchatov had chosen such people, the USSR would never have produced the atom bomb." I said that it would be embarrassing for the USSR to announce the results of those experiments. I also pointed out that many good proposals were being rejected because of the limits of available space on the satellites for scientific devices.

Even though he had an important meeting to attend right after ours, Keldysh followed my argument carefully, and he did not interrupt as he did at public meetings. As usual, it seems, he understood me well, but he said, "Why didn't you tell this to X and Y? They were the directors of the institutes that approved these projects." I answered, "But they discuss these problems only with the members of their own institutes. They use their authority only to endorse the experiments conceived in their institutes." And I continued, "Why must I speak to X and Y? They are not professionals in the ionosphere and magnetosphere field. They should have to deal with me on these problems, not me with them!" After this conversation nothing changed. Throughout the 1970s and 1980s, incorrect scientific results had to have been obtained from the experiments I discussed with Keldysh.

Nevertheless, it appeared that Keldysh was doing his best to find optimal solutions for the scientific research problems of space missions. Distinguished physicists were often invited to his meetings. On one occasion Peter Kapitsa and Yakov Zeldovich took part in the discussions. Keldysh informed us at that meeting that a space probe would be launched to the planet Venus. He asked for ideas for scientific experiments. Close to the end of the meeting I proposed the following rather simple experiment for what is now popularly called searching for extraterrestrial intelligence (SETI).

The frequency of the alternating electrical current used everywhere in the world is in the range of 50–60 Hz. This is because any electrical system including alternators, dynamos, and electrical lines achieves its highest efficiency at these frequencies. This optimal solution was found at the beginning of our century. It is a general law of electrical engineering. Consequently, it should be known to any technically developed civilization. The radiation of these electrical installations can, in principle, be found far from their sources.

But to prove the validity of this idea, it has to be known if the radiated power of such closed electrical systems can be detected at remote distances. I roughly estimated the energy content of the 50–60 Hz emissions for the entire world. I concluded that this was sufficient for reception above noise at very remote distances from the earth, as, for example, where the tail of magnetic field lines still exists. The earth's magnetic field lines guide these electromagnetic oscillations. Years ago the 50–60 Hz emission of electrical current was found at the bottom of the ocean despite the very strong absorption of these waves in the highly conductive water of the sea.

The second point is more fundamental. How can these extra-low-frequency electromagnetic waves reach remote distances from a planet and still be detected through space, where no organized magnetic field lines exist? Indeed, a magnetic plasma with a density of several units of electrons per cubic centimeter will cut off all the electromagnetic waves with frequencies of less than several kilohertz if magnetic lines do not exist. The waves will not leave the planet and will not propagate into distant space. The answer is that the emission could reach remote distances from a planet by virtue of the magnetic field lines frozen in huge plasma clouds. The clouds would capture the radiation of the electrical stations and bring it into deep space. These clouds are formed in a planet's magnetic tail, where the magnetic lines are opened. In general, these clouds, traveling at great distances in space, may also contain important scientific information on different kinds of electromagnetic phenomena. To try to obtain this information would appear to be worthwhile.

Near the end of our meeting, Keldysh asked Kapitsa to give his opinion about our discussions. I was pleased to hear Kapitsa say, "The most interesting idea was presented by Alpert. It should be checked out on that mission." Months went by, and Keldysh did not ask me to prepare a detailed proposal for the experiment. So why had he invited those distinguished experts to discuss the problems? Was it only for show? I never again offered ideas for space experiments, because it seemed futile to do so.

Another event illustrates the situation. Once there was a discussion about the scientific devices that should be placed on a new satellite mission. The meeting was not held under Keldysh in Moscow, but in Leningrad. While explaining a proposed experiment, a young man from the Institute of Cosmical Investigations made an incorrect scientific statement. I did not interrupt him; I wanted to discuss the matter with him privately. After the meeting I asked the young man why he had not corrected his statement. His answer was a cynical one: "I did so to save my experiment. The chair did not understand the matter. But I know my mistake, and I shall improve the experiment, if it is approved."

Despite the great interest of many scientists in the USSR in the new and exciting field of space research, there were those who, one by one, refused to collaborate with the people who regulated the space program. They did not want to work in that uncertain atmosphere. By the late 1960s I did the same. In general, political, military, and career considerations prevailed in this area. Often the people responsible for placing scientific experiments on the satellites were not those best suited to the task. Different experimental designers were awarded with prizes, orders of merit, and so on for their alleged success. In fact, I do not know many especially significant scientific achievements gleaned from those experiments of the 1970s and after. In contrast, soon after the launching of its first small satellite, *Explorer I,* the United States took the lead in scientific space research. I remember when the first scientific delegation approved by the KGB and the party bosses went to France to present the scientific results obtained from satellites. The choice of this team was yet another highly compromised decision. I was told that many scientists at the French meeting asked about the absence of people from whom they had expected scientific presentations. Mstislav Keldysh did not object to the roster of those who were allowed to go abroad; he did not oppose the official decisions of the party bureaucrats or the pressure of the KGB.

Some space missions were more exercises in flag-waving than serious scientific efforts. That happened with the Halley's comet mission in the 1980s. At that time, I had not had any connection with the activity of space research for many years. Besides, I was a refusnik — someone who had applied for emigration and was not permitted an exit visa, an enemy of the USSR in the official view. Still, some foreign scientists who collaborated on this project with the Institute of Cosmical Investigations of the Academy of Sciences (Roald Sagdeev was its director) visited me and discussed its program; they even asked me to think about it professionally. The mission to Halley's comet would be an exciting scientific event and an excellent chance to explore many phenomena produced in the space plasma. It was an opportunity to learn many of the peculiarities of magnetoplasma in general and also to learn the behavior of the solar wind on the path of the space probe on its very long voyage to the comet.

I prepared a small, simple program of such experiments. It included measurements of important new characteristics of magnetoplasma and deduced some theoretical formulas for the treatment of these data. Without mentioning the source of the ideas, my foreign colleagues and friends tried to discuss them with their Soviet colleagues, without success. The only aim and interest of the Soviet manager of that project was to reach the comet and procure photographs of it. After that mission there were many awards and medals. Roald Sagdeev even became a Hero of the Soviet Union for the "scientific" achievements of that mission. Yet the only worthwhile science associated with the mission was the work involved in getting the space probe to the comet. The engineers and technicians were the ones who truly deserved credit and gratitude for that mission, as for many others.

Many important and advanced elements were omitted from Soviet radio rocket experiments. The U.S. radio experiments with sounding rockets were scientifically far superior to ours. In addition, for other kinds of experiments by that team on satellites with Langmuir probes, the scientific results produced in the USSR were often wrong. Yet those results were not only published, they were advertised as constituting an important achievement of the Soviet space research program! Moreover, those involved became its official heroes. They were the protégés of the KGB, which supported them and chose them to go abroad to represent the Soviet scientific community to the West. Initially, Western scientists did not protest when the many other Soviet scientists they had invited were not permitted to travel to the West to attend their meetings. That Soviet reality, the preferential selection of people and of space science projects, which began soon after the launch of the first sputniks, steadily diminished the scientific achievements of the USSR in space research. In my mind, that situation, and not technological difficulty, was the most important cause of the regression of Soviet space research with rockets and satellites.

The Soviet Union possessed the expertise and technological resources required for space science. At IZMIRAN in the early 1960s, for example, we built a network of devices for radio phase satellite experiments. The radio beacon placed on the satellite was a small and lightweight device. The receiver and the recorder of the Doppler-shifted radio waves were designed together with the design bureau of the Ministry of Communication by a good radio engineer named Alexander Kutyakov and by one of my young associates, Vladimir Belyansky. At that time our device was unique, the first of its type. We tested

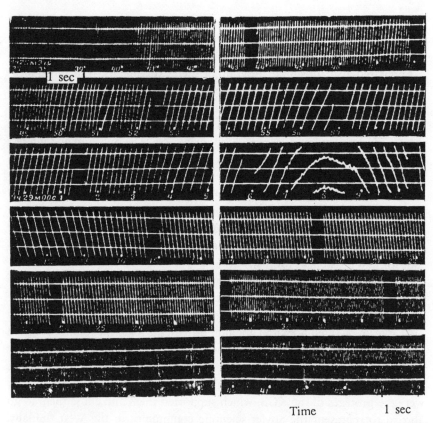

13. The phase difference of two Doppler-shifted radio waves radiated by the *Cosmos* satellite and recorded near Moscow at IZMIRAN, 1964

this new device with radio beacons flown on helicopters. The clarity and precision of our satellite data surprised many visitors from the West who saw them (figure 13).

In recognition of our preeminence in this field, and also because I was not permitted to go to the West, an international symposium of the Committee of Space Research of the International Union of Radio Science was organized in my department at IZMIRAN in 1974. The main subject is reflected in the symposium title: "Radio-Beacon Investigations of the Ionosphere by Satellites." That symposium was attended by about eighty people, including thirty-one from thirteen countries in the West, from Europe, the United States, Cuba, and Australia.

Our experiments were performed through the early 1970s. We learned from them the altitude dependence of electron concentration, that is, the extent of ionization of the upper part of the ionosphere, its "cloudy" structure, and we observed different new wave processes in the magnetoplasma. The results of these experiments were summarized in dozens of papers. At that time, however, I gradually ended my activity with experimental investigations by satellite. My withdrawal began earlier because of the situation with Keldysh's committee. But it was also inspired when Soviet tanks invaded Czechoslovakia in 1968. I became convinced that we in the USSR were living under a system of deceitful politics and fascist ways, precisely the things that had led to the occupation of foreign states. Those times are the subject of the next chapter.

11

The Era of Refusal, 1975–1987

Soviet Tanks in Prague

On 21 August 1968 Soviet tanks entered Prague. The Kremlin took and announced this action, in defense of Marxism-Leninism and the Czechoslovakian people, two days after Soviet party leader Leonid Brezhnev embraced the progressive Czechoslovakian leader Alexander Dubcek in a friendly meeting. A photograph of that embrace appeared prominently in *Time*'s coverage of the Soviet move.

On 25 August 1968 seven Soviet citizens demonstrated against this tragic event. At noon that day Konstantin Babitsky, a linguist; Larisa Bogoraz, a philologist; Vadim Delone, a poet; Vladimir Dremliuga, a worker; Pavel Litvinov, a physicist; Victor Fainberg, an art critic; and Natalia Gorbanevskaya, a poet and philologist, assembled in Red Square. At the sixteenth-century circular stone monument known as Lobnoye Mesto, where the tsars' repressive decrees were announced, they held placards reading, For Our and Your freedom!, Shame to the Invaders!, Hands off Czechoslovakia!, and Long Live a Free and Independent Czechoslovakia! Within minutes the Russian police — the Militsia — surrounded the protesters, beat them savagely, and brought them to the Militsia building.[1]

1. There were actually nine people in the protest group that day. Natalia Gorbanev-

Like most Russians, I did not learn until much later of this heroic protest of noble young people against the re-Stalinization of the Soviet regime. In the tightly controlled USSR, at first only those who were in Red Square at the time, the small dissident community, and the Soviet authorities knew about the protest. In his memoirs, published posthumously in 1990, Andrei Sakharov, who also learned of the demonstration long after it occurred, called it "a miracle that restored the honor of the country."[2]

But I did learn soon enough of the tanks in Prague. It sickened me to know that Soviet troops held the Czechoslovakian people at gunpoint, "protecting" them from their own desire for a more open society. For two weeks I did not go to my laboratory. I stayed alone in a small country house, listening constantly to the "Voices," as we called the radio broadcasts from the West, for news of what was happening. Radio Liberty, the BBC, the Voice of America, Deutsche Welle, Radio Sweden — I switched between them as the hours passed. One of my close friends, a physicist, told me later that when he learned through the Voices of the Soviet move on 21 August, he walked to his institute, about three miles distant, and was not able to stop his tears. Many people shared these feelings. But many other people said of the Czechoslovakians, "Tak nado" ("It must be so"). That was the stereotypical answer of Soviet citizens who justified (though perhaps only by words) any political or social action of the Soviet leaders and of the Communist Party. For example, Nikolai Pushkov, the director of the institute IZMIRAN, where I worked, said this to me, as did Irina's sister and many other people. This destroyed my relations with them.

At the end of August 1968, on a brilliantly sunny afternoon on the Baltic seacoast, where I had gone on vacation with my first wife, Irina Chernysheva,

---

skaya had her three-month-old son with her in a baby carriage. The police only beat Gorbanevskaya in the van taking the protesters away, after separating her from her child. The ninth person was a young history student, Tanya Baieva. Wanting to keep her career from being ruined before it started, the other protesters told the police that Baieva was only a passer-by. Of the seven protesters, three were sentenced to internal exile, two were imprisoned in the Gulag for two years, and two, Fainberg and Gorbanevskaya, were incarcerated in a mental hospital in Khazan. These were thought to be relatively light sentences. Pavel Litvinov was the grandson of Maxim Litvinov, who as the USSR's foreign minister for many years was one of the original Narodny, or People's, Commissars. He was the Soviet ambassador to the United States in 1941–43. Maxim Litvinov's widow wrote to Anastas Mikoyan on behalf of her grandson; Mikoyan in turn suggested to Brezhnev that a show trial and heavy sentences would be a great propaganda opportunity for the West.

2. Andrei Sahkarov, *Vospominaniya* (New York: Chekhov Printing House, 1990), 385. The translation from the Russian text is my own.

our good friend Eugene Lifshitz and his wife, Zina, I heard Andrei Sakharov's essay "Reflections on Progress, Peaceful Co-existence, and Intellectual Freedom" read by an announcer on BBC Radio. I stood by the receiver and listened to Sakharov's words as to my own inner voice. Shortly before I heard the essay, the distinguished dissident Andrei Amalryk had transferred it to the West. In their reports on Soviet affairs and the Soviet military intervention in Czechoslovakia, the radio programs from the West discussed the many arrests and trials during the 1960s of people who fought for human rights in the USSR.

Step by step, the conviction that the USSR was a fascist country became stronger in my mind. The regime was inescapably totalitarian and anti-Semitic. The lie of the system pervaded all of public life and spoiled private life too. I have written about similar ideas and feelings that I had many years before. At this juncture I understood that I could not and should not be reconciled with the Soviet system any longer. I knew I had to make a choice. It was a crucial time of choice for many Soviet citizens.

Soon I learned about the refusnik movement. I knew that for people who were involved, as I was, in research programs on satellites and space rockets it would be hard to win permission to emigrate. But in my mind in 1968 I made the choice to apply for an exit visa. It was clear to me that I would, at the least, be dismissed from all my positions and be barred from working in the Academy of Sciences. That had already happened temporarily in 1951; this time I expected the bar to be permanent. Still, I did not think much of possible consequences. I decided to seek to emigrate and be done with it. That was my protest, as it was for some others.

This was not an action I could take immediately, however. First, I felt, I must gradually withdraw from all confidential work on rockets and sputniks and all consulting on military research projects. My hope was that this would speed things along when I applied to emigrate, because the authorities would recognize that I was no longer involved in matters of state secrecy. For example, I deflected invitations to attend rocket launches, which in the USSR were highly secret affairs. I kept on with my research and continued to publish papers and a new book, but I no longer participated in secret projects and I ceased going to Keldysh's Wednesday morning meetings.

There were other reasons for not acting right away. In 1969–70 I fell in love with Svetlana Pivkova. As soon as I realized that this had happened to me, I spoke to Irina. We separated, in peace, after twenty-five years together as husband and wife. For many years before that we were friends, and we have remained friends to this day. At that time Irina was a full professor and chair of the Department of Lexicology and Stylistics at the Moscow Institute for Foreign Languages. She is well known as a leading professional in her field and has published books in Russian and German. In 1986 she gave me her last book, *Lexicologie der Deutschen Gegenwärts Sprache,* inscribing it, "To Dear Yanya, in the hope that he will never leave his homeland."

In 1972 Svetlana and I married. Two years later, six years after my initial decision to try to leave the country, we decided to apply to emigrate from the Soviet Union. It was a difficult decision for Svetlana to try to leave her family and her homeland. Svetlana is the youngest daughter of Maria Evdokimovna, who came to Moscow from a small village about eighty miles away. Maria Evdokimovna lost her husband at the beginning of World War II, and she never remarried. An uneducated woman from the countryside, she supported herself and her three daughters by sewing military uniforms. She was a strong person indeed. She died in November 1998, at ninety-six years of age. Her first daughter, Zoya, seventeen years older than Svetlana, became a nurse. The second, Lida, fifteen years older, became a ballerina of the Bolshoi Theater in Moscow.

When we decided to apply to emigrate, Svetlana was a senior engineer at the Institute of Medical and Biological Problems in Moscow. There she designed devices for the study of certain life conditions on space rockets, and she was part of a team that studied the behavior of different plants and animals in experiments later performed in collaboration with the United States. Svetlana also took part in experimental observations of the behavior of three people who spent a year isolated in a special chamber. They performed tests there, for example, cultivating plants and doing exercises. In a sense those experiments simulated the behavior of people in space on satellites.

Svetlana was employed at that institute in 1964. But her working life started in 1958, when she was seventeen years old and continues up to now. She was awarded her degree as a research engineer in 1966 at the Moscow Power Institute (MEI), which had an extension school with evening classes. Because Svetlana had heart murmurs — I wrote earlier about her open-heart surgery in 1980 — the Medical Commission of MEI did not accept her at the institute as a regular student. She was considered a disabled person. But the extension school of MEI did not require a medical exam. Thus the bureaucracy put Svetlana, with her weak heart, in the circumstances of working eight hours a day and attending evening classes four days a week!

With the decision to seek to emigrate, Svetlana and I entered the world of the dissidents and the refusniks, two distinct but related, and sometimes overlapping, groups. It was at this time that we learned much more about the early dissidents who struggled for freedom and human rights in the USSR, particularly about the trials of Vladimir Bukovsky, of Peter Galanskov and Alexander Ginzburg, of Anatoly Marchenko, and of Yuri Daniel and Andrei Sinyavsky, among a number of other brave and noble people who were the first in this holy movement in the 1960s and even earlier. Some of these people spoke out against the regime when they were only eighteen or nineteen years old and spent half their lives and more in prison, or even died there. Anatoly Marchenko, for example, who was married to Larisa Bogoraz and who died in prison, was a young industrial worker when he first demonstrated for human rights. Later he became a writer.[3] He was on trial for crimes against the Soviet state on 21 August 1968. Among those keeping vigil outside the closed courthouse was Pavel Litvinov, who told every passer-by, "The tanks of Russia are in Czechoslovakia." Much has been written about the early dissidents, but not enough can be said to honor their sacrifices.[4]

Becoming Refusniks

The refusniks were so named because anyone who applied to emigrate was immediately refused. The tortuous emigration process was administered by the Soviet Office of Visas and International Relations (OVIR). The first step in the process was to secure a letter from a relative in Israel, inviting one to settle there. At this time even non-Jews leaving the Soviet Union could only go to Israel, and when the authorities expelled someone from the country they gave him or her visas to Israel. In 1973 I asked for such a letter and in due course received one.

The writer of the letter claimed to be my uncle, but in fact he was not a relation and I did not know the man. This happened as follows. When we decided to emigrate, Svetlana and I came into contact with the refusnik community. Among the first refusniks we got to know well were Tanya and Benjamin Levich, whom we met in 1973 while we were on vacation in Sukhumi, on the Black Sea. Benjamin Levich was a corresponding member of the academy and well known as a physicist. The Leviches did much to welcome us into the refusnik community and its links with foreign scientists and journalists. The Leviches' two sons and their wives were also refusniks. On one occasion at the Leviches' home, I met the man who was president of Israel's Academy of Sciences. I asked him to arrange a letter of invitation for me, and he did so. (I

3. Anatoly Marchenko's *My Testimony* was published in many languages. The English version was translated by Michael Scammel (New York: E. P. Dutton, 1969). The original version was first made available in Russia only in 1981 through *samizdat,* the dissident community's underground distribution of material banned by the Soviet regime. The first samizdat "Chronicle of Events" appeared in 1969.

4. An essential source for information on the dissident movement is Ludmilla Alexeyeva's *The History of the Russian Dissidents* (Middletown: Wesleyan University Press, 1985). Alexeyeva was one of the founders of the samizdat movement. She was also one of the first to join Yuri Orlov when he founded a Helsinki Watch Group in Moscow, and she is now the head of that group.

also gave him copies of the American editions of two of my books on the ionosphere and the propagation of radio waves for the library of Tel Aviv University.) The refuseniks and the Soviet authorities alike understood that the letters of invitation from Israel often contained an element of fiction; it was all part of the complicated and serious game that the Soviet system forced us to play.

The authorities began to act on my letter of invitation as soon as it arrived in the Soviet Union, but before it reached me personally. On my going to work at IZMIRAN one day, I discovered that the glass sign that read Chief of the Department, Professor Yakov Alpert, had disappeared from the door of my office. I soon learned that I was also dismissed from the institute's scientific council and was relieved of all duties. For some reason I was not fired outright but made a "senior scientist" with a reduced salary. The authorities also treated Sakharov in this way. He was a "senior scientist" with a salary from PhIAN all the time he was in internal exile in Gorky.

In any case, I was told that my schedule was free. The KGB and the leadership of the institute did not want me to associate with the other members of my institute, lest I "infect" them. As it happened, the director of IZMIRAN, Pushkov's successor, was none other than Vladimir Migulin, who had been one of my bosses at PhIAN. I once said to him, "I understand that if they tell you to do so, you will immediately throw me out of IZMIRAN." He did not contradict me.

After the letter was delivered to us a few days later, Svetlana encountered even worse at the Institute of Medical and Biological Problems. When she came to the institute one day late in October 1973, the guard at the entrance stopped her, saying that she could not enter the institute because he did not have her identification permit. Except when employees were actually at work, identification permits were kept at the entrance booth. On entering the institute an employee would say her or his number, and the guard would hand the person the identification permit. Svetlana came home in tears, and from that day she was never allowed inside the institute. Her professional activity was completely stopped.

Later in 1974, when we decided to apply for exit visas, the administration of the institute refused to give Svetlana the reference that had to be included in the package of application documents for emigration. Weeks went by, and then months, with no success. The answer to Svetlana's telephone calls to the chief of her department was, "It is forbidden to give you a reference." That meant that the KGB had forbidden it. I decided to call the director of Svetlana's institute. He was a very well-known scientist, the academician Oleg Gazenko. I had met him from time to time at Keldysh's meetings. Gazenko remembered me and said that the matter did not depend on him, that it was a matter for the vice-director, the institute's personnel manager. At that time colonels or generals of the KGB held such positions at prestigious institutes. Gazenko gave me his telephone number.

That day I was sick in bed with a fever and a cold. I told the vice-director the purpose of my call and said, "Such a step by the institute is against Soviet law." I added that the Communist Party Committee for that part of Moscow — I had called them before — had said that it was the duty of the institute to give such a document upon the employee's request. I concluded, "If the requested reference is not given to my wife, I will organize a press conference for foreign journalists and tell them about the decision of the institute's administration." The vice-director did not interrupt me. He asked only that I call him again in two hours. In two hours I was told that Svetlana could pick up the document. She called a taxi, and we went to her institute. The chief of the Communist Party organization of the institute, the party secretary, brought the reference to Svetlana outside the institute, handed it to her, and said, "You are a brave woman, Svetlana." It is curious that the document praised Svetlana's job performance and her social behavior.

Finally, on 3 October 1975, we could officially apply to emigrate. It was the third turning point in my life. We became refusniks. During the next twelve years we would apply to OVIR twenty-four times, because we had to reapply for exit visas every six months to maintain the status of having been refused. My hope that I could hasten this process by carefully withdrawing from secret work proved to be vain indeed. And, in fact, from the very beginning I never expected that we would really be allowed to emigrate. I expected the Soviet authorities to treat us harshly. Yet the decision to apply to emigrate eased my mind. I no longer needed sleeping pills, which I had been relying on for some time beforehand.

Once our refusal era began, our lives changed completely. We never before met or spoke so often with so many people of different characters. There were people of different professions and positions, of different ideologies and morals, and of different sympathies. It was an active, interesting, and sometimes hard life accompanied by terrible events. But we were fortunate because we did not have the burden of making ends meet. To be sure, my salary was reduced, and taking into account that Svetlana had been fully discharged from her job, and that she did not have a job during the twelve years that we were refusniks, our income became less than half what it was. But it was enough to pay our modest living expenses. We even saved some money for vacations. It was very helpful that we had saved a little bit of money from the royalties from the books I published in the United States. Personal gifts brought from abroad were also helpful. It was important that we remained disciplined in our spending. Thus, during all those years we were not in need. When in 1981 I retired and the administration of IZMIRAN moved me to another position, to that of "scientific consultant," we also were not in need. My pension and the again-diminished salary covered all our modest expenses.

The Scientific Seminars of Refusniks

During the years we were refusniks, we had many meetings and discussions with other refusniks and with Westerners, both journalists and others. These encounters took place on the street outside Moscow's central synagogue, among people keeping vigil outside the courthouse where a refusnik was being tried, in Western embassies, especially those of France and the United States, and in the hotels where foreign visitors stayed. On Saturdays we often visited the U.S. ambassador's residence, a palace built by a capable architect in the old times, where there was a regular gathering of refusniks, dissidents, and their families. The embassy provided light refreshments and screened American movies. I remember, for example, *Children of a Lesser God*. The ambassador and his wife often attended these gatherings. But by far the largest part of our refusal activity was connected with the unofficial scientific seminars held by refusniks in their homes. Indeed, the seminars were our club and our work.

From the point when Svetlana and I applied to emigrate until Andrei Sakharov's 1986 return to Moscow from internal exile in Gorky, I stopped attending official scientific seminars at PhIAN. Since being fired from PhIAN in 1951 I had in any case been there only two or three times. The story of one visit may illustrate why in general I did not want to go there.

In 1953 or 1954, when I worked at IZMIRAN, I was invited to a seminar of the oscillation laboratory, where I had worked for about sixteen years. A former student of mine from Uzbekistan presented the results of his dissertation for his Ph.D. degree. At that time, after my discharge from PhIAN, his adviser was Sergei Rytov, a corresponding member of the academy and, in fact, a good professional physicist. The subject of the dissertation was the same one I had proposed to him and that I began to develop with the student in 1950. It was not in Rytov's field. Unfortunately, from the very beginning of the report, I realized that there was a key mistake in the work. The calculations assumed that the Fresnel zone of the ionosphere, which reflected radio waves back to the earth, was composed of very small ionized clouds, equivalent in size to or smaller than the length of the radio waves. But in fact the clouds are much larger than the length of the waves. Because the task was not set forth properly, the results could not be right. Rytov immediately understood and agreed with me. My other old colleagues made quite a stir about my having immediately found this mistake. Nonetheless, I was discouraged. Why had

Sergei Rytov not asked me in due course about the main points of the problem? Was it because General Malyshev had expelled me from PhIAN and Rytov was afraid to collaborate with me? I would be sorry to think so, but it seems to be the only possible answer to the question. That is what I learned from the acts of many other physicists at that time. Such behavior was even more common during my refusal time.

It was largely to avoid such problems that in 1974 I stopped attending the prestigious and very interesting Wednesday evening seminars that Peter Kapitsa held at his institute. I didn't want to put the seminar participants in the position of having to choose to collaborate or not to collaborate *with that refusnik*. Until then I attended the seminar often and presented talks at it from time to time. After each session Peter Kapitsa invited a few people to his large office for roundtable discussions over tea and cookies. I regularly participated in the roundtable discussions, in which the main speaker was usually Kapitsa himself. He told fascinating stories and anecdotes about physicists and politicians. One of my last visits to the seminar and the subsequent roundtable was in 1973, when the famous English physicist Paul Dirac presented a talk.

Throughout the 1970s and 1980s hundreds of people from abroad visited the refusnik seminars or otherwise made efforts to meet and assist the refusnik scientists. In addition to distinguished scholars in many fields, they included representatives and leaders of scientific organizations. But whether our visitors were important people or unimportant people in the eyes of the world, they were all vitally important to us. These people encouraged the refusnik community with their visits. They were a link to the outside world. And their brave presence at our seminars and gatherings told the Soviet hierarchy that the world was watching and that it cared about the fate of the refusniks. For those of us who battled the Soviet system from the inside, every visitor's name evokes a story of our long struggle. Without the generous interest of these people, the situation of the refusniks would have been much worse than it was.

An extensive list of some of those who attended the seminars is given in appendix D, together with a selected list of some of their lectures. But to convey a sense of the refusnik experience in general and for Svetlana and me in particular, I must select here only a few stories out of many.

The Seminars at the Homes of Alexander Voronel and Mark Azbel

In general the history of the seminar of physicists and mathematicians which I describe here, and which can be called the Moscow Refusnik Seminar, splits into two periods. In the first period, from 1972 to 1977, the seminar met at the homes of the physicists Alexander Voronel and Mark Azbel; in the second period, from 1977 to 1987, it met first at the home of the mathematician Victor Brailovsky and then in Svetlana's and my apartment.

It all began in 1972 at Alexander Voronel's home. Shortly thereafter the organizing committee of the seminar started to plan an international conference for 1–5 July 1974. This plan met with an enthusiastic response. One hundred and thirty physicists from the United States, England, France, Israel, and other countries, including several Nobel laureates, and thirty refusnik and dissident scientists, including Yuri Orlov and Andrei Sakharov, expressed a desire to present papers at the conference. Among the most active organizers of the conference were the physicists Mark Azbel, Alexander Voronel, and Benjamin Levich and the mathematician Victor Brailovsky.

In the middle of May 1974, however, the members of the organizing committee of the conference were arrested. They were held in prisons in Moscow and the surrounding region until 5 July 1974. The wives of these men were under house arrest at the same time. Although the KGB scuttled the international conference, the seminar itself continued at Alexander Voronel's home; on his emigration to Israel, it moved to Mark Azbel's apartment. I began to attend the seminar on a more regular basis in 1975–77, during the period when it was hosted by Azbel.

I had not attended the seminar much before that for a specific reason. As I mentioned at the close of the previous chapter, from 1971 to 1974, the International Union of Radio Science was organizing, through its Committee on Space Research, an international symposium on radio investigation of the ionosphere by satellites to take place in my department at IZMIRAN. Because I was not allowed to travel to the West, my foreign colleagues in radio science decided that they would come to me. Had I become open at this time about my hope to emigrate, the KGB would have destroyed the symposium. And I would have let down many scientists from the West, who went to great lengths to organize the symposium.

The Seminar at the Brailovskys'

At the end of 1977 Mark Azbel was allowed to leave the Soviet Union and go to Israel. He had first applied for an exit visa in 1973. Because of the change in Azbel's circumstances, the seminar shifted to the home of Victor and Irina Brailovsky at the end of 1977. In 1982 Azbel published a book on his experiences, *Refusnik: Trapped in the Soviet Union.*[5]

From time to time until his exile to Gorky, Andrei Sakharov visited the

---

5. Mark Azbel, *Refusnik: Trapped in the Soviet Union* (Boston: Houghton Mifflin, 1981).

seminar at Mark Azbel's and Victor Brailovsky's; after his return from exile, he also attended the seminar at our apartment. I remember also a most interesting lecture presented at Azbel's home in 1977 by the oncologist Howard Temin, winner of the Nobel Prize in medicine for his cancer research. And it was a great honor for the seminar when on 18 December 1978 the American physicist Arno Penzias, fresh from having received the Nobel Prize in physics in Sweden, repeated his prize lecture at the Brailovskys'. The next day he visited Svetlana and me in our apartment.

Another visitor to the seminar at the Brailovskys' in December 1978 was the physicist Ives Quéré, of the Ecole Polytechnique. At present he is a member of the French Academy of Sciences and is responsible for the academy's international relations. Ives also visited the seminar after it had moved to my apartment, in 1982, 1986, and 1987. All through these years he was active in efforts to help the refusniks. When he visited the seminars, he always brought gifts from different people in France, particularly from Nicole Cartan, to be distributed among refusniks who were in need.

On 25 December 1978, a Sunday, the Rutgers University mathematician Joel Lebowitz, then president of the New York Academy of Sciences, and the physicist James Langer, at that time a professor at Carnegie-Mellon University in Pittsburgh, both came to the seminar. In 1979 Lebowitz published "Letter from the President: Moscow Sunday Seminar" in the May–June issue of *The Sciences,* the journal published by the New York Academy of Sciences, and Langer published "Journey to an Unauthorized Scientific Meeting" in *Physics Today.* These papers motivated many more scientists to visit the seminar, among them many members of the American Physical Society.

Joel Lebowitz visited again in 1979 and in April 1980. After those meetings, he played a major role in the development of the seminar. He arranged for many other scientists to visit us. And it was his idea to gather the refusnik scientists' papers for publication by the New York Academy of Sciences. Beginning in 1980 he edited five volumes of *Reports from the Moscow Refusnik Seminar.* The volume published in 1983 was dedicated to Victor Brailovsky, and the one published in 1987 was dedicated to me. These proceedings had intrinsic scientific value. They also showed our independence and that we ignored the censorship rules of the Soviet system.

Joel visited the seminar in April 1980 after attending an international congress on mathematics in Hungary. Before he left the United States, he called Svetlana and me and gave us the address of his cousin Herman in Kazakhstan. He asked us to let Herman know when he would be in Moscow. Joel naively thought that Herman could easily travel to meet him there. Behind Joel's call lay the following story, which we learned different parts of from both Herman and him.

In May 1944, when Joel Lebowitz was fourteen years old, he was deported together with his family and other Jews from his birthplace, Taceva, a small village in the Carpathian Mountains, to Auschwitz, the terrible German concentration camp. He was the only foreign visitor to our seminar who was a survivor of the camps; on his arm was the identification number tatooed by the Germans. At that time Taceva was part of Romania, and before 1939 it was part of Czechoslovakia. Joel was later moved to Bergen-Belsen, and among the prisoners there he met his cousin Herman. In April 1945 British and American troops liberated Bergen-Belsen. Joel and Herman were in the part of the camp overseen by the British. Joel was then very sick and weak, and Herman left the British-liberated part of the camp to go the American-liberated zone to look for food for him. Herman never came back.

Joel then spent a year in Germany before emigrating to the United States in August 1946. In 1955, ten years after Herman disappeared, Joel received a letter from him. Herman was now a miner in Karaganda, a city in Kazakhstan in the southeastern part of the Soviet Union. Just as Herman was looking for food in the American-liberated sector of Bergen-Belsen, a Soviet military detachment arrived there with authorization to take all Soviet prisoners. Herman was a stranger to that part of the camp and he spoke only Yiddish. The soldiers captured Herman and took him to the USSR. After a long and difficult journey, during which he was often accused of being a spy by the military detachment, Herman reached Karaganda. Eventually Herman became a Soviet citizen, married, and had a son. Then, in the mid-1950s, Herman's relatives in the village of Chust, which at that time was part of the USSR, gave him Joel's address in the United States.

Following Joel's call, in which we learned only a part of this story, we sent a letter to Herman, and soon Herman telephoned, telling us that he had been given permission to come to Moscow for three days. There was a problem, however: he could not buy a round-trip ticket in Karaganda, and without it he could not go to Moscow. If he were not able to return to Karaganda on time, he explained, he would lose his job and would be punished. And we could not buy a ticket for him in Moscow without being able to produce his passport when we did so. I decided to go to the chief of the ticket office of our region. I told him who Herman was and how Joel and he had been prisoners in the German concentration camp. Then I asked him to let me buy Herman a ticket without his passport, which was breaking a strict rule of the Soviet regime. And it happened that everything worked out. The official bent the rule and let me buy Herman's ticket.

On 14 April, early in the morning, Herman came to our home from Karaganda. In a matter of hours Joel arrived in Moscow and called us. We asked him to come to us but did not tell him that Herman was already at our apartment. Herman met Joel at the door. It was an overwhelming surprise for him. The reader can imagine the feelings of the two men. Thirty-five years to the month had passed from the time of their liberation from the German concentration camp. Herman stayed at our home until his return flight to Karaganda. He and Joel had several meetings and spoke together in Yiddish.

After this event Joel Lebowitz tried to come to the seminar many times, but his applications for a visa to the USSR were always denied. Many dozens of times over the next years, until Svetlana and I left Russia, he called us. Through his work in publishing the refusnik seminar papers and in many other ways, all the participants of the seminar felt his support and help.

In December 1979 the organizing committee of the seminar held an international session. Before the session, Victor Brailovsky was detained by the Militsia. It seemed that he was under arrest. He was held for five hours. Then the Militsia released him and *advised* him to stop the seminar at his home. But the international session took place as planned: twenty-six scientists from the West and twenty refusniks presented papers, including in absentia Yuri Orlov, whose paper was brought from the labor camp at Perm' by one of his visitors, and Andrei Sakharov, whose paper was brought from his exile in Gorky. The physicist Yuri Golfand, a doctor of physical and mathematical sciences who did pioneering work on supergravity, read the papers by Orlov and Sakharov.

On 13 November 1980 Victor Brailovsky was arrested and the refusnik seminar at his home was terminated. At that time many other seminars of refusniks in Moscow terminated their activities because of KGB pressure, and some refusniks doubted if seminar activity could be continued at all. For example, the mathematician Alexander Lerner, who had applied for an exit visa to Israel in 1971 and subsequently made his home a nucleus of refusnik activity, closed his home to all seminar and refusnik activity for a time. The KGB terrorized him into doing so, threatening to arrest his son if he did not stop meeting his fellow refusniks in his own home. In general, the persecution of refusniks escalated after the arrest of Anatoly Sharansky in 1977 and then again after the arrests in 1979 of the Jewish activists Vladimir Slepak, Ida Nudel, and Joseph Begun. At this time the Soviet authorities prevented scientific communication in general.

We tried to continue holding the seminars at the Brailovskys' apartment. In a sense, it was our protest and demonstration against Victor's arrest. KGB agents closely watched his apartment building, however, stopping both refusniks and visiting scientists from the West on the street before they got there. At first we responded to this crackdown by trying to organize an international conference that would take place in different refusniks' homes and bring attention to the plight of Victor Brailovsky and other imprisoned refusniks and dissidents. But the KGB literally closed in around us and stopped these efforts. Svetlana and I and many other refusniks were under house arrest for several days. When Svetlana and I went out to buy a loaf of bread or take a walk, we were followed. The KGB kept this up, in our case, for days.

We knew we had to abandon hopes for a conference at that point, but by the end of 1980 the physics-mathematics seminar began to meet again occasionally at the homes of the mathematicians Alex Ioffe and Naum Meiman and in our apartment. From the beginning of 1981 it met regularly in our home. Alexander Lerner joined the seminar in our home and visited it often.

Before turning to the seminar in the years when I organized and hosted it, I must mention a few more of the visitors to the seminar at the Brailovskys' in the late 1970s and early 1980s. Dorothy Hirsh, a noble lady and the executive director of the Committee of Concerned Scientists, first visited the seminar in October 1979. She visited again in May 1981, bringing with her the Boston University mathematician Nancy Kopell. Dorothy became an ardent advocate for the refusnik community, lobbying American politicians, government leaders, and scientists on our behalf and arranging meetings with them for us.

The distinguished American mathematicians Martin Kruskal and Norman Zabusky presented lectures at the seminar in November 1979 and April 1980. Zabusky was again in Moscow in 1983. He wanted again to present a talk at the seminar, but because of his collaboration with the refusniks he was expelled from the USSR before he could do so, as we will see.

Joseph Birman, a distinguished scientist from the City College of New York, visited the seminar in November 1978, October 1979, and in 1982, 1985, and 1987. He made many efforts on behalf of the refusniks.

James Arnold, the director of the Space Research Institute of the University of California at San Diego, presented a review of recent investigations of planets with space probes at the seminar in 1980. The French scientist Alfred Romani of the Ecole Polytechnique visited the seminar in April 1980 and again in April 1982. During his visits he went to the presidium of the Academy of Sciences of the USSR and to other officials on behalf of the refusniks. For example, he tried to help the Brailovskys to obtain exit visas.

Seminars at Our Home

Every week or two from early 1981 through 1986 and somewhat less frequently in 1987, Svetlana and I hosted the refusniks in our home. Usually we met on Saturday evening from 6 or 7 P.M. to 10 or 11 P.M., but sometimes we met on Sunday afternoon. Organizing the seminars was a hard task, taking two or three full days a week and often more. We were kept very busy on the telephone, making calls to foreign visitors in Moscow and other refusniks. We frequently had to guide strangers to and from our apartment, meeting them at subway stations and bus stops and even at their hotels. This was made a little extra difficult by the fact that we sold our car on going into refusal. We were reliably informed that the KGB had arranged more than one car accident for refusniks.

Fifty to fifty-five Moscow physicists and mathematicians, all refusniks, belonged to the seminar, although not everyone came to every meeting. Usually the attendance was between fifteen and twenty-five people. These persons of diverse personalities and backgrounds would not have come together except for the shared experience of being refusniks. It was a delicate problem to distribute the gifts that foreign scientists and others gave to the seminar. Alex Ioffe, who is now in Israel, assisted us in distributing calculators, cameras, clothing, and shoes. We distributed the gifts to the families of imprisoned dissidents as well as to refusniks. The people receiving the gifts either used them or sold them at the so-called commission shops for money for living expenses. Many people needed this help because they had lost their jobs by becoming refusniks. It was important that this process be completely transparent, so that misunderstandings did not arise.

From 1981 to 1987, about 350 people from the West visited the seminar, including 154 scientists (see appendix D). Most of the scientists were physicists, but their number also included mathematicians, biologists, and medical researchers; they came from Europe, the United States, and in the case of Luis Carbonell and his wife Julie, from the Institute of Research in Caracas. Many distinguished scientists and professionals were among our guests. I am pleased to list here some of the visitors. The titles of a number of their lectures can be found in appendix D; readers who are professionals in the relevant fields will note that the talks were often in the most exciting fields of development of modern research. Joel Lebowitz said of the seminar in the paper cited above, "The audience is eager and the discussions are most stimulating. (Nobelist A. Penzias says it was his best audience.)"

Among the scientists from the United States were the mathematicians Norman Zabusky (then at the University of Pittsburgh), Louis Nirenberg, Eugene Trobowitz, Melvin Kalos (Courant Institute in New York), Mitchell Feigenbaum (then at Los Alamos National Laboratory), and Leonard Berkovitz (Purdue University). In the 1980s the American physicists Miriam Sarachik (City College of New York), Gordon Hamilton (Lawrence Livermore National Laboratory), Arno Bohm (University of Texas), Daniel Friedan (University of Chicago), David Gross and Edward Witten (Princeton University), John Kogut (Loomis Laboratory, Urbana, Illinois), Robert Jaffe (MIT), and many others came to the seminar. Some of them attended the seminar several times.

From England came Oliver Penrose (Department of Mathematics, Open University), Michael Green (Queen Mary College), and Bernard Shutz (University College in Cardiff).

Paul Kessler, a French physicist, came to the seminar twice, in 1982 and 1983. He made many efforts to help refusniks, especially the mathematician Vladimir Kislik, who was arrested in Kiev. In February 1983 Kessler came directly from the European Center for Nuclear Research and presented a talk in Russian. Another French physicist, Seneor Roland of the Ecole Polytechnique, visited the seminar in 1983 and 1984. The distinguished French scientist Louis Michel and his wife visited on 28 November 1982. Scientists from France were among the most frequent visitors to the seminar. From the Ecole Polytechnique alone came Ives Quéré (five times), Seneor Roland (twice), Alfred Romani, Daniel Lallough, Jean-Louis Poloche, and Dominique Gressillon.

In 1981 the well-known physicist John Ziman (University of Bristol, England) came to our seminar. He gave me his interesting book *The Force of Knowledge: The Scientific Dimension of Society* . In 1981 the physicist Freeman Dyson (Princeton University) sent me his book *Disturbing the Universe*, which he inscribed, "To Yakov and the Scientific Seminar, a token of deep respect." It is obvious that the refusnik seminar was popular in the West and was broadly supported by the scientific community.

Many scientists came to the seminar from Sweden, Denmark, and Norway. Among them were Jens Larsen (Niels Bohr Institute, Copenhagen), who attended three times, Thome Fried (Research Institute of Physics, Stockholm), Ian Åman and Eisen Hanno (Institute of Theoretical Physics, Stockholm), Rolf Stuller (Institute of Theoretical Physics, Oslo), and Gunnar Berg and Stan Kayser (Department of Mathematics, University of Uppsala).

One of the most frequent foreign visitors to the seminar was the Swedish scientist Inga Fisher, the vice-president of the Swedish Royal Academy of Sciences. She visited us five times in 1981–86. Inga Fisher did a lot to help the refusnik movement. On 1 and 2 December 1983 in Stockholm she convened an international conference on collective phenomena devoted to the Moscow Refusniks' Seminar. The Conference Committee included Kristoffer Gjjoetterud (Norway), Joan Dale (Great Britain), Joel Lebowitz (United States), Ives Quéré (France), Luis Carbonell (Venezuela), and Alexander Voronel (Israel). Four of the two-day conference's five sessions were devoted to the research fields in which Victor Brailovsky, Alexander Lerner, Naum Meiman, and I were active. Recently Svetlana and I had a most pleasant meeting with Inga Fisher in Stockholm, during our vacation in Scandinavia in July 1995.

The Swedish physician Magnus Nasiell, Heidi Fried, a psychologist in the Jewish community of Stockholm, and Kristoffer Gjjoetterud, a member of the Norwegian Acadmy of Sciences, frequently helped refusniks in their fight for emigration. Kristoffer Gjjoetterud was very active in the human rights move-ment. He visited us only once, in October 1984, and thereafter was denied a visa whenever he requested one. But he directed many people to us and often called us to keep informed of our activities. Recently we met Kristoffer in Oslo. Unfortunately, we were not able to see Heidi Fried during that trip, because she was out of Stockholm at the time. But I would like to tell here a little about Heidi.

Heidi Fried was born and raised in a small city in Rumania. In 1944, when she was twenty years old, the Germans placed her family and her in the ghetto and then in Auschwitz. All her family died in the camp, except for her sister and her. After the war the Red Cross took Heidi and her sister, who was then very sick, to Sweden, and Heidi settled there. She became a psychologist after the death of her husband in 1962. In 1990 she published a powerful book, *Fragments of a Life: The Road to Auschwitz,* which was translated into many languages (an English version was published in 1990 and a Russian version in 1993). When Heidi learned of our recent trip to Stockholm, she sent us a copy of her book with a moving inscription.

It is sad to note here that Magnus Nasiell was killed in a car accident in Stockholm in 1984. At a seminar meeting at our home on 21 October, two of his Swedish colleagues presented lectures in his memory. Astrid Graslund (Department of Biophysics, University of Stockholm) spoke on the interaction between the chemical carcinogen benzo(a)pyrene and DNA, and Morten Rosengvist (Department of Medicine, Huddinge University) spoke on modern trends in cardian pacings. The refusniks Irina Brailovsky and Inna Meiman also presented short talks in Nasiell's memory.

From time to time biologists, medical professionals, and physicians visited the seminar and presented interesting talks. Two biologists from Sweden, Anders Elenberg and Lars Ernster, came to us in October 1981. Astrid Graslund first visited us on 21 May 1983. And Marc Fellous and Herlund Marko-vic (then at the Institut Pasteur in Paris) visited on 9 November 1984.

Some sessions of the seminar took on a special character. One such session took place on 24 June 1982, when six American participants in the International Cardiology Congress, then being held in Moscow, came to the seminar at our home with their wives and other participants in the congress. The famous American cardiologists David Joffe, Frank Marcus, and Douglas Zipes, who presented a talk at the seminar, were among them.

An impressive event took place on 22 January 1985, when two members of the American National Academy of Sciences, MIT professor Walter Rosen-blith, the academy's foreign secretary, and University of Illinois professor Hans Frauenfelder, came to the seminar. They were delegates of the Special Commission of the National Academy, which had come to the Soviet Academy of Sciences to discuss a new agreement between the academies. That meeting of two members of the American commission with fifteen members of our seminar was a demonstration of support for the refusnik scientists. They brought us a copy of the "Protocol of Discussions between the Two Academies." It seems that those two members of the American delegation were sitting with us in our apartment at the same time that the two presidents of the academies and other members of the American and Soviet commissions were meeting at the presidium of the Soviet Academy.

The largest session of the seminar at our home took place on 15 February 1986. It was a celebration of the 850th anniversary of Maimonides and the 100th anniversary of Niels Bohr. The great medieval Jewish philosopher Moses ben Maimon (Maimonides, 1135–1204), physician to the Sultan Saladin and leader of the large Jewish community in Egypt, applied a scientific turn of mind to codifying Jewish law, the writing of his own medical and philosophical treatises, and the debunking of astrology. The Dane Niels Bohr (1885–1962), winner of the Nobel Prize in physics in 1922, was one of the greatest physicists of the twentieth century, a pioneer in the field of atomic theory. Forty-one people, including Jens Larsen from the Niels Bohr Institute in Copenhagen and Fyrind Gron from the University of Oslo's Institute of Physics, crowded into our small apartment for that seminar (see appendix D).

The last meeting of the seminar at our apartment was held on 27 June 1987. The seminar was visited that day by distinguished members of the French Academy of Sciences: the mathematicians Henri Cartan (with his wife, Nicole) and Laurent Schwartz and the foreign secretary of the academy, the physicist André Guinier.

Henri and Nicole Cartan, Laurent Schwartz, and many other French people of good will were very active in the international campaign on behalf of our people. They tried to help dissidents and refusniks and stimulated the French government, including the president of France, to speak about us and to write letters on our behalf. Nicole Cartan, Jeanette Zupan, and Janine Atal frequently sent parcels for the families of refusniks and imprisoned dissidents. Henri Cartan, Laurent Schwartz, and Ives Quéré were among the fourteen members of a "Commité en favour du Professeur Yakov Alpert." The others were the Nobelist Alfred Kastler; the French academicians Pierre Auger, André Blanc-LaPierre, Pierre-Gilles de Gennes, Louis LePrince-Ringuet, Louis Michel, and Jean-Claude Pecker; René Pellat, a corresponding member of the French Academy of Sciences; the astrophysicist Catherine Cesarsky; Jean-Paul Mathieu; and Evry Schatzman.

Within two days of our seminar meeting Henri Cartan had a special appointment with the president of the Academy of Sciences of the USSR, the academician Gury Marchuk, to encourage him to make active efforts to accelerate the permissions for emigration for the mathematician Naum Meiman and me. The day after that meeting, the scientific secretary of the French embassy brought me a note in French. President Marchuk had told Henri Cartan, "There are no security reasons not to allow Yakov Alpert to emigrate. The final decision does not depend on me, and I will again communicate with the appropriate organizations." Previously, in 1980 and 1981, a commission organized by Marchuk's predecessor, Anatoly Alexandrov, had investigated my security clearance and concluded that there was no reason to refuse my request to emigrate. I emphasized this when I was summoned to OVIR in 1982, as I discuss in the next chapter. But the officials answered that until then I had known important secrets and so could not be allowed to emigrate.

Other Events and Meetings

I mentioned above that Joel Lebowitz edited five volumes of papers that the refusniks gave at the seminar for publication by the New York Academy of Sciences. To get these papers abroad we could not use the Soviet postal service. Instead we had to find sympathetic people willing to carry the papers to the West for us. One of the people who helped us in this way was Eliza Klose, the wife of the journalist Kevin Klose. The Kloses lived in Moscow from 1978 to 1981 while Kevin was reporting for the *Washington Post*. I met him for the first time on the tiny street outside the courthouse where the refusnik Anatoly Sharansky was being tried in June 1978. Of the many Western journalists we met with in these years, most were from the United States. Those meetings took place in the streets, close to the Moscow synagogue, at our apartments, and at such places as we could find. Kevin stood with us for hours while Sharansky's trial was going on. I gave him a letter for publication in the West on behalf of the famous dissident Yuri Orlov (see Chapter 13). Later Svetlana and I became friends with Kevin and Eliza and their children: a daughter, Nina, and two sons, Brennan and Chandler.

Many times our papers were carried abroad by the foreigners who participated in our seminar. They also took to the West papers written by refusniks in other cities in the USSR. From time to time refusniks came to our seminar in Moscow from Leningrad (at present St. Petersburg), Minsk, Kiev, and Kharkov. But one refusnik from Kharkov, the physicist Eugene Chudnovsky, became a regular member of the Moscow refusnik seminars from 1979 to 1987. After his first visit to the Brailovskys he came to Moscow many times, especially for the sessions at our apartment, and made many presentations.

Chudnovsky, a gifted physicist, was one of the most active refusniks in Kharkov. Unemployable simply by virtue of being a Jew, he lectured on mathematics and physics in his home to young people who were denied admission to the university because of their Jewish origins. Over that long period he was the link between the Moscow and Kharkov refusniks, whom we in Moscow tried to help. Not many foreign visitors or journalists could go to Kharkov. Later Svetlana and I became close to his wife, Marina, and their daughter, Julia. They came to Moscow to say good-bye to us before their emigration in March 1987. Through Chudnovsky we also became close to another refusnik from Kharkov, Yuri Tarnopolsky, who was arrested and spent three years in a labor camp. I will tell you a little more about him and his family in a later chapter.

The members of our seminars took part in different actions of the refusnik movement, particularly demonstrations of support for imprisoned refusniks and dissidents, such as the distinguished convicted refusniks Joseph Begun, Ida Nudel, Anatoly Sharansky, and Vladimir Slepak. One of the last such demonstrations of the refusniks, one that drew many people, took place on the Arbat, the crowded, pedestrians-only street in Moscow, on 13 February 1987. The demonstration was on behalf of Joseph Begun, who had been in the Gulag for more than a dozen years. He was released soon after, and on 23 February, ten days after the demonstration, he was in Moscow.

We had meetings at home and at other places with members of the U.S. Congress, representatives of the American embassy, members of the British House of Commons, and members of the parliaments of Canada, Denmark, Norway, and Sweden. I shall list here some of the meetings.

On 19–20 March 1982 the Swedish parliamentarians Anita Grabin, Val-lord Lundgrem, and Gerald Nagler visited the seminar. Two other Swedish parliamentarians visited us in 1983: Nika Emberg on 12 November (with Stive Gustavsson) and Karen Nasiell on 20 November. And the Swedish parliamentarians Karin Andersoon, Gunell Morell, and Robert Söderboon visited us on 19 May 1984.

We had meetings with Kyell Bohlin, a member of Norway's parliament, Elizabet Fleetwood, and Brita Hammasbreleen on 27 November 1984. The Norwegian parliamentarians Irene Levin and Reivle Steen attended our seminar on 10 November 1985.

A meeting with five members of the United States Congress was held at our home on 15 October 1985. One of them was Bill Nelson of Florida, who later flew on the space shuttle. The others were Manuel Lujan (New Mexico), Bob Young (Missouri), and Larry Couglin and Don Ritter (Pennsylvania). Two of their wives and two representatives of the American embassy were with them. They came to us in a special minibus from the American embassy. It was an exciting meeting: twenty-five people gathered in our one-bedroom apartment. When they left, Bill Nelson's wife, Grace, wrote on a card that she gave me,

"God bless you. We will pray that God will give you the *wisdom* to know how to unlock the gates. One in heart with you, Grace Nelson."

In May 1987 a group of American citizens from a religious delegation to the USSR visited us. A missionary, Charles Miller, who had spent several years in Africa, was among them. Hester Munden, one of three evangelical Methodists in the group (along with Barbara Blackstone and Twick Morrison), sent us photographs she took at that meeting. Later we corresponded with her in the United States. She presented lectures about her visit to us and to other re- fusniks in Moscow. We have not heard from her for a few years, and in 1995 there was no reply to a greeting card we sent her.

We met often with other people from the West at the apartments of other refusniks, for example, in the homes of Alex Ioffe and Alexander Lerner, at the French and American embassies, and outdoors near the synagogue. For exam- ple, in 1985 we had discussions with Mark Chilly Fisher, a member of the British House of Commons for Northern Ireland, and his wife at the home of Alexander Lerner. In December 1986 we met Senator Gary Hart at a party at the apartment of an official at the American embassy.

I had short discussions with Henry Kissinger and Cyrus Vance in February 1987 at the American embassy. Mario Cuomo, then governor of New York, was at a meeting of many refusniks at the apartment of Alexander Lerner one evening during Rosh Hashanah in September 1987.

The refusniks Joseph Begun, Vladimir Slepak, and Victor Brailovsky, who spent years in prison and internal exile, joined Inna Begun, Irina Brailovsky, Benjamin Charny, Alexander Lerner, Masha Slepak, Svetlana, and me at the American embassy in August 1987 at a meeting between a large U.S. delega- tion, including two members of Congress, and many refusniks.

In October 1986 Svetlana and I spent a lovely evening with the winner of the Nobel Prize for peace, Elie Wiesel, a distinguished fighter for freedom and justice, and his wife, Marion. We met them at the synagogue during the Jewish holiday of Simchat Torah, and he invited us to his suite in the Hotel Russia.

From time to time students from different countries visited us. A student from England, Martin Penrose, the mathematician Oliver Penrose's son, came in April 1982. In January 1986 two beautiful young women from Norway, Kristen and Gerda, came to see us. It was nice to learn that one of them recently converted to Judaism. Two American students, Jacob and Ariel, who were among a group of young amateur musicians who gave concerts in Moscow, visited us in April 1986. And in May 1986 Nina Klose also came to see us.

The Americans Gene Sosin and his wife, Gloria Donen-Sosin, were among the people of good will who visited us in 1986. They came when Gene Sosin retired from Radio Liberty as director of program planning for Radio Free

Europe-Radio Liberty. They were very sensitive to the refusniks' problems. They greeted Svetlana and me at Kennedy Airport in New York in 1988, on our arrival in the United States. Later we had a few meetings with them, in particular in April 1988 at Temple Beth Abraham in Tarrytown, New York, where I was nominated as an honorary member. The temple newsletter for June 1988 ran a short article on me with the title "Veni, Vidi, Vici."

Unworthy Actions

The cornerstone of the Soviet response to the dissident and refusnik scientists, as we have seen, was to isolate them as much as possible from the rest of the scientific community, especially foreign scientists, and from society as a whole. The chief agents of this policy of isolation were often other scientists.

At the end of September and at the beginning of October 1976 an international conference on plasma physics was held in Tbilisi, capital of the Soviet Republic of Georgia. Sometime in 1975 I was invited to present a paper at that conference. I accepted the invitation and sent an abstract of my paper and later the registration fee. That happened before Svetlana and I submitted our first application to OVIR on 3 October 1975.

Then, on 22 or 23 September 1976, days before the opening of the conference, I received a cable from Tbilisi saying that because of the overloaded program of the conference my talk had been canceled. My registration fee was returned and our hotel reservation in Tbilisi was canceled. Ironically, Svetlana and I were considering canceling our trip to Tbilisi because I had a bad cold and was in bed with a fever. But that cable convinced us not to do so. We understood that the real reason for the cancellation of my talk was my refusnik status, which the conference organizers had obviously just learned about.

The next day Svetlana and I went to Tbilisi despite my fever. Before leaving I called one of my associates in Tbilisi. He was a member of a team that I had organized there for observations of the radio signals of sputniks. When I told him what had happened, he offered to find us a place to stay in Tbilisi. He then met us at the airport and brought us to the home of friends who gave us their apartment for several days while I tried to recover from my cold.

A day before the conference opened I went to the chair of the conference, Elefter Andronikashvili, a physicist, and said, "You see, I am here despite your cable. If I have any trouble now, I shall call a press conference with foreign journalists and scientists. The public will know about the story." Acting as if he accepted my presence at the conference, Andronikashvili called one of his assistant organizers, a physicist named Lominadze, and asked him to find a hotel for us. It was not the prestigious Hotel Iveria, however, where most of the other participants, including those from abroad, were staying and where a room had originally been reserved for us. Lominadze still hoped to distance us from the foreign scientists at the conference. But some of them, including the distinguished American plasma physicist Norman Rostoker, came to visit us at our hotel.

The conference organizers were not happy about our meetings with scientists from the West, and they did not invite us to attend the various social events held in connection with the conference. For example, there were bus trips to the mountains and other places of interest near Tbilisi. Lominadze saw us in one of the buses and held the bus. But when he saw that many foreign scientists got on the bus and remained with us, he let it go.

A similar event occurred in September 1981, when Gustav Engelmann, a physicist from the University of Utrecht and the chair of the Physics Department of the European Physical Society, arrived in Moscow to attend the International Conference on Thermonuclear Synthesis. On his arrival he visited us and told me that Andrei Sakharov and I were invited to present talks at the conference. Yet we had not been informed about this. The Soviet chair of the organizing committee was the academician Eugene Velikhov, and Engelmann was the co-chair. On behalf of Sakharov and me he delayed the opening of the conference for two days. He demanded our presence at the conference. At last, Velikhov and Engelmann achieved a compromise, and the conference began. One day after that Engelmann called me and said that I could come to the conference in a couple of days and that he would meet me at the entrance of the Armand Hammer Trade Center, where the conference was being held. The evening before the appointed day, however, Engelmann telephoned me again and asked me not to come. He had just learned that I would not be allowed to enter the building. Velikhov had deceived him.

And here is another story. In 1978 a workshop of Soviet and U.S. plasma physicists was organized in one of the resorts of the Academy of Science in Zvenigorod, close to Moscow. The physicist Roald Sagdeev chaired the Soviet group. The U.S. group comprised eleven physicists, including Frederick Mayer and Eli Yablonovitch. Meyer and Yablonovitch visited the Brailovskys, where the refusnik seminar operated at that time, and arranged that on the next Sunday the entire U.S. team would visit the seminar and present talks. On that Sunday we gathered at the Brailovskys' at noon and waited for the U.S. scientists. Andrei Sakharov and other well-known physicists and mathematicians were among us. An hour went by, and another, and still the U.S. scientists had not arrived. We decided to leave at about 2:00, but close to that time, Mayer and Yablonovitch finally arrived in one of the black Volga cars used by the Academy of Sciences.

They explained to us that that morning Roald Sagdeev, together with eight other Soviet scientists, aggressively lobbied the U.S. group, urging them to stay away from the refusnik seminar. Sagdeev insisted, "Don't think that I am an anti-Semite, my wife is Jewish." His line was that there were no scientists at the seminar (he knew many of us personally) and that it was risky to go there (see also appendix C). Singling out one of the leaders of the dissident community, the physicist Yuri Orlov, the founder of the Helsinki Watch group in Moscow, Sagdeev said, "Orlov is only a politician, not a scientist." Such deceitful rhetoric amounts to slander.

The notion that it was risky to attend the seminars was a curious one. Soviet scientists who loyally served the system and were rewarded with opportunities to travel abroad and to collaborate with Western scientists often told their foreign colleagues that it was risky to go to the seminars.

It is sad to note that some Western scientists believed such disinformation. For example, a U.S. physicist, Timothy E. Toohig, who participated in experiments conducted by the FermiLab in the United States and the Joint Institute for Nuclear Research in Dubna, wrote in the January 1984 issue of *Physics Today,* "I tried to understand the dissidents' situation. Regret was expressed about Sakharov, though it is stated he is no longer a physicist." Toohig also quoted claims that Orlov is "crazy. He molests the women he works with. He should be in jail." In writing these words Toohig no doubt repeated the poisonous statements of his Soviet colleagues.[6]

Here I must tell you about one more regrettable incident of the refusal time. In October 1983 the American mathematician Norman Zabusky visited the Second International Workshop on Nonlinear and Turbulent Processes in Physics, held at the Institute for Theoretical Physics in Kiev. On his way to Kiev he stopped in Moscow, and he came to see Svetlana and me at our home. Zabusky had given a talk at the seminar in 1980, when it still met at the Brailovskys' apartment. We agreed that he would present a second talk at the refusnik seminar on 5 November, after the conference in Kiev. In due course Zabusky returned to Moscow. A few days later he was informed that on 2 November the American embassy in Moscow had received a telephone call from an official of the Academy of Sciences who said that Zabusky's conduct was "inconsistent with his status as a guest of the Academy" and that he had to leave the USSR by noon on Saturday, 5 November. The official added that if he

6. Timothy E. Toohig, "View from the Volga — Updated," *Physics Today,* March 1984, 108.

did not leave, the academy could not guarantee his safety. Zabusky's purely scientific lecture at the refusnik seminar was scheduled to take place on the evening of 5 November at our apartment.

This is not all. Zabusky was traveling with his wife, Charlotte, and their daughter Stasya. Eugene Lifshitz, a collaborator of the great physicist Lev Landau, had invited the whole family for dinner on the evening of 1 November. But during the day on 1 November, the day before the American embassy was informed that Zabusky was being kicked out of the country, Lifshitz telephoned Zabusky to say that they could not meet. This was Zabusky's first inkling that something was not right. I was greatly disappointed when I heard of Lifshitz's behavior. I knew Eugene well. For many years he was one of my best friends. It was important for me to know how Lifshitz had been induced to do what must have been for him a most shameful and stressful action. Later I learned the following.

Days before the scheduled meeting with Zabusky, Sagdeev convinced Lifshitz to withdraw his dinner invitation. I do not know their conversation in detail; I know only that Sagdeev persuaded Lifshitz to telephone Zabusky. Although I am sorry to say so, I know that Lifshitz was afraid to do anything that might prevent his traveling to scientific meetings in the West. This incident represents typical behavior for certain Soviet people and scientists. The Soviet system distorted the integrity of many people.

In response to the Soviet declaration of Zabusky's "inconsistent" status, Walter Rosenblith, the foreign secretary of the U.S. National Academy of Sciences, sent a cable on 5 November to Georgy K. Skryabin, his counterpart at the Soviet academy, asking for additional information. Only a month later did Skryabin reply, repeating verbatim the original one-sentence charge that Zabusky's conduct was "inconsistent with his status as a guest of the academy."

... and Worthy Ones

During the refusal time there were periods when Svetlana and I were in most difficult circumstances. Nevertheless, our refusal activity was instructive and interesting. All in all, it was indeed an unforgettable and important period in our lives because of the following.

First, during that time we maintained our self-respect, we followed our choices, and we became free from inner conflict.

Second, we were most fortunate to have met and become friends with many humane and well-intentioned people from everywhere in the world. If we had not been refusniks, we would never have met those human beings. Many of them became our good friends.

We were also lucky that we survived that time so well, and it was important to put an end to the conflict that continually shattered the lives of many Soviet people for so many years.

Many foreign colleagues who were working in my fields of research, and whom I had never met or been in touch with before, displayed a keen interest in Svetlana and me during all the time of our refusal. They initiated meetings and appeals for help; they distributed information about our status; they mailed me journals, reprints, and so on. One of these people was the physicist Owen Storey, from Cambridge, England, who lived and worked at that time first in France and later in the United States. Owen and I met in 1979 when he came to see me in Moscow and presented a talk at the refusnik seminar at the apartment of Victor Brailovsky. But even before that he made himself my ally.

In 1978, at its international congress in Helsinki the International Union of Radio Science devoted a session to my scientific contributions: "40 Years of Research on VLF Propagation: A Tribute to Professor Ya. L. Alpert." Of course, I could not attend. The American physicist Robert Helliwell of Stanford University stopped in Moscow in his way to Finland. He visited me and took my report, written especially for the congress, to the meeting. Owen Storey gave a brief talk about me at the session, and the French physicist Roger Gendrin read my report.

In the months leading up to that session I received more than forty letters from scientists in different countries in the West, the largest number coming from the United States. I do not know how many more letters were not delivered to me by the Soviet censors. Many colleagues wrote in those letters very pleasant words about my pioneering contribution to that field. I knew of only a few of them, and had never met any of them. Those congratulations and the general recognition of my research were an unexpected pleasure and encouragement for me. But they did not gratify the Soviet officials.

Attending the congress was a large delegation from the USSR — composed particularly of people from IZMIRAN (where I worked) — Czechoslovakia, East Germany, and other so-called socialistic countries. The head of the delegation was Vladimir Migulin. Protesting the session devoted to me, Migulin threatened to have all delegations from socialistic countries leave the congress if the session took place. The union ignored his protest, and Migulin in turn ordered his delegation not to attend the session. He sent one scientist, Yakov Likhter of IZMIRAN, as an observer. That event again illustrates the Soviet reality.

During the first years of refusal I wrote a book, *Waves and Satellites in Near-Earth Plasma*. The doors of all the publishing houses in the USSR were closed to me then, however, and I had no way to submit the manuscript to a publisher in the West. Owen Storey presented it to publishers in the West for me. Written in Russian, it was published in English in 1983 by Cambridge University Press. I was not able to see the translation or the proofs. Owen revised the translation, speaking with me by telephone from France for many hours while doing the proofreading of my book. He, his wife Françoise, and my colleague from Cavendish Laboratory in Cambridge, the distinguished radio physicist Kenneth Budden, a member of the Royal Society, whom I had never met, were my official representatives at Cambridge University Press. Budden also checked proofs for me and did the subject and name indexes of the book.

Before they could do all this work for my book, I had to get the manuscript out of the USSR. The manuscript made a bulky package: it was two volumes and comprised about seven hundred pages. I decided to ask an American I knew to help me. This man was an official at the American embassy and had lived in Moscow for about three years. I waited for a chance meeting on the street to talk to him. From time to time he escorted U.S. visitors to meetings with refusniks outside the central synagogue. He was not there for several weeks, but at last he came one Saturday evening. We had to speak quickly and quietly, away from other people. He agreed to help and asked me to bring the package to his home. He lived in one of the buildings that were exclusively for foreigners and were supervised by Soviet guards, who questioned every visitor.

Despite all the precautions we took, including my not even discussing the matter with Svetlana at home, we were not sure whether the KGB knew that I was planning to bring my manuscript to someone for transfer to the West. We decided that Svetlana would follow me to the American's home. We did not stand together at the trolley bus stop, and when the trolley bus came I boarded at one entrance and she boarded at another. We did not sit together and we also got off the trolley bus separately. As we walked to the American's building, Svetlana stayed a good distance behind me. We thought that if I were stopped and arrested by the KGB, or if I failed to come out of the building, Svetlana could immediately run to telephone foreign journalists to tell them what had occurred. Nothing of that sort happened, however. When I entered the apartment house, the guard asked me whose apartment I was visiting but did not stop me. My American acquaintance was waiting for me. On my entering the apartment he turned on some music to mask our conversation from KGB bugs.

I was inside for quite some time. Meanwhile Svetlana waited outside, increasingly nervous that something had gone wrong. When I finally came out of the building, we embraced and went home, relieved that so far all had gone well. And fortunately, everything went as planned. Following my instructions, the American mailed my manuscript to Senator Dennis DeConcini, whom I had met in Moscow. The senator in turn mailed it to Owen Storey in France.

The American was taking a risk to help me. At minimum, discovery would almost certainly mean being forced to leave the country under a cloud and suffering some damage to his career. The Kloses ran a similar risk when Eliza Klose carried refusnik seminar papers out of the country; Kevin Klose could not have continued to report for the *Washington Post* from Moscow if the authorities had intercepted these papers.

Soon after publication of the book, I asked Kenneth Budden to collaborate with me on my theoretical study of the propagation of radio waves in a magnetoplasma. To solve that problem, which I had begun studying earlier with a young colleague named Boris Moiseyev, complicated computer calculations were needed. Budden repeated the analytical calculations to prove our final equations and began the study. He then composed a set of complex computer programs, did many numerical calculations, and mailed the results to me. I received from Budden many hundreds of such computer printouts. That work continued for about two years. It was astonishing that all the letters and sheets with figures sent by Budden reached me. Although, in general, correspondence with the West was cut off, the censors did give me my mail from Cavendish Laboratory. Why? I do not know the answer. Kenneth Budden, Boris Moiseyev, and I published a lengthy paper on the results of our common study in *Proceedings of the Royal Society*.

Thus, during the refusal time, scientists and others from the West helped me to survive as a researcher, as they helped many other refusniks and dissidents. It was wonderful to meet such good people and friends. I cannot say this too often.

Refusniks and dissidents who were permitted to emigrate or who were exiled from the USSR were often seen off by many of their comrades-in-arms and other friends, a tradition that was regularly observed. One or two evenings before their departure, a party would be organized in their or their friends' apartment. Many dozens of people visited those parties. They were served wine, vodka, and good food prepared by the hosts and brought by many of us. The doors of those parties were open to any visitor. On the day of departure there were often many dozens of people seeing the émigrés off at the airport. There were journalists and representatives from Western embassies, mostly from the American embassy. In some measure those events were demonstrations of our solidarity and a form of protest in themselves. Everyone in the environs of our gathering (usually it was at an airport) learned about the phenomenon of the refusniks. Unquestionably there were also KGB people there, but they did not interfere directly with us. If that ever happened, I did not know about it. But the KGB often troubled us in other ways, as I will relate in the next chapter.

In conclusion I must say that many people of good will, religious and secular, scientists and students, high-level politicians and parliamentarians, were involved in the various battles for human rights and freedom of the people of the USSR, of dissidents and refusniks. All the people who supported and helped us, particularly those cited in this narrative, deserve high respect and gratitude not only from us but from all humankind. *Membra Sumus Corporis Magni:* All of us are members of one great body.

12

The Vigilance and Intrusion of the KGB

During the time of refusal the KGB kept us under surveillance and generally intruded in our lives. It sometimes seemed that they followed our every step. It was obvious to us that a special department or departments had been organized by the KGB to "take care" of dissidents and refusniks. We knew many of the KGB agents by sight. We saw the same faces watching us again and again during the long days of the trials of Anatoly Sharansky, Ida Nudel, Vladimir Slepak, and others, when many of us stood outside the courthouse, waiting and giving our support. Periodically a black Volga car appeared carrying a person who seemed to be the chief. The KGB people gathered around him as he gave instructions, and then he disappeared. These same people blocked the way to Victor Brailovsky's house when we tried to continue our seminars there after his arrest in 1980.

In the period immediately following Victor's arrest, as I related in the previous chapter, Svetlana and I tried to organize an international conference in our apartment. In consequence we were put under house arrest, along with other members of our seminar. A KGB agent stood in the hallway outside the door of our apartment all through the day, smoking cigarettes. Knowing full well who he was, Svetlana looked out the door at one point and harangued him: "What are you doing here? What do you want? Why are you smoking here?" I told Svetlana, "He is working on orders. It is his duty." Svetlana vented her feelings fully. The man had a pocket radio transmitter and communicated with another man who was outside, close to a black Volga that we could see from our window. In the evening we were free to go for walks, but the black Volga always followed us.

This continued for days. Then one morning we looked outside the door, and the KGB man was gone. We were free to come and go as we pleased. But even then we often saw one of the KGB's black Volgas behind us on the street, for example, whenever we took foreign visitors in a taxi to meet other refusniks.

Of course, our telephone was tapped all through the refusal time. Clicks and other noises on the line told me that. Knowing the surveillance we were under, of both permanent and intermittent varieties, we endured it and as much as possible we ignored it. That was our life. We knew that the KGB could cause trouble for us anywhere, any time, as they did for many refusniks. We did not dwell on those possibilities, however, or speak about them much. We made our choice and followed our path without looking back. We knew we were not always watched or overheard. Our ability to deliver my manuscript to the man who mailed it out of the country showed that. But we could rarely be sure that we were not being observed or recorded.

Like all Soviet citizens we grew up knowing that the KGB might touch our lives, or the lives of people we knew, at any time. In the normal course of events there were KGB watchers in every apartment building, neighborhood, and place of work, "black cats" of the kind that Bulat Okudzhava sang about. And any contact with a foreigner might attract the intervention of the KGB. The experience of my friend Geza Penzesh illustrates this aspect of Soviet life.

The Story of Geza Penzesh

One day in 1933, Irina Chernysheva and I were crossing Krymsky Bridge, close to Gorky Park, and speaking German. Suddenly three men jumped off the trolley car that was slowly passing over the bridge, exclaiming, "Sie sprechen Deutsch?" They had arrived in Moscow only that day. One of them was Geza Penzesh, a Hungarian architect; the two others were German. In the 1930s the Soviet government hired many architects, engineers, and other professionals from the West to take part in rebuilding the country. At that time Hungary was, according to the Soviet perspective, a capitalistic Western country.

We became good friends with Geza. He learned Russian by speaking with me, and I improved my German by speaking with him. He was a tall, handsome man and an intellectual. I learned much from him about the West, about the architecture of Paris, Rome, and so on. I loved architecture. We spent many hours and days together. Our meetings, however, became rare in 1935. At that time I was working a great deal at PhIAN, and Geza was working hard on his projects. One day in 1936 I met him by chance on a trolley. He told me that the next day he was leaving for Spain; he was going to join the People's Front international brigade in Spain's civil war, fighting on the Republican side against the fascists. The next morning I went to his home thinking it would be a nice surprise for us to have a last meeting, but he was not in. I had copied out Byron's "Translation of the Famous Greek War Song" for him. The poem exhorted,

> Sons of the Greeks, arise! . . .
> Then manfully despising
> The Turkish tyrant's yoke,
> Let your country see you rising,
> And all her chains are broke.

I slipped the poem under his door.

I never found out if Geza saw that poem, but in 1937 I received a letter from him, written from a hospital in Paris. He was recuperating after being wounded in the war. Geza asked me to send him cigarettes and chocolate. He also wrote that the letters he was writing to his lover in Moscow, an actress at the popular Moscow Comedy Theater, were going unanswered. He could not reach her by telephone either. At that time, all international calls were answered at the Moscow international telephone station. The caller made an appointment to call again, and notice of that date and time was then given to the intended recipient, who had to come to the international telephone station in order to take the follow-up call. Geza had tried to reach his friend by telephone several times, but she was never there when he made the follow-up call. He gave me her address and asked me to visit her.

Before this I had no knowledge of Geza's romantic life. I sent a small parcel of chocolate and cigarettes to him in Paris. He confirmed its receipt by sending me a Spanish postcard. The famous slogan of the defense of Madrid against the fascists, No Pasarán! (They shall not pass!), was on the front of the card. I went to the house of Geza's friend and knocked on the door. A lady immediately opened it and, looking at me, said, "You are Yanya," which was my childhood nickname. I was much surprised. She explained that Geza had told her a lot about me and so she recognized me. She showed me their son, about one year old, in his baby carriage.

She told me that the KGB agent at the Moscow Comedy Theater had "recommended" that she not answer Geza's letters or speak with him by telephone. He was brief and to the point, telling her that it would be better for her if she followed his instructions. She was understandably frightened. In 1937, a Soviet citizen who had connections with foreigners risked being arrested, and she now had the child to care for. Such a warning as Geza's friend received was one of the methods of the KGB: to frighten people by threatening them. Yet the KGB did not warn me in 1937. It did, however, cut off my brief correspondence with Geza.

I thought I might not hear from Geza Penzesh again. But "one never knows the ways of the Lord." In 1963 I received a letter from Geza from Hungary. He addressed the letter simply, "International, Yakov Alpert, Professor, Moscow, U.S.S.R., Soviet Union." Remarkably, the Moscow central post office found me and delivered what was for me a very dear message. The letter was dated 15 June 1963, one day after the launch of the Russian satellite carrying the first female cosmonaut, Valentina Tereshkova, together with Valentin Bykovsky. Immediately after that event I was interviewed for a foreign broadcast by the Soviet information agency, TASS. Geza heard the interview and mailed me a moving letter, enclosing his photograph. He had gone through the war years in Hungary and almost been killed by the Germans. He wrote, "I have been arrested many times and have been in prison. . . . I was nearly shot. . . . Because of the Soviet army I am still alive." He also wrote that his son, whom I saw when he was only a year old, had become an architect and was with him in Hungary. Later I received two other letters from him written in Russian and in German. I mailed him two letters. He invited me to come to Budapest, but I did not even try to apply for the trip, which would never have been allowed. Soon after Geza's letter of 12 November 1963, our mail was stopped, intercepted by our "trustee," the KGB. To this day I have kept all the letters I received from Geza Penzesh.

Conversations with the KGB

As I related in Chapter 1, the KGB's General Malyshev withdrew my security clearance and dismissed me from my position at PhIAN in March 1951. About six years before that, however, at the end of 1944 or soon after the war, in 1945, a tall, good-looking man in his thirties knocked on the door of my laboratory at PhIAN, where I was working alone. The man smiled and said roughly the following: "I am a representative of the KGB at this institute. I have come to meet you as well as other members of the institute. If now or at any time in the future you have a problem, I am here to help you." After that I saw him at the institute from time to time. I responded to his greetings as briefly as possible and carried on with my work. Months passed and he again came to my laboratory. This visit was not a courtesy call. He wanted to know my opinion of the chief of PhIAN's Theoretical Department, Igor Tamm. He asked me to put in writing what I thought about Tamm.

The academician and Nobelist Igor Evgenievich Tamm was a distinguished physicist and a splendid man. In his youth Tamm was interested in political struggles, and in 1917 he was a member of the Menshevik, or minority, faction of the Russian Social Democratic Party. They opposed the Bolshevik, or majority, faction organized by Lenin. Tamm published his first scientific paper only when he was twenty-nine years old, in 1924; people said that for a theoretician it was late. Nevertheless, he soon became a well-known physicist. He educated many theoretical physicists, including Vitaly Ginzburg and Andrei Sakharov. Igor Tamm was a good friend of the brilliant physicist Leonid Mandelshtam and belonged to his scientific school.

I understood which way the wind blew when the KGB man spoke to me about Tamm. In 1945 Tamm, as I learned much later, was involved in the atom bomb project and must therefore have been under intense KGB surveillance. I knew well that Tamm was a distinguished human being. I also realized that the KGB wanted to find some hold on him. After some hesitation I decided to write about Tamm's honesty, about his deserved intellectual reputation, and in short about his being someone the USSR could and should be proud of. I wrote about two pages and gave them to the KGB man. It is good to note here that Igor Tamm was never arrested by the KGB and that he died as an honored Hero of the Soviet Union for his contributions to Soviet science.

The KGB man continued to appear often at PhIAN. He watched us, and sometimes he spoke to me, although I do not remember his questions. I never protested or became defensive. I did my best to shrug off and evade his questions while still being polite. I even remember that I did not feel hatred for him. That man was part of our institute; he was part of the Soviet reality. Unfortunately, he, or his boss, could not abide my tactics. Once, when I had ignored one of his questions, he said: "Why do you not want to help us? Why do you avoid me, and why are you rebelling? Many members of the academy are helping us. You will also become an academician just as they have. You will attain a high position at the academy." At this, despite my generally expansive nature, I was restrained. I again answered his declaration with silence. It seems to me today that in this way I built a protective wall for myself.

Following this conversation the KGB agent came to me and said that his boss wanted to see me, but not at PhIAN. He asked me to come to the corner of Dzerzhinsky Street and Kuznetsky Most, outside the KGB headquarters and within sight of Lubyanka Prison and the statue of Felix Dzerzhinsky, the founder of the Soviet secret police apparatus from which the KGB derived. In 1991 a crane worked for several hours to remove that symbol of the Red Terror from its pedestal.

We walked along the street. The boss was in his fifties, a thickset man with a pleasant round face. He spoke slowly, as if he were measuring every word. The scope of his discourse was the importance and necessity of helping the KBG to save the country from infiltration by enemies from the West. Suddenly he stopped and asked me, "Who was the foreigner Geza Penzesh with whom you corresponded when he was in Paris in 1937?" At that moment I did not comprehend that this question was intended to frighten me. As I mentioned above, unofficial relations with foreigners were considered a major sin against the USSR. The KGB arrested people for having such contacts. In fact, I am sure that the KGB well knew everything about my meetings with Geza, and that they had copies of our letters. But at that moment on the street I simply told the KGB boss about Geza and about the No Pasarán! postcard I had received from him in 1937. "It would be interesting to see it," he said. Our brief conversation was over.

Only later did I realize that the KGB asked me about the postcard only to startle me. They could use such a document of my collaboration with the West against me if they decided to arrest me. The location of the meeting, close to the KGB building, was also intended to frighten me. The Russian people knew what sorts of events transpired in that building. Thus, the whole meeting was a provocation. After a few days I showed the postcard to the younger KGB man when he came to my laboratory at PhIAN. He took it and I never saw him or it again.

General Fyodor Malyshev, however, continued to watch and to "guide" PhIAN. Certainly, he knew of my conversations with his people, since it was he who was in charge of KGB activity at our institute. No doubt he had a dossier of KGB reports about me when he dismissed me from PhIAN in 1951.

When I began to host refusnik seminars in my home, various agencies of the Soviet regime began to press me to stop them. In 1981, I was summoned to the office of the Soviet prosecutor, and later to the offices of the governor and vice-governor, of the Gagarin district of Moscow, where I lived. I received similar summonses in 1982 and 1983. During those meetings officials charged me with generating anti-Soviet propaganda. They said we were using the seminars to tell people to emigrate. They began by saying that our activity was unacceptable. Gradually they tried to intimidate me. I knew that their actions were initiated and controlled by the KGB. I denied the charge of anti-Soviet activity and invited them to visit one of our seminars. They declined, saying that the subject of our seminar was not in their range of interests.

In 1982 I was summoned to the Soviet immigration service, OVIR. Svetlana accompanied me, as usual. On entering the office we saw a Militsia captain and three KGB representatives in civilian clothes. I recognized one of the KGB men from the street close to the courthouse. The captain said that because of my having had a security clearance we were again being refused visas to emigrate. I noted that the Academy of Sciences said that there was no security reason for denying me a visa, but this meant nothing to them. Then one of the KGB people said that my refusnik activity was a violation of Soviet law. The other two KGB representatives joined in, threatening that I would be arrested and imprisoned just as Brailovsky and other refusniks had been. I listened to them quietly and did not interrupt them. Then I said, "Cowardice is bad for us and for you too." The two KGB men who were threatening me started to shout and to threaten me more and more. But their chief told them, "Shut up." On that note our conversation ended. All the while Svetlana had sat in silence. I was never again summoned to meet with Soviet officials, at least not until the end of our refusal time, which was at the end of 1987. On our leaving OVIR's offices, we passed a car with the same three KGB men inside. Their chief called Svetlana and me over to the car and said that they would drive us home. We turned our backs to them and went toward the subway.

Why at these and other crucial moments in my life did the KGB not square accounts with me completely by arresting me? I have no answer. Who could ever fathom the decisions of the KGB? I was merely lucky! Several of my colleagues have told me that they had similar feelings and questions about their own situations. Was my behavior brave or foolish? Again I can only say that I was and am a very lucky man indeed. I acted in accordance with my nature; such was the reaction of my "organic." That is the word Joseph Brodsky used when a journalist asked him about his behavior in similar circumstances. I managed to overcome the stumbling blocks of my life without losing my self-respect. Any other losses are trifles, the little nothings of life.

SOS
Sakharov, Orlov, Sharansky

In 1978 an executive committee of "Scientists for Orlov and Sharansky" was formed in the United States. Soon after Sakharov was sent into internal exile in Gorky in January 1980, the committee was renamed SOS, for "Sakharov, Orlov, and Sharansky." I take the liberty of writing here about my contacts with these exemplary figures of the dissident and refusnik era, who firmly entered the history of civilizations. Of the three I met and spoke most often with Sakharov; I had less contact with Orlov, who was for dozens of years in prison and internal exile; and I met Sharansky only a few times before his arrest.

The lives and actions of these three men, of very different social origin, show the greatness of human spirit and courage. Everyone feels this on reading their books: *Fear No Evil* by Natan Sharansky, *Memoirs* by Andrei Sakharov, and *Dangerous Thoughts* by Yuri Orlov.[1]

Yuri Orlov

By birth the talented physicist and dissident Yuri Orlov is of "worker and peasant" origin, as the Russian idiom has it. In his eloquent autobiogra-

1. Except where noted, this chapter's quotations of Sharansky, Orlov, and Sakharov are taken from the following: Anatoly Sharansky, *Fear No Evil* (New York: Random House,

phy he remembers how his grandmother Pelageya, a peasant woman, often took him to sell potatoes at Drovin railway station when he was four years old. He recalls how once on their way home hungry wolves chased them, "racing to cut [their horse] Blacky off with powerful leaps across the snowy field" (15).

Orlov had been given into his paternal grandmother's care in a small country village by his mother, who on "doctor's orders . . . brought me there when I was six months old and dying of the whooping cough. Later when I had nearly died of other illness, my mother carried me to Moscow and gave me her blood" (17). Orlov grew up in the village under the care of his grandmother alone, his grandfather having died before he was born. Only when Orlov was seven did Pelageya bring him to Moscow to his parents. An almost entirely self-educated engineer, his father Fyodor was a gifted man of strict manner. He lived a hard life and died of consumption when he was thirty. Yuri's mother Klavdia, an uncommonly beautiful woman, became an orphan and homeless when she was ten. Klavdia and Fyodor met when they were fourteen and eighteen, respectively. The mother's whole life was difficult, and she died when she was forty-nine.

Orlov relates how during one of his frequent walks with Pelegaya in the forest, shortly before he went to Moscow, she told him very sad stories about her and others' hard life at the end of the civil war and also at present. "Everything was destroyed, burned to the ground," Pelegaya said. But as she told Orlov this, she "was smiling slyly," and she went on, "It is possible to live, Yegorushka. Just work, work, work. God will provide." Orlov adds, "I myself thought we were living wonderfully. And it was true that during those two years of long marches with milk and berry lunches in the forest, I became much stronger and stronger" (27–28).

On 4 October 1986, Svetlana and I spent the evening at a farewell party at Yuri and Ira Orlov's apartment in Moscow. The next day Yuri was to be expelled from the USSR. We knew that he had been brought out of internal exile to a prison in Lefortovo, in Moscow. One of his sons met him at Lefortovo. Yuri's wife, Ira Valitova, was to go with him to the United States on the same flight. We could not be sure, however, that they would really be allowed to depart safely. Nevertheless, the next day we saw Yuri's back as he walked behind the airport border guards to the plane. We recognized his figure and the distinctive mop of hair on his head. He and Ira were indeed able to leave Moscow for the West.

1988); Andrei Sakharov, *Memoirs* (London: Hutchinson, 1990); and Yuri Orlov, *Dangerous Thoughts* (New York: William Morrow, 1991). Page references appear in the text.

I first met the physicist and dissident Yuri Orlov at the time of his activities with the Helsinki Watch Group. In 1976 Yuri founded that international movement in Moscow. Soon afterward, the Helsinki movement for freedom and peace began in many countries. In 1973 he had co-founded the Moscow chapter of Amnesty International. At the same time he also wrote a letter to Leonid Brezhnev to support Sakharov and to argue for *glasnost* as well as for economic reforms.

In general, Yuri Orlov was an exceptional human being. He was fired from the Institute of Theoretical and Experimental Physics of the Academy of Sciences in Moscow in 1956, after a meeting at the institute when Yuri spoke out about the necessity for democratic reform in the USSR and criticized the politics of the Communist Party. Soon a highly confidential meeting of the presidium of the Central Committee of the Communist Party was organized concerning "Orlov's provocative statements." At the age of thirty-two Orlov became unemployed, and his fruitful research in physics at the Academy of Sciences in Moscow was stopped. Afterward he worked at the Yerevan Physics Institute in Armenia and did research at Andrei Budker's institute in Novosibirsk. He received his "candidate" and doctoral degrees in physical and mathematical sciences in 1958 and 1963 and was elected a corresponding member of the Armenian Academy of Sciences in 1968. He received a full professorship in 1970.

In 1972 he returned to Moscow and actively joined the dissident movement. Soon he was again unemployed for several months. At the end of 1972 he became a senior scientist at IZMIRAN, where I had been working for twenty years. At first, however, I did not learn that Orlov was at the institute, and I never met him there, perhaps because my laboratory was in a building of its own away from the main building. I was not acquainted with Orlov personally; I knew a little bit about his dissident activity, but that was all. Then the following happened.

Some time in December 1973 I went as usual to a meeting of IZMIRAN's scientific council. Close to the end of the meeting the director, Vladimir Migulin, said that PhIAN and Moscow State University had jointly nominated Orlov, Drs. Kolomensky and Lebedev of PhIAN, and Dr. Ternov of Moscow State University for the State Prize in Physics of the USSR (formerly the Stalin Prize) for their investigations of electron emission in an electromagnetic field. Migulin said that IZMIRAN was being asked to second the nomination of Orlov because he now worked at our institute. It was clear that Migulin did not wish to do this. He did not speak frankly and straightforwardly; he equivocated, his words had a fetid smell. I immediately stood up, objected to Migulin's remarks, and proposed that the institute second Orlov's nomination. After some discussion, the scientific council voted to support the nomination. But at the beginning of 1974 Orlov was fired from IZMIRAN. No doubt Migulin knew this was going to happen before the meeting in December.

Later Kolomensky and Ternov met Orlov privately. Ternov said, "Listen, Yura, we were warned that if we did not exclude you from the list of nominees for the Prize . . . we would not get the Prize." Kolomensky added, "There is just one way out. Yuri, you have to remove your name from the list. We were told that you had signed some sort of a collective document. You know yourself what that means. . . . You signed some sort of document against the state." Yuri answered them, "No, I do not know what it means. . . . It is just a paranoid state. . . . I will not play" (171–72).

In 1977 members of the KGB interrogated several people about Orlov, including Mikhail Leontovich and Vladimir Migulin. During his interrogation Leontovich emphasized that Orlov was continuing to do good work in physics and to publish papers, and he asked the KGB to include this statement in their report. Leontovich understood very well that the system and its puppets liked to dismiss people such as Orlov by saying, "They have ceased to be scientists, they are now only politicians." But as Orlov later learned, Migulin contradicted Leontovich in a separate report to the KGB. Migulin claimed that Orlov had not worked in physics for a long time and had not published any papers after 1963.

None of these events made Orlov stop his activities for human rights; in fact, he continued and expanded them. As a result he was arrested in February 1977. His trial took place in 1978 in Lublino, in the greater Moscow area. He was sentenced to the maximum term for the charge under the "Article of Law," namely, seven years in a strict labor camp plus five years in internal camps. Because of pressure from the West, and particularly because of the SOS Committee, Orlov was removed from the Gulag in October 1986, after serving about nine and a half years of his sentence. He was stripped of his Soviet citizenship and deported from the USSR.

Today Orlov is a senior scientist at the Cornell University Laboratory of Nuclear Science, working actively on theoretical and experimental problems. A member of the American Academy of Arts and Sciences, he studies particle accelerator design, beam interaction analysis, and quantum mechanics. He also continues his extensive activities for human rights. Recently Orlov won the 1995 Nicolson Medal for Humanitarian Service from the American Physical Society.

Now and then before Yuri's arrest I visited the unofficial seminars at his home in Moscow. The last such visit took place about a week before his arrest. It was Monday, 2 February 1977. After his seminar we walked around his apartment building. During our long conversation, I remember that I told him that we were both in the same harness. I explained that I had not joined the Helsinki Watch Group because I had earlier applied for emigration. To be involved in those two roles of freedom activity was, to my way of thinking, inconsistent. Political dissidents did not ask to emigrate.

I was happy to meet Yuri in Washington recently. We had a long, frank conversation in my hotel room at midnight. It was our first conversation in the United States. I reminded him of our last conversation in 1977. He said, "Certainly, you were right." I was glad to hear that. I tell you about that event to emphasize again what the motivating force was in my applying to emigrate and my refusal activity. It was my protest against the Soviet reality and my fight for human rights.

During the long years of Yuri Orlov's imprisonment and internal exile, Svetlana and I often met his wife, Irina Valitova. Many times she told us about her rare meetings with Yuri in prison, in the camp, and in exile. Ira was courageous and steadfast all those long years of Yuri's imprisonment. I still have a photograph of Yuri taken in exile in 1984 and given to me by Ira.

Anatoly Sharansky

At the beginning of his book Anatoly, or Natan, Sharansky writes, "In the evening of March 15, 1977 I was abducted by the KGB . . . on Gorky street. The KGB charged me with espionage. I spent the next 9 years in prison and labor camp . . . including more than four hundred days in punishment cells, and more than two hundred days in hunger strikes. . . . My captors were determined to break me" (1). It is frightening to read these lines.[2]

Natan Sharansky's book is mainly about those nine years, but he also relates how he grew up in a Jewish intellectual family, "completely unaware of the religion, language, culture, and history of my people." His father, a journalist, occasionally told him and his brother tales from the Bible. His grandfather "was a religious Zionist who had dreamed of moving to Palestine. . . . But like most of his generation, Papa . . . believed that the Revolution would solve the Jewish problem, and that the destiny of the Jews was to work together with other people to create an earthly paradise." At the same time Sharansky's book says about his father that when Stalin died, "He told me and my brother Leonid, who was seven years old [Anatoly was five], that Stalin had killed many innocent people, that in his final years he had begun persecuting Jews,

---

2. This account refers variously to "Anatoly" and "Natan" because Sharansky became "Natan" after his emigration to Israel.

and that we were very fortunate that this terrible butcher was dead. Papa warned us not to repeat these comments to anyone" (9).

Is not it strange to see how contradictory was the Soviet people's perception of reality? Soon Anatoly concluded that "in order to survive in the Soviet society you had to function on two levels at once: what you really thought and what you allowed yourself to tell to other people. I lived with this dual reality until 1973, when I joined the aliyah [the emigration] movement of Jews" (10). During this period he was graduated with a degree in computer sciences from the Physical-Technical Institute in Moscow. His thesis was about computer simulations of the chess endgame. From his childhood he played chess very well and loved it. In his book he writes that often he used the logic of chess to solve many delicate problems in his relations with his torturers.

Sharansky applied for an exit visa in April 1973. I learned about him for the first time some time late in 1974, when I heard that he was a very active refusnik and that he had lost his job after applying for emigration to Israel. According to Soviet law, a jobless person could be arrested for being a sponger, a parasite. This happened to many refusniks. Another refusnik, Lev Ulanovsky, asked me to hire Sharansky as my secretary, so that he could not be accused of being a parasite. According to Soviet law, my status as a full professor, a doctor of physical and mathematical sciences, allowed me to have a private secretary at home and to pay him a salary. This employment had to be registered with a special Soviet body. Of course, I agreed to do that, and fortunately I could afford to pay the modest salary that was stipulated for the job of secretary. I fixed a day to meet Sharansky and register him as my employee. But in the meantime, Anatoly met the well-known mathematician Naum Meiman, and Meiman made him his secretary. Meiman applied for emigration in 1975. After several years he entered the Moscow Helsinki Watch Group. Meiman told me that he thought that membership in the group would hasten permission for his emigration. That did not happen. He was permitted to emigrate only a couple of months after Svetlana and I emigrated. (I must mention here that the first Jew who applied for an exit visa to Israel and who was refused was Benjamin Bogomolny in 1966. In the *Guinness Book of World Records* he is described as "the most patient refusnik." Bogomolny emigrated in 1986.)

During the next fourteen months, I met Sharansky only a few times on Saturday evenings near the Moscow synagogue. I do not remember any of our personal discussions, but I would like to tell here about one event in particular at the end of 1976 or the beginning of 1977. Twenty to thirty refusniks had come together at the synagogue that morning. We decided to go together to the house of another refusnik for a cultural meeting several miles from the synagogue. Andrei Sakharov also joined us at the synagogue. Sharansky opened the meeting by speaking against the Soviet suppression of the Jewish cultural movement. His talk was impressive. It was at that meeting that I first learned that Sharansky was a strong, clever, and brave man.

I wrote in the previous chapter about the KGB's presence at refusnik and dissident gatherings. On leaving this meeting I saw many KGB people near the house and a few black Volga cars. The KGB was watching the exit of the house and its elevator. By chance, just when I was leaving the building together with Solomon Alber, another refusnik, Sakharov came out of the elevator. Apparently alerted by a KGB man inside, a black Volga immediately came to the front of the house from where it had been parked among the identical black Volgas of the KGB. It was a car from the garage of the Academy of Sciences. The car's driver knew Sakharov, having served him before. (Some academicians used the academy's car service for their private needs and called for a car by telephone.) The scene I observed was a revealing example of the omnipresence of the KGB and the close watch that was kept on the refusnik and dissident community.

Sharansky was arrested in March 1977, about a month after the arrest of Yuri Orlov. At that time he was twenty-nine. He was arrested because of his refusnik activity, but he was also among the first members of the Moscow Helsinki Watch Group. (Recently Orlov told me that he invited Sharansky to become a member of that group.) His trial was held in Moscow soon after Orlov's, at the end of June 1978. That trial was especially severe because Sharansky was accused of being a spy. We were afraid that he would be sentenced to be shot. Instead he was sentenced to three years in prison plus ten years in strict labor camps. The trials of Orlov and Sharansky, and of some other Russian dissidents, filled the world with indignation. Perhaps precisely because of the activity of the SOS Committee, Orlov was at the Gulag for nine and one-half years instead of the twelve years of his sentence. Sharansky was there for nine years instead of thirteen.

Anatoly Sharansky was released in February 1986, about eight months before Orlov's departure from the USSR. On 11 February 1986 he crossed the Clienicke Bridge, which was at the border between East Germany and West Germany. A photograph of that moment was published in an English newspaper. We posted that page of the newspaper at our seminar.

I would like to mention here that in June 1987, the members of the SOS Committee were asked in a letter from its secretary, Philip Sigelman of the Department of Political Sciences of San Francisco State University, to discuss initiatives that could be taken on my behalf. On my coming to the United States in 1988 I read a copy of that letter. The refusnik Yuri Tarnopolsky, who had already immigrated to the United States and lived in Chicago, initiated that action of the SOS Committee. At that time Orlov was in the United States, Sharansky was in Israel, and Sakharov was in Moscow, his exile to Gorky having ended in 1986.

After the release and departure of Sharansky, his mother, Ida Petrovna Milgrom, waited for about six months for permission to follow her son to Israel. She was a brave and wise woman of seventy-eight. For almost a decade during the detention and imprisonment of her son, she fought for his freedom. We met her often at different places — in private homes, at the American embassy, at hotels when meeting with foreigners who fought for Anatoly's freedom, in an alley close to the Moscow synagogue, at our apartment, and elsewhere. During the trial Svetlana and I stood with Ida Petrovna in the narrow street near the courthouse where Sharansky was convicted. We were often the first to arrive and stood from about 9:00 in the morning until the end of the trial session late in the afternoon. All that time the street was full of many people.

Our last long meeting with Ida Petrovna was in April 1986 at her apartment in the Moscow suburb of Istra, soon after Anatoly's departure for the West. We spoke then about the detrimental actions of some refusniks. Svetlana and I were dismayed by the moral and humanistic shape of some people in the refusnik community. We spoke openly and frankly with Ida Petrovna, and she shared that concern.

At the send-off party for Ida Petrovna, which was on the evening of 23 August at the apartment of her second son, Leonid, she asked me to go out on the balcony with her. In general many of us never discussed delicate problems inside an apartment, there being many listening ears and often also listening devices. During this last conversation she asked me, "What you would like me to say to Tolya?" She remembered our conversation at her house months earlier about the refusnik community. I told her, "Tell him that our refusnik activity is a holy affair, indeed, and that the unpleasant actions of some refusniks were merely scum on the surface of water."

Ida looked at me with astonishment and asked, "Indeed, do you think so?"

"Yes," I answered, "that is my honest opinion." Two days later we saw her off at the airport. Whether she ever told Anatoly about our conversation I do not know. I recount it here to explain the stimulus of refusnik activity. During those twelve years I never thought about what would happen to us. We did what we had to do and did not look back. When the KGB agents threatened me with arrest in 1982, I immediately responded, "Cowardice is bad for us and for you too." Cowardice often provokes treachery.

As I write these lines, Natan Sharansky is a leader of a new political party,

Yisrael Ba-Aliyah ("Israel in Ascent"). He is also a minister of industry and trade in Israel.

Andrei Sakharov

Nature is full of enigmas and miracles. Some miracles are simultaneously also enigmas, as, for example, the creation of such different yet exceptional people as Albert Einstein and Nicolò Paganini. How could it happen? What combination of life processes, of origins and nature — in the language of physicists, of nonlinear feedback processes — could create such phenomena? I do not even know how to phrase such a question. That is essentially the problem I encounter when I think about Andrei Sakharov. He was a man who could not be measured in ordinary terms. A line from an excellent Russian poet, Fyodor Tyutchev, says, "Arshinom obschim ne izmerit" — you cannot measure everything with the same measure. Sakharov was a singular individual. Such people cannot be put in a line according to their height. Certainly, I do not want to do that, and I did not do that when I mentioned Einstein and Paganini. Rather, it is the common characteristic of such individuals that they are each unique. Sakharov was such a creation of nature. At the same time he was an ordinary human being. Still today some of his actions and ways of thinking are unclear and contradictory. Many questions remain unanswered. This is a task for his biographers.

At the beginning of Chapter 11 I spoke of the impact of Sakharov's essay "Reflections on Progress, Peaceful Co-existence, and Intellectual Freedom" in the fight waged by Soviet dissidents and refusniks for human rights and freedom. I would like to continue here with a few brief reminiscences about Sakharov. First, for his origin: Sakharov relates in *Memoirs* that his maternal grandfather, Alexei Sofaino, was a professional soldier. He became a general during the Russo-Turkish war. After the war with Japan he retired with the rank of major general. He died at the age of eighty-four in 1929.

Andrei Sakharov's paternal grandfather, Ivan Sakharov (the son of a village priest), became a successful lawyer in Moscow. He was a man of liberal views for his time. There were many advanced and distinguished people among his acquaintances, such as the writers Vladimir Korolenko and Vikenty Veresayev. Andrei's father, Dimitri, was a many-sided man. He began with medical education and did very well. Then he transferred to the Physics-Mathematics department of Moscow State University. He became a teacher of physics and author of several books and popular science publications. His most important work was "Problems in Physics," which went through thirteen editions. Andrei wrote, "My father made me a physicist" (*Memoirs,* 21). But his father was also accepted at the Gnessin Conservatory and was graduated with a gold medal. Despite his acknowledged talent, the elder Sakharov did not become a professional musician. But throughout his life he continued to play the piano and write piano sonatas and songs. He often played his favored Beethoven, Chopin, Skryabin, Rimsky-Korsakov, and others for his own enjoyment. I give this very short sketch only to show Andrei Sakharov's roots and the atmosphere in which he grew up.

For all the years of the refusal era the prominent Sakharov supported the refusniks in many ways. Let me begin with an occurrence on 6 September 1972, when Sakharov took part in a demonstration of Jews in Moscow. That demonstration was held to condemn the murder of Israeli athletes by Arab terrorists at the Olympic Games in Munich. As a punishment for the demonstration Sakharov and the other demonstrators were taken by police to the cells known as drunk tanks. Such places were used to keep drunks overnight. Many years later refusniks would say, "When I met Sakharov in the drunk tank . . . ," or "Sakharov and I met for the first time in the drunk tank." That story and many others are described in a useful and interesting book by Martin Gilbert, *Sharansky: Hero of Our Time*.[3]

On 25 October 1970 Andrei Sakharov was outside the Supreme Court in Moscow among those protesting the Leningrad Court's death sentences for defendants Edward Kuznetsov and Mark Dymshitz, a pilot. Both were among a group of twelve refusniks who tried to hijack a commercial flight from Leningrad to Priozersk on 15 June 1970. They planned to force the plane to fly to Israel, but they were arrested at the airport in Leningrad. At trial Kuznetsov told the court, "All I wanted was to live in Israel." That year the number of Jews who were refused permission to emigrate grew. Before that event Sakharov founded the Soviet Committee for Human Rights together with Valery Chalidze and Andrei Tverdohlebov. It was in September, in the midst of the "hijacking affair," as the newspapers called it, that Andrei Sakharov first met Elena Bonner at a meeting at the home of Valery Chalidze.

The well-known Russian mathematician and corresponding member of the academy Igor Shafarevich later told Sakharov at a meeting of the academy that he wanted to join the Committee for Human Rights. Many years passed, and in the 1980s Shafarevich adopted an anti-Semitic form of "slavophilia." He became an ultra-Russian nationalist. His terrible anti-Jewish book *Russophobia*, published in Munich, is well known. It is sorrowful, but c'est la vie!

In May 1971, Sakharov's Committee on Human Rights protested in an open letter to the Supreme Soviet the unlawful refusals of Jewish requests for

3. Martin Gilbert, *Scharansky: Hero of Our Time* (New York: Viking, 1986), 268.

exit visas. In a message to Israel Radio Sakharov said, "I feel a great sense of warmth toward these people [Jews who had left the Soviet Union] in order to build new lives in their modern ancient homeland." In September 1973 in an open letter to the U.S. Congress, Sakharov argued in support of "tens of thousands of citizens of the Soviet Union, including Jews, who want to leave the country and who have sought to exercise that right for years and decades at the cost of endless difficulty and humiliation."

Jewish cultural and educational seminars on Jewish art, Bible study, and other topics were suppressed by Soviet bodies in the 1970s. At that time many house searches took place at the homes of active refusniks. Many materials — such as Hebrew textbooks, books on Jewish history, prayer books, and tape recordings of Jewish music — were confiscated. In an open letter of November 1976 the refusniks wrote, "That blow was directed against the Jewish spiritual renaissance." Indeed, any move against the Jewish refusnik seminars clearly violated the Helsinki agreement. Although the USSR had signed that agreement, the refusniks' three-day Cultural Symposium in Moscow, which took several months to prepare and was scheduled for December 1976, was suppressed by the Soviet government. In support of that symposium, Andrei Sakharov joined the demonstration of Jews in 1976 of which I wrote above. Yuri Orlov was arrested in February 1977, Anatoly Sharansky one month later.

It is worth noting in this connection that the anti-Semitism of the Soviet authorities stimulated the very activity that they wished to suppress. Many Jews became refusniks not for religious reasons but because of anxiety over what rising anti-Semitism would mean for their children, who were increasingly being kept out of the universities and institutes. It was during the period of refusal that their religious identity and activity became strong.

When U.S. secretary of state Cyrus R. Vance visited Moscow in 1977, Sakharov declared at a press conference, "If President Carter is really serious about a human rights campaign, he must come to the support of Anatoly Sharansky. . . . [Any] hesitation will have very tragic consequences." In a statement in the fall of 1977 Sakharov called upon Western governments to delay the opening of the Belgrade Conference on the Monitoring of the Helsinki Agreements, demanding that Orlov first be discharged. On 8 July 1977 Sakharov's signature was among those of leading human rights activists on a very moving letter to the West on Sharansky's behalf. The letter said in part,

> He appeared about five years ago among those Moscow Jews who were waiting for repatriation. . . . Anatoly Sharansky became quickly a universal favorite. . . . The whole history of Jewish emigration in recent years was pierced by his personality like a laser beam. . . . He demanded not only the

right of emigration, he insisted on fundamental human rights. . . . We who know him are convinced of his innocence. . . . We call upon you to defend Anatoly Sharansky. . . . People, react! Speak! Write! Demand! Shout!

In a similar vein, after Sakharov was sent into internal exile in Gorky and went on a hunger strike there in 1981, seven other scientists and I gave the following letter to journalists from the West.

To the Scientists of the World:

The hunger strike of Andrei Dmitrievich Sakharov and his wife, Elena Georgiyevna Bonner, which has been going on for ten days, has an absolutely tragic character.

Andrei Sakharov is a founder of one of the most important deeds of our time — namely, the realization of thermo-nuclear guided synthesis. "Sakharov pointed the way to solving one of the mighty atomic problems of the 20th century — how to obtain inexhaustible energy by burning ocean water" (*Kurchatov,* by I. N. Golovin, Moscow, Atomizdat, 1967).

For more than twenty years now, research in this field has been open and conducted in close international collaboration. Is such collaboration compatible with persecution of Sakharov and his family?

We appeal to scientists for general support of Sakharov, and in particular to ask their governments and parliaments to support Sakharov in his current tragic situation.

Academician Sakharov must be returned to Moscow. The practice of holding him and those close to him hostage must be stopped.

We call for decisive and immediate actions; in a few days it may be too late.
December 1, 1981
Physicists: Ya. Alpert, B. Altshuler, Yu. Golfand
Mathematicians: I. Brailovskaya, A. Lerner, N. Meiman, G. Freiman
Biologist: V. Soifer

At the same time I asked a few prestigious scientists who visited me to give a message to six great physicists in the West, among them five winners of the Nobel Prize, asking them to resign their honorary memberships in the Academy of Sciences of the USSR to protest the deportation of Sakharov to Gorky and to support him in his hunger strike. I reminded them of the letter of the great English physiologist Sir Henry Dale, who won the Nobel Prize in 1936, together with Otto Loewi of Austria, for their work on the chemical transmission of nerve impulses. Dale was the president of the Royal Society of London from 1940 to 1945, and he was made an honorary member of the Academy of Sciences of the USSR in 1942. That same year the Royal Society elected Nikolai Vavilov as one of its fifty honorary foreign members. In 1945 Dale learned that Nikolai Vavilov had died, and he began to make inquiries about his fate.

As I mentioned above, Vavilov had fallen victim to Stalin's terror. In 1948, when this became clear to Dale, he wrote to the president of the Soviet Academy of Sciences to resign his honorary membership. Dale's letter, which was quoted in the *Times* of London on 26 October 1948 and in other Western newspapers, said in part, "I believe that I should do disservice even to my scientific colleagues in the U.S.S.R., if I were to retain an association in which I might appear to condone the actions by which your academy, under whatever compulsion, is now responsible for such a terrible injury to the freedom and integrity of science."

The response of the academy, published in the *Times* of London on 28 October 1948, was to condemn Dale for being "an obedient instrument of the anti-Democratic forces." What is sad for me to note is that in 1981 none of the academy's honorary foreign members emulated Sir Henry Dale's noble act of protest. None of them resigned their memberships or in any way lodged protests with the academy over the harsh mistreatment of Andrei Sakharov. About that I can only say, *tempora mutantur et homines mutantur* — times change and people change with them.

Some Reminiscences

A lot has been said about Sakharov, a brilliant physicist and distinguished fighter for human rights. Many books, articles, and reminiscences have been and will be published about him. He has firmly entered the history of the twentieth century, and there he will remain. What I have related about his humanity and brave actions represents only the smaller elements of his achievements. Now I shall talk about a few of my meetings and conversations with him, and I shall begin with an event connected with what I have related about Anatoly Sharansky. This story again shows Andrei Sakharov's face.

One day Sakharov stood on a tiny street outside the Moscow courtroom where Sharansky's trial was taking place. It was 14 July 1978, Bastille Day. Meanwhile, the trial of the famous and brave dissident Alexander Ginsburg was taking place in Kaluga. Elena Bonner and Andrei Sakharov had been present in Kaluga every day of Ginsburg's trial, except for that day. On that day they were in Moscow with all of us to hear Sharansky's sentence. Throughout the day many people gathered behind the barrier that separated them from the courthouse at the end of an alleyway. Ida Milgrom, Anatoly's mother, was there, as well as perhaps a hundred or more refusniks, and many dissidents. In the crowd were also scores of journalists, dozens of uniformed police officers, and certainly many plainclothes KGB agents.

Only Leonid, Anatoly's brother, was allowed in the courtroom. Even Anatoly's mother had been forbidden to attend the trial. At the end of every trial session Leonid told those waiting outside what was happening inside. On the last day of the trial Ida Milgrom again asked in writing for permission to enter the courtroom to witness the sentencing of her son. She received no reply to her request. We stood in tense silence waiting for the sentence. It was impressive to see Andrei Sakharov, generally a quiet man with a pastor's disposition, literally throw himself with clenched fists at the Militsia. He screamed at them to say why they did not let Sharansky's mother enter the courtroom. Although Svetlana and I did not hear his words, a U.S. journalist wrote that Sakharov declared angrily, "You are not people. You are fascists!" And he also said to the crowd, "What is happening is pure sadism, a mockery of a mother's feelings."

We waited hours for the sentence. Then, in the late afternoon, a black Volga arrived. A man from the car crossed the barrier and strode with confidence to the courthouse. It was obvious that he carried the decision of the Kremlin with him. Soon afterward, Leonid Sharansky walked out through the barricade and said with a voice full of agitation, "Thirteen years!" When he had been somewhat calmed down, he repeated Anatoly's sentence to the crowd. Then many people near the barricade sang the Jewish and Israeli anthem, "Hatikvah" (Hope). Meanwhile, we saw that a khaki-colored prison van had appeared near the courthouse and then quickly departed. The crowd realized that Anatoly had been taken to prison. In unison the crowd shouted, "Tolya! Tolya!"

I met Sakharov for the first time at the beginning of 1945, before the end of the war. Igor Tamm had admitted Sakharov there to work on his Ph.D. dissertation. In those days I encountered Sakharov only rarely and never had any scientific discussions with him. We were members of different departments. Moreover, Vavilov organized a highly confidential scientific group shortly after Sakharov joined the staff. The office of the group was closed to outsiders. Today we know that they were working on theoretical calculations for the creation of the hydrogen bomb, which was also being discussed in the United States at that time. In the beginning the group comprised Semyon Belenky, Andrei Sakharov, and Igor Tamm. Later Vitaly Ginzburg and Efim Fradkin joined them. Now we know that within two months of the start of the activity of the group, Sakharov proposed a new line of hydrogen bomb research. It is known that the fathers of the hydrogen bomb were Sakharov in the USSR and Edward Teller in the United States. Both were the creators of that monstrous power. It is also known that later Ginzburg also proposed an important idea connected with the hydrogen bomb project.

Soon Sakharov and Tamm were taken from PhIAN into the ultraconfidential places where that and other atom bomb projects were realized. Andrei Sakharov was the only one of that group who was there from start to finish, continuously developing new ideas during the project. In Moscow he worked behind firmly closed doors at PhIAN for two years. From 1950 to 1968, he worked in a strictly closed confidential city.

Humankind knows well what happened at the end of that long period. In 1968 Sakharov's landmark essay "Reflections on Progress, Peaceful Coexistence, and Intellectual Freedom" appeared. Soon after he was fired from his high-security job. In 1968 he became one of the world's most distinguished dissidents and fighters for human rights and freedom.

I did not meet Sakharov again until 1970 in the dining hall of the Academy of Sciences. That dining hall was open every day from 1 to 5 P.M. exclusively for academicians, corresponding members of the academy, and some other privileged people who worked at the Academy of Sciences. I had that privilege as a doctor of sciences and head of a department at IZMIRAN. I was having my dinner when Sakharov approached my table with a lady. He said with shining eyes, "Yakov Lvovich, here is Elena Bonner, my wife." I do not remember the subject of our conversation during dinner, but thus it was that I again met Sakharov twenty-five years after our short encounters at PhIAN in 1945. After that event we met briefly on different occasions, in particular at the refusnik seminars.

Late in 1978 Andrei Sakharov and Elena Bonner were at a meeting of five refusniks with Senator Edward Kennedy at the apartment of the well-known and active refusnik, the mathematician Alexander Lerner. I was at that meeting, too. The senator came to Lerner at night, close to 1:00 A.M. We had discussions for about two to three hours. I vividly remember that dark night, when at about 4:00 A.M. I crossed the streets of Moscow after that meeting alone on foot, not being able to find a taxi. Svetlana and I lived about three miles from Lerner's house. I was afraid that I would be stopped and beaten. Certainly the KGB knew about our meeting. Svetlana was anxiously waiting for me at home. It was usual to see KGB people on such occasions, but I did not see any of them around Lerner's house, nor did I see anyone following me. Perhaps the Soviet government had decided to show the senator their indifference to the activities of refusniks, which was often a false and intricate tactic of Soviet policy. Kennedy had meetings with several Soviet authorities of the highest level during his visit to Moscow. It was after such a meeting that he joined us.

It is well known that Sakharov's exile in Gorky began on 22 January 1980 and ended on 22 December 1986. In *Memoirs* Sakharov describes how a telephone was hurriedly installed in his apartment in Gorky on 16 December 1986. The following day Gorbachev telephoned him and said that "they" had decided that Sakharov could return to Moscow and continue his "patriotic deeds." Who "they" were, Gorbachev did not say. Three days later the president of the Academy of Sciences, Gury Marchuk, went to Gorky. Sakharov wrote in his book *Gorky-Moscow and Beyond, 1986 to 1989,* "We had a long tête-à-tête meeting at the Gorky Institute of Physics," to which he had been brought in the car of the director of the institute.[4]

On the morning of 19 December I received a telephone call from physicist Boris Altshuler, Sakharov's good friend, who did much to help him and Elena during the seven years of exile. Boris said that he had just finished speaking by telephone with Sakharov and gave me the telephone number in Gorky. After some minutes I reached Sakharov. It was my good luck, for during all the following days of his stay in Gorky his telephone was always busy. Sakharov told me about his conversation with Gorbachev in detail. Now, reading the description of that conversation with Gorbachev in Sakharov's book, I can see that he told me everything, including how he interrupted Gorbachev when he spoke about Elena Bonner, saying, "She is my wife, and her name is not Bon*nar* but *Bon*ner." (Gorbachev had mispronounced her last name). Sakharov also told me that at the very beginning of their conversation he spoke with Gorbachev about those who were mistreated in the prisons especially the distinguished human rights defender and writer Anatoly Marchenko, who had died in the prison eight days before that conversation, on 8 December, after a hunger strike he had begun in August. He was only forty-eight years old. Sakharov, moreover, was the first to say to Gorbachev, "Do svidaniya" (goodbye), thus breaking off the conversation.

On 23 December 1986 Sakharov and Elena Bonner were back in Moscow. The following evening Svetlana and I went to visit them at their home. There we were surprised to find a crowd of journalists; it was Sakharov's first press conference after his exile. We had not called ahead. Refusniks and dissidents rarely did that when they visited one another. Remember that our phones were regularly tapped and we did not want to give the KGB advance notice of our movements. Another pleasant meeting also took place that evening at the Sakharovs' apartment with Mustafa Jamilev and his wife, who had come unexpectedly that same day to Moscow from Siberia after having been in exile. That brave man, a prisoner of conscience, was convicted many times and in total spent, with only short intervals, about thirteen years in various prisons and in exile. The next day Mustafa and his wife visited us.

Jamilev was one of the most active people fighting for the rights of the Crimean Tatars to return to their homeland. In 1944 Stalin forcibly transported

4. Andrei Sakharov, *Gorky-Moscow and Beyond, 1986 to 1989* (), 30–31. Future references appear in the text.

many thousands of Tatar women, children, and elders to Uzbekistan. At that time most Tatar men were at war. Crimea became a republic known as Taurida soon after the revolution in 1917–20 and was renamed the Autonomous Soviet Republic of Crimea from 1920 to 1944. In 1976 Andrei and Elena went to Omsk (Siberia) for one of Jamilev's trials, and in 1979 Andrei went alone to Tashkent (Uzbekistan) for another. Crimean Tatars, friends of Jamilev, visited me in Moscow, and I introduced them to Sakharov, as happened, for example, in 1987. From time to time we were in correspondence with Jamilev's wife, who was a schoolteacher. Svetlana sent her gifts for her children. To this day we have five small volumes of collected poems of seventeenth-, eighteenth-, and nineteenth-century Eastern poets, gifts to us from the Jamilevs from Tashkent. A volume of the collected poems of the famous fourteenth-century Tadjic philosopher and poet Jamee was among those books, and also a book of the nineteenth-century enlightener Zakurdan Furkat.

During the years of Sakharov's exile we often visited Elena Bonner. The Militsia personnel, who sat outside the door of her apartment and "protected" her, recognized Svetlana and me and often did even not check our passports, as the rules required. We usually sat in the kitchen, and Elena told us many stories of her life and the circumstances of their social activity. She gave us a copy of a photograph of Andrei Sakharov taken in 1981 after his well-known hunger strike. She told us, "Don't show it. They [the authorities] don't know I have it."

Once she told us about a good friend from her childhood and youth, Vsevolod Bagritsky. She read us some of his verses. Bagritsky was the son of the popular and talented Russian poet Edward Bagritsky. At the beginning of the war, Elena and Vsevolod joined the army as volunteers. Vsevolod died, I learned, in the small village of Kuzminki on 26 February 1942, after being shot accidentally. Sakharov wrote that Vsevolod had played an important role in Elena's life. After the war Vsevold's poems were published, and Elena was one of the compilers of the book. Many of the poems were published from her memory. Elena Bonner is indeed an exceptional human being.

After Sakharov's return from exile at the end of December 1986 and until December 1987, when we received permission to emigrate, we saw him from time to time at his home. We spoke with him and Elena by telephone, although Sakharov rarely telephoned us. Both he and Elena were very involved in their human rights activities then, and we also had many troubles over our refusnik seminars. During one such meeting with them at their home, I told Sakharov for the first time about Vavilov's conversation with Stalin regarding the nomination of the new president of the academy. As I related in Chapter 1, Stalin told Vavilov that the choice would be between him and prosecutor Vyshinsky.

When Sakharov wrote of that incident in his book, he mixed up the names of the people involved. During another meeting I told him the story of how I had been fired from PhIAN by the general of the KGB in March 1951. It was curious to hear from Sakharov that almost at the same time the same general of the KGB, Fyodor Malyshev, the commissioner of the board of the ministers of the Central Committee of the Soviet Communist Party, invited Andrei to join the Communist Party. We know that Sakharov did not do so.

The meeting I had with Sakharov on 7 July 1987 was the most important of my meetings and conversations with him during that period for many reasons. At the end of June I called and told him that I could not hide from him my serious misgivings about some of his actions. I had not mentioned these thoughts to anyone. In a couple of days we spoke together at his home. I began our conversation with the statement that his support of some of the actions of Mikhail Gorbachev had surprised and distressed me, as it had some others. Especially troubling was his support for Gorbachev's persistent and vociferous statements against the Strategic Defense Initiative (SDI), or Star Wars weaponry, that had been developed in the United States. I told him that such a project had been attempted in the USSR decades earlier, but that it had been at a much lower technical level. I do not remember if I also told him what I thought about Gorbachev's responsibility for the terrible consequences of the Chernobyl disaster. Gorbachev delayed making an announcement about the catastrophe immediately. The official announcement misrepresented the level of radiation, saying it was hundreds and even thousands of times lower than it truly was. Only after a week had passed did Gorbachev officially tell the people about the disaster; and when he did so he lied, saying that similar events had taken place in the West, specifically in the United States. Another detestable statement that Gorbachev made was during his meeting with Dubcek in Prague, when he told him that Soviet tanks entering Prague had been a necessary and right step by the USSR.

But that night the main point of my conversation with Sakharov remained the SDI problem, and we spoke not as we usually did, in the kitchen, but in another room. Elena Bonner was sitting silently to the side in an armchair. Only once did she speak, and that was to say, "Andrei, I said the same thing to you." Sakharov followed me in his usual quiet manner, and then he asked me, "What are the people saying about it?" I answered that they were saying, "Sakharov is no longer Sakharov." He only shook his head. When I was about to leave, he said, "But I think that I am right in what I am doing, although it is clear you think otherwise."

What is remarkable is that one of Sakharov's rare telephone calls to me occurred two to three days after that meeting. He said, "For a long time you have not been to our home. Perhaps you will visit us with Svetlana." It seems by that call he wanted to say that nothing had changed between us after our most recent conversation.

Shortly before that meeting, Svetlana and I met him at the French embassy on 29 June during a special ceremony at which medals and the diploma of the Académie des Sciences of France were presented to the famous mathematician Vladimir Arnold and to Sakharov. Henri Cartan and his wife, Nicole, also attended the ceremony. Two days earlier they visited us at our home.

In July and August 1987 Svetlana and I were away from Moscow on vacation for about two months. Soon after that a radical change took place in our lives. At about 7 P.M. on the evening of 6 November we were officially informed by OVIR, the Soviet immigration service, that we had been granted permission to leave the USSR. Both of us had waited for nearly twelve years for that permission: the time of our refusal. I had waited for about twenty years, since the time when Soviet tanks entered Prague.

The lieutenant who telephoned us from OVIR asked us to come to begin to draw up our visas on 9 November, the following Monday. On the morning of that day, about an hour before our going to the immigration office, we got another rare call from Sakharov. He invited us to visit him and Elena. He was the first person I told about OVIR's call. He immediately said, "It was a sign from God that moved me to call you today."

On 20 October 1988 Andrei arrived in Boston. I telephoned him, and I again had good luck in reaching him. He and Elena were living at the house of Efrem (in his book, Sakharov calls him Rem) and Tanya Yankelevich; Tanya is Elena's daughter. During our short conversation I told him, "It is a miracle, Andrei Dmitrievich, that you are here!" He immediately replied, "Yakov Lvovich, it is a miracle indeed too that you are also here." I blushed in embarrassment. But the truth is that I was also proud and pleased to hear Sakharov's words.

Svetlana and I met Sakharov in Boston twice. Once was at the American Academy of Arts and Sciences on 18 November 1988 at a meeting of the International Fund for the Survival and Development of Mankind, a creation of Eugene Velikhov, who had involved the American physicist Jerome Wiesner in the project. The board of the fund included twenty to thirty well-known persons. Its announced goals were to support dissidents, refusniks, and prisoners of conscience. In 1987, at Wiesner's urging, Sakharov became involved. It was hoped that his involvement would bolster the fund's image and attract contributions. Sakharov later wrote in *Gorky-Moscow and Beyond* that "it was . . . a sad story." He thought that his "entrance to the International Fund would be a logical continuation of my previous activity." He concluded, however, "It was a big mistake" (78–82). In any case, in November 1988 he presented a talk at a meeting of the International Fund.

It was not as if Sakharov did not know whom he was dealing with, at least in Velikhov's case. In *Gorky-Moscow and Beyond* Sakharov relates how Velikhov came unexpectedly to his home in February 1987 with the Italian physicist Antonio Zicici and his wife. Sakharov expected only the Zicicis. Sakharov notes "how familiar yet respectful" Velikhov's manner was. Sakharov adds, "That was rather amazing, especially when one remembers that not long before Velikhov, like other administrators of the Academy, told tales about my well-being, including at the time of my hunger strike." Velikhov even told such tales to one of Sakharov's foreign friends, not knowing about Sakharov's relations with that man. In Sakharov's view, Velikhov "established a record in that genre" (49).

Now I ask myself, how could it happen that Sakharov believed Velikhov's claims for the International Fund for the Survival and Development of Mankind? Did he believe them because, as the saying goes, even Homer sometimes nods? Like some other Russian scientific figures who were involved in the fund or similar projects, Velikhov served the system and himself.

Another meeting with Andrei in Boston took place on 25 November, before his departure to Moscow. We were invited to a farewell party, which was held at Efrem and Tanya's home. That evening, when Andrei stood in a crowd of people, I asked him, "Do you remember our conversation about Gorbachev?"

Sakharov replied, "Certainly I do."

I continued, "Now everything is clear about Gorbachev." Gorbachev was then resisting further reforms of the Soviet system. Sakharov shook his head, and I said, "But Elena Georgievna agreed with me."

"Elena is 'dushka,' " Sakharov said. I cannot translate that sweet intimate Russian word into English; "darling" would be a very rough approximation.

It was the last time we saw Andrei. Before we left the party, he gave us a 1989 calendar made in Canada and titled "Blessed Are the Peacemakers." It featured pictures of world figures in human rights activity. The calendar was dedicated to Sakharov and showed him on the cover as well as on one of the months inside. He wrote on the cover of the calendar, "To dear Yakov Lvovich and dear Svetlana for good memories, A. Sakharov, 28/XI/88." We saw him again only on television in 1989, when we were in Boston. It was a taped session of the Supreme Soviet of the USSR. We saw how Gorbachev interrupted Sakharov and waved papers in front of him and turned off the microphone. The auditorium did not hear Sakharov's words. On 14 December that year Andrei died. That sad news reached us the same evening.

On 18 January 1990, when Svetlana and I were in Moscow for a week,

Efrem Yankelevich visited us in our hotel. He told us that on 14 December 1989 Andrei went to his office at home to work and told Elena that he was going to prepare his speech for the next day's session of the Supreme Soviet. He added, "Tomorrow there will be a battle." In a few hours Elena began to wonder why Andrei had not returned. She entered his office, which was in another apartment a floor below, and saw that Andrei was dead.

The day before he died, Sakharov finished the epilogue to his memoirs. The epilogue says, "This book is devoted to my dear and lovely Lyusya [Elena]." And the last words read,

Life goes on.	Жизнь продолжается.
We are together.	Мы вместе.
13 December 1989	13 декабря 1989 года,
Moscow	Москва

When I read that later I began to tremble. Another coincidence that seemed like an almost mystical phenomenon shocked Svetlana and me. In the calendar he had given us, as I said, Sakharov was pictured on the cover and for one of the months inside. The month was December 1989.

14

Denouement, October 1987

At about 6 P.M. on Friday, 6 November 1987,[1] as I mentioned in the previous chapter, a lieutenant from OVIR telephoned. She said that Svetlana and I should come to the immigration office for our exit visas on Monday morning. Because the celebration of the October revolution was the next day, my immediate reaction was to ask, "Is it an award to celebrate the seventieth anniversary of the October Revolution?" and then to add, "Congratulations on the holiday to your supervisor and to you." The lieutenant did not answer. Did she understand the irony in what I said?

All that weekend Svetlana and I were a little nervous, anticipating our visit to OVIR. We had been there so many times, so fruitlessly, in the previous twelve years. We wondered if the call might be a hoax. Thus we did not tell anyone about the call until Andrei Sakharov unexpectedly rang, as I also mentioned above, an hour before we left for our appointment.

The call was not a hoax, and the very next day we began preparing for our departure from Moscow. The lieutenant told us that we could expect to leave Moscow in no later than six to seven weeks. There was much work to do to be ready for our departure. Simply buying plane tickets to Vienna sometimes

1. The October Revolution occurred when Russia still observed the Julian calendar. When the country switched to the Georgian calendar after 1918, the event began to be commemorated in November.

meant waiting in line at the international ticket office for days and nights. Although it happened that we did not experience that all-too-usual delay, our preparations were typical enough.

First, we had to sell our apartment. We knew it would not be difficult to find a buyer. Many of the inhabitants of our huge apartment building (consisting of seventeen floors with about four hundred apartments) wanted to change apartments. Ours was a comfortable one-bedroom apartment with a balcony and a large living room and entrance hallway. We kept about half of our home library, consisting of about two thousand volumes, in the living room. Bookcases with sliding glass doors ran along an entire wall of the room and went from the floor to the ceiling. The rest of our home library lined the entrance hallway. We also had a small storage room with shelving, where we kept our clothes in a large wardrobe. Thus it was a good apartment, especially for Moscow, where housing conditions were not the best. But the process of selling an apartment usually took up to two months, and we needed money quickly. Fortunately, we obtained the money we needed within a few days.

The people we dealt with knew that we were emigrating to the United States, and they knew that the Soviet agencies considered us to be enemies. There was a watcher at the entrance of our building twenty-four hours a day. Our building manager and staff had seen foreign visitors arrive in embassy cars, signs of relations that were forbidden for the Soviet people. Nevertheless, many Soviet people treated us not as enemies but with kindness during these last weeks in Moscow, just as they had during the twelve years of refusal. Once a strange man went to the apartment of our neighbor, a talented film producer named Vladimir Motyl', who lived on the same floor as we did. (His film *The White Desert Sun* was generally recognized as one of the best of the Soviet era.) Finding only Mrs. Motyl' at home, the stranger told her that the Alperts were making a great deal of noise in the house, that they had crowds of noisy visitors, and that they disturbed the rest of the people in the building. Mrs. Motyl' simply said, "Quite the contrary, we are the ones making noise here, not the Alperts. We often have very noisy guests, especially after the premieres of my husband's movies." The stranger went away with nothing to show for his efforts. Mrs. Motyl' came to us afterward to tell us the story. It seemed that our "watchers" had tried to establish grounds to expel us from the building.

Our Last Days in Moscow, December 1987

Svetlana and I wanted to take the major part of our library with us when we emigrated, but to do that we had to have the permission of a special commission of the Soviet Ministry of Culture, which operated out of the Lenin

Library in Moscow. Svetlana worked day and night to type a full bibliographic inventory of our books, including their number of pages and even their value; in all there were about eleven subentries for each book entry. It was a difficult and time-consuming job. We visited the special commission three or four times. They inspected our list slowly, and finally gave us their decision only after four or five weeks, close to the day of our flight. In the end, our list was cut by four-fifths. The commission allowed us to take only about three hundred books, and we had to pay the commission for them — our own books! — at their current cost, which amounted to about 1,300 rubles. They forbade us to take the sonnets of William Shakespeare and the collected works of the poets Alexander Pushkin, Lord Byron, and others. We were also forbidden to take the collected works of Stendhal, Sholem Aleichem, and many other writers. Moreover, we could not take the volumes of *The Theory of Physics* by Landau and Lifshitz, even though those books had been translated into more than five languages and thus were already available outside the USSR. Some of these volumes were signed by the authors and were very dear to us. This was a strange and foolish decision, but so the commission ruled. We were also forbidden to take many illustrated books of the work of famous painters. We were forced to sell them to bookstores, which bought up most of our books quickly and willingly. At that time such books were rarely available in bookstores. It turned out that we could have taken more books with us, but we learned that only when it was too late. Some of our forbidden books — for example, the rare complete collected works of Pushkin in one compact volume comprising 1,524 pages on extremely thin paper — were brought to the United States by foreigners who visited us.

During the long years that were our refusal time I never discussed with Svetlana what we would do to earn a living in the West. I never asked anyone in the West to look for a position for me. I was not speaking completely in jest when I answered questions about what work I would do with, "Well, I'm a good driver. I have been driving for thirty years! I could drive a taxi." At that time I was seventy-six years old.

We decided to take with us everything we could: our clothes, tableware, kitchen things, bed linens, and so forth. With three hundred books, there was a large quantity of things. We sent most things by ship, but we took a great deal of luggage on the plane with us. Everything had to be inspected by customs officials — a serious process.

We knew that the inspection of the luggage of refusniks at the airport took many hours, even days, and was conducted with much difficulty. In Chapter 11 I mentioned that through Eugene Chudnovsky and his family, Svetlana and I also became friends with another family of refusniks from Kharkov, the

Tarnopolskys. Yuri Tarnopolsky was a chemist and one of the most active and brave refusniks in Kharkov. He was arrested and spent three years in a camp in Siberia. His wife, Olya, often came to Moscow during his stay in the camp and tried to free him. We helped her to contact various officials and journalists and with other activities during her brave, selfless, and difficult struggle. We met Yuri only in Moscow, when he was on his way home from the camp. After his release, he again fought the regime.

We became friends with Olya and later with Yuri and their daughter, Ira. When they finally received exit visas, they spent the last two days and the night before their emigration at our apartment in Moscow, together with their friendly, lovely dog. They got the dog as a puppy, and it really became part of the family. In order to take the dog abroad with them, the Tarnopolskys had to secure a document from a veterinarian attesting to the dog's health. With that in hand, and quantities of luggage, the Tarnopolskys and their dog went to Sheramentyevo Airport for the flight to the West. We went along to see them off. At the customs checkpoint, the officers said, "The dog cannot go." No reason was given.

Yuri came to me and said, "Yakov, they will not let the dog go. So I cannot go either."

I went to the chief customs officer and identified myself as a refusnik scientist from the Academy of Sciences. "If the dog is not allowed to leave," I warned, "I shall immediately organize a press conference with foreign journalists, and they shall report all over the world that Soviet customs officials denied a family the right to take the family dog to their new home." At this the customs officer asked me to leave her office. Fifteen or twenty minutes later she asked me to come to her office and told me that everything was okay. So the Tarnopolskys flew away with their dog. It is an amusing story, to be sure, but it has a serious side, does it not?

We packed our belongings in fourteen suitcases and boxes. The items to be delivered by ship had to be packed in special containers at the customs office by custom officials. Besides, we had many files, scientific notes, and photographs, the strict inspection of which could delay our clearance by many hours, even days.

To facilitate our customs process, a couple of weeks before our departure I called the superintendent of the international airport at Sheramentyevo and asked for an appointment. I did not tell him the purpose of my visit. After a day I went to see him with three suitcases of photographs, scientific slides and files, and some other things. I introduced myself, told him that I was a physicist and a professor, that I had been working at the Academy of Sciences, and that my wife and I had received permission to emigrate. He listened to me attentively and did not interrupt me. He was a fatso in his fifties. I explained to him that I knew how difficult it was to go through customs before a flight, that we would have to spend several days and nights at the airport during the customs inspection. I said that at my age it would be very difficult for me, and I asked him for two things: first, to inspect the things I had brought with me that day; second, to allow me to bring our other suitcases for inspection a couple of days before our flight. He was compassionate and considerate toward me. He spoke with me about our situation and even asked me whether I had any heart problems. He said that he had heart disease and was taking the heart medicine Sustak. It happened that I was also taking Sustak, although in milder form, as a precautionary measure on the advice of my doctor.

The superintendent said that he would order the early inspection of our things. He called a customs officer and told me to bring our suitcases to him. It took a couple of hours to examine the things that I had brought with me that day, and the officials asked me to bring all our suitcases to them in a few days. When we went to the airport that day, the officer asked my name and immediately started the inspection. The customs officers looked through all our suitcases very carefully. They also reinspected the suitcases that I had brought earlier. Svetlana and I realized that if we had included the forbidden books by Landau and Lifshitz, we would have been allowed to take them with us.

I have already said that our standard of living in the USSR was satisfactory. We had enough to meet our needs. Even during the time of refusal we had enough money for subsistence and to take a vacation, and I have lived within my means since I first began earning my living, when I was eighteen years old. Svetlana is also the same kind of person. Yet in just four to five weeks before our departure we became "wealthy." We sold our apartment, many books, and some of our furniture, and in all we collected 22,000 rubles, about $36,000 at that time. We had never had so much money in our savings account before. We were allowed to take only $299 with us to the West, however, and those dollars cost us only 180 rubles at the bank.

Where did the rest of the money go? A good deal was spent simply in preparing to emigrate. It was a difficult job to ready all our things for departure. A young refusnik helped us to pack all our suitcases for the airplane and all our things for shipment by sea. He worked with us for several days, and we paid him well and gave him some of our Finnish furniture. He also helped us to deliver all our packages to the customs office and to the airport. We often took taxis to visit embassies, consulates, and our friends and relatives and to shop. On some days we hired a taxi for the whole day, and it sometimes had to wait for us for hours. It was not easy to find a taxi when you needed one. Yet we had enough money to pay for one. We also spent our rubles by buying a lot of nice souvenirs and gifts for our friends in the West and for people in England, France, and the United States who had visited us in Moscow. We bought new clothes for Svetlana and me. We paid six thousand rubles for a fur coat for Svetlana. Never could we have bought such an expensive fur coat before. About one-half of the money we gave to Svetlana's mother and to a few good friends.

Our last hurdle before departure was the customs inspection of the things that would be shipped to the United States by sea. It was a curious event. Our appointment with the Moscow customs office was at 4 or 5 P.M. two days before our flight to Vienna. Svetlana and I took the cargo of our belongings to be inspected. When we unloaded our things in the customs hall, an officer told us that only I could remain during the inspection and repacking. For all those long hours Svetlana had to wait in the lobby. Two customs officials began their task by warning me that I must stay seated at a distance and threatening to stop the inspection if I touched anything, even with a finger. They showed me a chair where I was supposed to sit. Long hours of inspection ensued, as the officers checked boxes with china, plates, cups, and other household effects. They inspected every book, and when they realized that the major part of our luggage comprised books, they asked me about the subject of the books. I told them that I was a physicist and explained about the subject of my research. And I answered their questions about some novels and about sociological books.

The customs officials saw that our luggage did not contain expensive things. And they were astonished to see our collection of toys and our model sailboat packed in a large custom-made wooden box. (On the recommendation of a friend, that box was designed and constructed for us by a carpenter from Vakhtangov's Theater.) The problem was that they had to check the inside of the heavy keel of the model ship with X rays. They took it into another room where they had a special X-ray system. They did not find gold or diamonds, only pieces of lead. That model ship was the symbol of our apartment. We bought it in a toy store and assembled it ourselves. We still have that ship in our apartment in Boston. The customs officials were also astonished to see a collection of colorful sticks that I made myself from driftwood I found while walking along the Baltic shore during our vacations.

Thus, piece by piece, they found us to be unusual people. After a couple of hours they asked me why I was leaving the USSR and where we were going. It was an unusual situation. Our exchanges had given them the sense that they could be open with me and that I would not betray them. I told them about the refusniks and about Andrei Sakharov. Soon I was working with them, helping them to repack our books and other things! If I could have foreseen that happening — something I could not have imagined — I would have included in those boxes many books that we had been forbidden to take. The whole business of inspection and repacking was completed at about 1 or 2 A.M. Our two containers weighed about a ton.

That story and other similar events and situations that I have related show that the Soviet people themselves did not condemn us. They did not consider us to be traitors of the homeland because we were leaving the country. Perhaps some of them even envied us. And when they realized that they could trust us, they even helped us and treated us with respect and a sympathetic attitude.

15

Farewell Meetings

Thus, the days of farewells came. They were the days of parting from our homeland, from the people who had shared sorrows and joys with us over that land, and from our good friends. In 1987, the power of the Soviet state still seemed to be stable. We were not sure whether we would ever be able to see our loved ones again or even to correspond with them. It was time to tell them good-bye. Since my childhood the term *good friend* has been all-encompassing for me. From the age of ten I had such friends, with whom I shared my thoughts, enthusiasms, and dreams. For any of us it is hardly possible to meet many such people during our lives. At this point it is my heartfelt obligation to recall a few of those good friends.

In writing earlier about my childhood I talked about Tolya (Anatoly) Grinberg, one of my most intimate friends. He passed away about sixteen years ago. He was a physicist and worked in Leningrad (St. Petersburg) at Ioffe's Physical Technical Institute for about forty to forty-five years. During those years we met only a few times. Initially, I received long letters from him, of ten or more pages, some of which I have kept. For all those years we maintained a mutual understanding and feelings, but we were seldom together and lived far from each other. Slowly, gently, we parted from each other.

The Indissoluble Four

At the beginning of this book I spoke about the friendship that blazed up in the late 1930s and endured for many decades between four physicists: Syoma (Semyon) Belenky, Borya (Boris) Geilikman, Vitya (Vitaly) Ginzburg, and Yasha (me). Unfortunately, those unforgettable years of friendship ended, just as everything in the world must end. When the truly wise and talented physicist Syoma Belenky died in 1956, it was too soon. He was only forty years old. Borya Geilikman, the most educated and gentle of us, was also a talented physicist. He passed away in 1973 at sixty-three years of age. Vitya is eighty-three years old now, and I am eighty-eight. Such is the fate of human beings.

I separated from Borya many years before his death. Generally we never quarreled, and we broke our relations without any fuss in the middle of the 1960s. It was stupid on both sides. Still, I think that if I had tried at the time to clarify our misunderstandings, it would not have changed anything. The break in our friendship was a perhaps inevitable loss of that time. What happened was that shortly before my break with Borya I ended my association with Vitaly Ginzburg. The reason was his ugly action against another physicist and the extent to which Vitya's behavior seemed dominated by self-interest at the expense of a sense of duty to other people. I did not quarrel with him; I stopped speaking to him and greeting him when we met unexpectedly. To various people at the academy he said, "Yakov does not even want to say hello to me." Nikolai Pushkov told me of hearing this from Ginzburg.

Borya Geilikman and Vitya Ginzburg became good friends during their student days at Moscow State University, before I met them, and Borya felt that I was too hard on Vitya. Still, I am sure that that was not the only reason for my split with Borya, and I think that perhaps Borya's view of me was poisoned by misinformation. In 1997 I spoke with his widow, Natasha, by telephone while she was visiting their son Misha in Canada, and I said, "I still have some questions for Borya. They often disturb me even today, but I can hardly expect that you can answer them. They will remain unanswered."

So, when Svetlana and I left the USSR, only two of "the indissoluble four" remained alive, and those two had been separated for about twenty-five years. One of Vitaly's closest friends told me that Vitya would never come to see me. In December 1987, however, before our departure, I called him, and he did come to see me soon after my call. We spent a pleasant evening together at our home. I gave him a nice book of Pablo Picasso's drawings, and I inscribed it, "In memory of our unforgettable, brilliant friendship. Perhaps those years were the best ones of our lives. In any case, I often think so." Nina, his wife, came to see us several days later. Svetlana gave her many pieces of amber that we had collected on the Baltic seashore. Recently I met Vitaly twice: once in Los Angeles and once outside Washington, D.C. For a time we still corresponded. He regularly sent me copies of his writings, and he was frank in his letters. Although we have remained on civil terms with each other, unfortunately many of Vitaly's current social actions are generally objectionable to me. He is like other scientists who cannot realize or acknowledge (even to themselves) what they were like in the past during that crucial time, nor what they are like today in the post-Soviet time. To do that demands fortitude, self-criticism, and a desire for the pure truth.

Vitaly has received great recognition and fame in his scientific career. I think more than he needed or deserved. Truthfulness and self-criticism on his part would be a great civic act for his compatriots, especially of the young generation, in this difficult transition time for Russia. Unfortunately, Vitaly's writings and published comments continue often to distort the true state of affairs. I am distressed to say that his repeated misrepresentations, particularly his unconscionable statements about Andrei Sakharov, most recently in a June 1997 interview in the Russian journal *Vestnik,* have separated us again.[1]

I also telephoned Natasha, Borya's widow, before our departure from Russia. Svetlana and I spent a pleasant evening over a good dinner at her home with Misha and her. We gave her a book by the Russian poet Maximilian Voloshin, and I wrote in it, "After many years of our unwarranted separation. In memory of our unforgettable friendship." Svetlana and I brought many photographs of our refusal time to show them and told Natasha and Misha many stories of our life during those years. Misha asked, "How did it happen that we were separated for so many years from Yasha?" Unfortunately, what happened was right. That belief is confirmed by many events in the far past and after. Those two meetings with Vitya and Natasha in a sense consummated the friendship of the Four. It is sad to say this because the friendship was a very important part of all our lives, at least for me.

For about twenty-five years, until our departure from the USSR, Lev Gor'kov and his wife Lyalya were our good friends. Lev and Lyalya stood by us during all the long years of our refusal time, which was by no means an ordinary occurrence. That was their choice. Many people, including relatives, were afraid to meet and even to speak to refusniks, who were outcasts. When we left the Soviet Union I gave Lev six volumes of the writings of the Jewish author Sholom Aleichem in the hope that our friendship would "remain to the end." Unfortu-

1. Vladimir Nuzov, "Interview with Vitaly Ginzburg," *Vestnik* 9.2, no. 14 (June 1997): 4.

nately, since the collapse of the Soviet Union these old friends of ours have chosen to remember and present their behavior as grander than it was. Their doing so separated us, but they do not acknowledge any responsibility for that.

Other Partings

I became friendly with Eugene Lifshitz at the beginning of the 1960s. We were drawn closer together in January 1962, when Lev Landau was suffering from multiple head and other injuries after an automobile accident. Eugene was Landau's co-author on the ten-volume *Theory of Physics* and for many years his closest friend.

Lev Landau made pioneering contributions in many crucial fields of physics. But in ranking twentieth-century physicists he said that Einstein and Niels Bohr belonged with Newton, and that Richard Feynman, for example, belonged in the first range after that. He put himself lower. I was told that Richard Feynman once heard this and said, "No, not me, Landau should be in the first range." It is also important to remember about Landau that he was imprisoned by Stalin in 1938 and was only saved by the personal intervention of Peter Kapitsa. Kapitsa told Molotov that of course Landau was a complicated and unpredictable person, but that he would be responsible for him.

In the first six to seven weeks after the accident, Landau was on an artificial respirator and he was actually declared clinically dead several times. Landau wound up spending almost two and a half years in the hospital, and it is sad to say that he survived but never fully recovered. Immediately after the accident Lifshitz organized a network of a dozen physicists, including me, to arrange Landau's care and take whatever action might be needed on his behalf. We each contributed five hundred rubles to a fund for special nurses and medicines, and one of us was always on call in case of an emergency. A special bed was even designed and built for Landau in Peter Kapitsa's institute.

It would take a lengthy chapter to touch on all the aspects of this episode. What may be interesting here is the leeway that the Soviet authorities gave the physicists who were trying to help Landau. For example, Lifshitz was allowed to procure medicines in England with the cooperation of Robert Maxwell, the publisher of the English translation of the Landau-Lifshitz volumes. And when the great Canadian neurosurgeon Wilder Penfield came to Moscow for an emergency consultation, Foreign Minister Andrei Gromyko took the extraordinary step of allowing Penfield to enter the country without a visa. After Penfield examined Landau, he said that all that could be done was being done and that "Landau was saved by the Soviet physicians and the Soviet physicists."

Another remarkable part of this story is that Landau won the Nobel Prize in physics that same year for his development of the theory of superfluidity, especially liquid helium. On 10 December 1962 the Swedish ambassador brought the medal to Landau in his hospital room, the first time that the prize had ever been brought to a recipient.

Over the next twenty to twenty-five years Eugene and I were good friends. Often we openly discussed social and personal problems. Once Eugene said to me, "I have never been so frank in talking about the circumstances of my personal life as I have been with you, Yasha." Eugene was an extraordinary person. He died in 1985, during heart surgery, when he was seventy years old, two years before my departure from the USSR. My refusnik status clouded somewhat the last two to three years of our exceptionally good friendship. Svetlana and I often remember him during these years in the United States, and we say to each other, "It is very sad that Zhenya [Eugene] did not live to see this crucial time." Indeed, I miss him and often wonder what he would say about the behavior of our people, especially of our colleagues and fellow physicists, during these times.

On the evening of 19 November, we sat in the kitchen of Elena Georgievna Bonner and Andrei Dmitrievich Sakharov and had our last meeting with them in Moscow. We visited them to say good-bye a little more than a month before our departure. We knew that we would be running around like squirrels in a cage that month. We left Moscow on 24 December 1987, exactly one year after our first meeting with Andrei and Elena after Andrei's release from Gorky in 1986.

One evening we were at the home of our good friends Katya (Kate) and Anatoly Pokrovsky. We had met them in Tsakhkadzor, in the mountains of Armenia, during our winter vacation in 1974. There was a camp and hotel there for the Soviet Olympic team. We became close friends. During the time of refusal, when many people were afraid to be in touch with us, nothing changed in our relationship. Anatoly is widely recognized as one of the best surgeons in Russia and in the world. He has performed many operations in Western countries, and a special article about them was published in the U.S. journal *America* (which is published in Russian). It was he who recommended that Svetlana have heart surgery in October 1980. He chose the surgeon, Vladimir Podzolkov, who did an excellent job. The Pokrovskys gave us moral support and much help during those days, and we shall never forget them. In the summer of 1991 they came to the United States and visited us in Boston. They were in Boston again in the summer of 1997.

The physicist Lev Pitaevsky and his wife Lyuba have been our close friends for about thirty-five years. Lev and I began our research collaboration at the beginning of the 1960s. We published a book and some papers on space plasma physics together, as I mentioned in Chapter 10. As circumstances demanded we came to each other's aid many times. Svetlana and I were moved when Lev and Lyuba came to us for our last meeting in December 1987 with a dinner Lyuba had cooked for us. They knew that we were overextended and exhausted. I gave him a book by the Russian writer Andrei Platonov, which I inscribed. We saw them again when we traveled to Italy in 1993. They came to Varena, where we were staying, for two days. At that time Lev was a visiting professor at the University of Trento. Lev also visited us in Boston in 1995, when he was a visiting professor at the University of Chicago. To this day we correspond.

We spent one morning before our departure with Svetlana's mother, Mariya Evdokimovna. At that time she was eighty-six. It was not easy to say good-bye to her. We often telephoned her after that and were glad to know that she remained in good shape mentally and kept her sense of humor almost to the end. She died very recently at the age of ninety-six. We had a somewhat difficult farewell meeting with one of Svetlana's two sisters, Lida Zotikova. She rejected us during all the time of our refusal. Her husband was a Soviet diplomat, and they spent many years in Austria and Finland. Lida was a ballerina at the Bolshoi Theater and visited many foreign countries with the dance troupe. But I am glad to say that in recent times we have become reconciled; Lida has even told me that she is ashamed of how she acted. I was glad to hear this; I hoped to hear the same from many other people. Svetlana's other sister, Zoya, was a medical assistant, and for all of my and Svetlana's years together in the Soviet Union, Zoya and her husband Nikolai, who died in 1981, were a part of our lives. They did not reject us after our request for visas to leave our common homeland.

One evening my brother, Israel, and his wife, Rosa, came to see us. Israel recently died at eighty-three. He was a modest and very goodhearted man who worked as a radio engineer. He was thirteen when I left my parents' house, and for all the intervening years our paths diverged. He retired at about seventy, and he then took up painting for the first time. About two months before his death, he sent me two oil paintings. One shows a green grove near my department's laboratory building at IZMIRAN and close to where Israel lived. The other depicts a beautiful sunset on a tree-lined lake. The paintings are very impressive. For me they are wonderful examples of my brother's character and of human beings' inexhaustible creativity.

I spent memorable hours with my former wife, Irina Chernysheva, a few days before our departure. For thirty-five years, from 1934 until 1969, we were each other's closest friend and for most of that time husband and wife.

Irina and I had a good, interesting, and productive life together. On our leaving the USSR, I made her a gift of a color television. (The television was made in Czechoslovakia; it was difficult to buy such a television in Moscow.) Irina often writes to me, and I regularly telephone her; we have remained good friends to this day. She is now retired and is also eighty-eight years old. She has more time to read novels in Russian, German, and English, and she still advises students on their Ph.D. and doctor of science theses.

We had a remarkable farewell meeting with our family physician, Svetlana Solovyova, who took care of us for many years. She was a young, pretty lady. It was she who, soon after our first meeting, warned us that Svetlana had serious heart disease and arranged an appointment for Svetlana with one of the most prestigious cardiologists in Moscow, Professor Kassirsky. At the end of the medical examination, Kassirsky told Svetlana, "I am astonished that you have survived till now with such a heart!" We are ever grateful to Solovyova for her help. As a remembrance of us we gave her an extraordinary art book of Russian icons, inscribing it, "We will always, always, remember you."

Before closing this brief account of our parting from people who played a great role in my life, I must mention a cast of players — actors, scriptwriters, directors, and producers — whom I met beginning around the time of the first Sputnik. A mutual friend introduced me to the actor Vladlen Davydov in 1957. Davydov and I became friends, and through him I met many other People's Artists of the USSR, as the Soviet government honored them.

My lifelong interest in art and literature gave me a common ground with these men and women. But what was more important to me, despite any superficial differences between art and science, was their fanatic devotion to their creative work. Over the years I had hundreds of meetings with friends in the Soviet theater and movie community. We spent time together in our respective homes, in theaters and studios, at premieres and private screenings, and on long walks in the countryside. After I applied to emigrate, we saw much less of each other. I did not want them to have to decide whether or not to be in touch with a refusnik. The situation of People's Artists depended even more on the caprices of the Soviet regime than that of scientists did. My friends' plays and movies were stopped often enough on their own account; they did not need the extra trouble with the authorities that contact with me might bring.

I had many social and political discussions with the film directors Alexander Alov and Tatiana Lioznova, who created dozens of absorbing films. Alov died some years ago. With co-director Vladimir Naumov, he made *Beg* (Running), based on Mikhail Bulgakov's novel about the defeat of the White Guard Army during the revolution, and *Skvernyi Anekdot* (Nasty Anecdote), based on a Fyodor Dostoyevsky satire on the tsarist era. The Soviet authorities perceived this movie as a satire on the Soviet regime, however, and accordingly it was banned for many years after its initial screenings. I saw the movie at a preview at the Mosfilm studio in Moscow.

Tatiana Lioznova's lyric melodrama *Tree Topolya na Plyuschike* (Three Poplars of Pluschich Street), is a very romantic story. It won first prize at an international film festival in Argentina. When Tatiana's thirteen-part television serial *17 Mgnoveniy Vesny* (17 Moments of Spring) was being broadcast, the newspapers reported that the streets of some cities were empty during those evenings. The serial concerned a fictional Soviet spy named Stirlitz, who infiltrates Hitler's inner circle without being caught. It was based on a novel by Julian Semyonov. Tatiana has often reminded me of Edith Piaf. She is now seventy-five years old. After about twenty-five years in which we had not spoken to each other, we recently had a conversation on the telephone, and it was as if we had spoken together every day of those years.

My acquaintance with Ruphina Nifontova, an actress at the famous Malyi Theater, continued for about twenty years. She played many leading classical roles and appeared in twenty-nine movies. One of her most famous performances was in the film *Kozhdenie po Mukam* (The Road of Calvary), based on Alexei Tolstoy's trilogy about the experiences of the Russian intelligentsia during the revolution. Ruphina Nifontova was an extravagant and clever woman, who always followed her own inclinations. She died very tragically some years ago; she had a heart attack while she was taking a bath.

Vladlen Davydov became a popular actor in 1949, when he was twenty-five years old, because of the film *Vstrecha na Elbe* (Meeting at the River Elbe). The Elbe River in Germany was where the advancing Soviet and American armies linked up at the end of World War II. He appeared in more than ten films, and his many stage roles included performances in productions of Chekhov's great plays. Our friendship with him and his wife, the actress Margosha Anastasieva, both of whom were members of the renowned Moscow Art Theater, continued for about thirty years. We last met them at our home in Moscow on my seventy-sixth birthday, on 1 March 1987.

I hope that many of my other friends will forgive me for not mentioning them here. This book leaves out many important aspects of my life, and many important friendships. I wish the best to all my friends and good acquaintances at this hazy beginning of the twenty-first century.

On Opposite Banks of the River

Throughout this book I have spoken about how the Soviet system poisoned the behavior of the Soviet people. Because of my own experiences as a scientist, I have concentrated on the ways in which many ex-Soviet scientists distort the history of the Soviet era and their own actions during that time.

Andrei Sakharov trenchantly noted that the Soviet reality challenged every scientist to "muster sufficient courage and integrity to resist the temptation and habit of conformity" to a repressive regime. In his own life Sakharov gave a shining example of how to meet the challenge of being both a good scientist and a good citizen. That challenge has an important dimension in the present, even after the collapse of the USSR. It applies, in fact, not just to scientists, but to all who were once citizens of the Soviet Union.

In Chapter 5 I described seeing Bulgakov's *The Days of the Turbins* as it was staged by the Moscow Art Theater in the 1930s. That great work dramatized how during the Revolution in Russia close relations, friends, and colleagues came to find themselves on different sides of the barricades or, as the saying goes, on opposite banks of the river. In the course of this book I have related a number of instances in which the community of Soviet physicists, and that of Soviet citizens generally, found themselves divided on opposite banks of the river, whether the cause of that division was Stalin's terror, the campaign against cosmopolites, or the treatment of dissidents and refusniks.

Today, we are experiencing a new and still-widening divide in connection with the crises of the past. Many people cannot bring themselves to be honest about their behavior in those times, whether their conduct was a matter of active collaboration with the KGB and other organs of a repressive state or passive acceptance of things as they were. In my opinion, no moral law required Soviet citizens to become dissidents or refusniks, let us say. Those who chose not to buck the system or decided to join the Communist Party to get ahead had the right to make that choice. What is poisoning our relations now is the widespread refusal to own up to the past for what it was. For careerists now to claim that they joined the Communist Party to help others, for example, is a travesty. It is only by owning up to the past that we can hope for the reconciliation that post-Soviet society desperately needs. And such reconciliation is possible.

Yuri Orlov told me that when he began his dissident activity he spoke about it to Arkady (Khadiya) Migdal, a distinguished Soviet physicist. Khadiya Migdal warned him, "You know, if you do that, your scientific work will be blocked. You will never have permission to go abroad." Migdal did not want to be an activist; he only wanted to do the science he loved, and so he made the choice not to buck the system.

Thirty years later, Orlov telephoned Migdal in America. Migdal was ailing, and in fact he did not have many months left to live. He was then on a visit to his son Sasha — Alexander — who was living in America. On the telephone Migdal asked Orlov, "Do you remember what we spoke about thirty years ago?"

"Certainly, I remember," Orlov said.

"You were right," Migdal told him.

In saying this Migdal did not extenuate or misrepresent the choice that he himself had made. He acknowledged the choice for what it was. The mutual honesty and respect of Migdal and Orlov enabled them to reach across the river.

I can add my own story about Khadiya Migdal. When Svetlana and I were getting ready to leave Russia, he called and said that he would like to come see us before our departure. He did that openly. Many others continued to shun us. We sat in the kitchen drinking cognac and I said, "Khadiya, you have the right to do what you are doing. Your honesty needs no apology. I don't know any step of yours that hurt others." As I mentioned above, we experienced a similar reconciliation with Svetlana's sister Lida.

What the post-Soviet time needs is neither apology nor recrimination. And we cannot all be friends, we cannot agree about everything. But we do need honesty, to acknowledge what has been done. Otherwise our common history will continue to lock us into conflict with each other. With this in mind I want to turn in the next chapter to a group of Soviet citizens, distinguished physicists, who in crucial events did not compromise their consciences.

16

Tribute to the Scientific School
of L. I. Mandelshtam

We left our homeland, its people, and the places where we were taught at the end of 1987. The legacy of the scientific school that I became part of and of some of the people with whom I collaborated was within me, however. It was a great privilege for me to live and work for dozens of years within that scientific and humanist community, especially for sixteen years at PhIAN. It was in harmony with my needs and my nature. I would like briefly to pay tribute to that unique scientific school and its guru, the great physicist Leonid Isaakovich Mandelshtam, one of the most distinguished scientists of Russia.

Mandelshtam was born in Odessa in 1879; he died in Moscow in 1944. His scientific works and lectures — *Theory of Oscillations, Basis of Quantum Mechanics, Selected Problems of Optics, Basis of Relativity Theory* — are on my bookshelves. Next to them are a large photo of Mandelshtam, the volume of memoirs dedicated to him on the centenary of his birthday, and the collected papers of Nikolai Papalexi, Mandelshtam's collaborator and closest friend of many dozens of years. The world scientific community lost a lot by the works of Mandelshtam not being translated into English and other foreign languages — especially his *Theory of Oscillations,* which fills up about two volumes of his collected works. I wrote above about those lectures.[1]

1. L. I. Mandelshtam, *Complete Works* (Moscow: Publishing House of the Academy of Sciences of the USSR, 1948–1955); S. M. Rytov and M. A. Leontovich, eds., *Academician L. I. Mandelshtam: The Centenary of His Birth* (Moscow: Nauka, 1979); N. D.

Mandelshtam began his research at the University of Strasbourg (Germany) with the famous physicist Karl Ferdinand Brown, who was the recipient of the 1909 Nobel Prize in physics together with Guglielmo Marconi for developing wireless telegraphy. Mandelshtam came to Strasbourg in 1899 to continue his education when he was expelled from the University of Novorossiysk because of his participation in student disturbances.

Mandelshtam's collected works show that he was equally familiar with all the branches of physics. For the reader who is a physicist or knows even a little about the history of physics, it will be interesting to know the following. Mandelshtam discovered theoretically, and with Papalexi confirmed experimentally, the inertia of electrons in metals in 1912 — four years before the classical experiments by Tolmen and Stewart in 1916! His wide-ranging ideas famously brought him into conflict with leading experts in several fields: arguing for the existence of radio side bands against Sir John Ambrose Fleming; debating Lummer on the nature of the optical image; and taking issue with two winners of the Nobel Prize in physics, Lord Rayleigh (John William Strutt) in 1908 and Max Planck in 1918, showing that light will be scattered even in a homogeneous medium because of the inevitable density fluctuations in the medium. Although not a mathematician by training, Mandelshtam found an error in the classical mathematical theory of the physicist Arnold Sommerfeld on propagation of radio waves along the surface of the earth. He showed very clearly in his lectures on quantum mechanics the faulty position Albert Einstein took in his famous polemic with Niels Bohr about the basics of quantum mechanics. Mandelshtam said, "Now the erroneous point of A. Einstein seems to be so trivial that it is even difficult to expound that this initial point of view was Einstein's indeed." Niels Bohr published some papers about that dispute. But when Mandelshtam's disciples asked him to publish his understanding of those discussions, he said, "Einstein is so great that he himself understands the matter."

In Chapter 7 I related how Mandelshtam and Grigoriy Landsberg lost a share of the Nobel Prize in physics in 1930, awarded to Chandrasekhara Raman for demonstrating the combinational scattering of light, because of Soviet censorship of scientific publication. Mandelshtam discovered that phenomenon theoretically in 1928. His deep insight into the unity of physical phenomena brought him to that understanding and is encapsulated in his maxim "Optics, Mechanics, Acoustics are speaking in their national languages. Their international language is the language of the theory of oscillations." Mandelshtam developed the quantum theory of the combinational

---

Papalexi, *Complete Works,* vol. 1 (Moscow: Publishing House of the Academy of Sciences of the U.S.S.R., 1948).

scattering of light with simple classical models of the oscillations of atoms and ions of different molecules and crystals, showing that the periodical variations of the distances between atoms are the cause of polarization of the electron envelopes. That creates the modulation of the scattered light by the atoms. The discovery of the combinational scattering of light, as Papalexi said, is equal to the great discovery of the basis of spectral analysis by Robert Wilhelm Bunsen and Gustav Robert Kirchof.

The brief sketch given here shows the diversity of the scientific thinking, activity, and teaching of Mandelshtam. "He was a romantic by his striving to share his conjectures, by his love of teaching, by the power of his word," said Alexander Alexandrovich Andronov, one of the most talented of his disciples.[2] I remember how flexibly Mandelshtam entered into and understood any problems discussed with him. At present, having just completed a long study of the electromagnetic oscillating nature of the background of the magnetospheric plasma, I often think about Mandelshtam. Were I to tell him the results of that study, he would like my new approach, which is to consider the magnetosphere as a resonance system. Resonances are one of the most typical characteristics of the international language of oscillations. Mandelshtam could strengthen my confidence in those conclusions or point out their weak peculiarities.

What also stimulated me to write this tribute was the rare harmony of Mandelshtam as a human being. He was a theoretician and an experimenter, a physicist par excellence, and a good mathematician. At the same time he was a man of exceptional high principles and nobility. He was full of indignation against people who put their own interests above everything. Mandelshtam combined goodness and sensitivity with rigor on matters of principle and intolerance of moral compromise. The distinguished Russian mathematician and naval engineer Alexey Krylov said about Mandelshtam, "He was a righteous man." Mandelshtam's scientific and human qualities attracted to him talented and noble people, both students and accomplished physicists. Among them were Grigoriy Landsberg, Igor Tamm, Alexander Andronov, and Mikhail Leontovich.

An expert in optics, Grigoriy Landsberg became a professor at the Moscow State University in 1923. It was mainly owing to his efforts that Leonid Isaakovich Mandelshtam was invited to join the faculty in 1925. Twenty years later Landsberg wrote, "I was not a young boy (35 years old) when I met for

2. The quotations from Mandelshtam's colleagues are taken from the volumes published in his and Papalexi's honor, *Bulletin de L'Académie des Sciences de L'U.R.S.S., Série Physique* 9, nos. 1 and 2 (1945), 12, no. 1 (1948).

the first time L.I. Now I am already an elderly man. . . . And yet it is not a shame for me to say . . . During two decades of my friendship with L.I. . . . I always ask myself what would be L.I.'s reaction to any of my or other's actions . . . I have never doubted the moral judgment of L.I. . . . , and for all my last years the recollections of L.I. will be the source of my moral power."

The theoretical physicist and Nobel laureate Igor Tamm met Mandelshtam when Tamm was twenty-five years old, teaching physics at the Polytechnic Institute in Odessa. Mandelshtam was the chair of the faculty. From their first acquaintance, Mandelshtam exerted a wide influence on the scientific evolution of Tamm, who did his first theoretical studies in classical electrodynamics under Mandelshtam's guidance.

It is also appropriate to emphasize that the extremely distinguished radio physicist Nikolai Papalexi, a man of high devotion to his duties and high morality, worked together with Mandelshtam and in his sphere for about forty years. They met in Strasbourg, where they began their common research under Brown's guidance. From that time on, their deep friendship and scientific collaboration, let us say their fates, were linked. They went together from Strasbourg to St. Petersburg in 1914, and they continued to collaborate until Mandelshtam died in 1944, predeceasing Papalexi by only three years. Their fates were even connected after their deaths, as we will see.

It was remarkable that most of the scientists who gathered around Mandelshtam and formed his scientific school were not only notable physicists but also people of great honesty with a high sense of civic responsibility. I shall illustrate that here by a few distinctive events when the moral temper of some of those people was tested and made manifest.

In 1936, in the midst of Stalin's terror, when hundreds of thousands of people, among them thousands of scientists and engineers, were arrested and lost in the Gulag, one of the victims was the physicist and historian Boris Gessen, a professor of Moscow State University, a corresponding member of the Academy of Sciences, and the vice-director of PhIAN. Gessen was arrested in August and shot in December of that year. One of Igor Tamm's most talented pupils, the physicist Semyon Shubin (see Chapter 9), and his brother, the chemical engineer Leonid Tamm, were also arrested that year. They, too, died shortly thereafter in prison. In 1956 Leonid Tamm and Boris Gessen were rehabilitated, according to the Soviet fashion. But twenty years before that the Soviet authorities, and specifically the KGB, falsely condemned them as political enemies of the Soviet land, as traitors and saboteurs. And the Soviet regime demanded that PhIAN endorse this barbarism by publicly repudiating Leonid Tamm and Boris Gessen.

For that purpose, in April 1937 a general meeting took place at PhIAN to discuss Gessen's case.[3] Many people at that meeting voiced the official line, condemning Gessen and harshly criticizing the decision to name him vice-director of the institute. Saying nothing against Gessen, Sergei Vavilov, the director of PhIAN, quietly took the blame for this decision and allowed that perhaps it was a mistaken one. At this Grigoriy Landsberg spoke up and said that the blame for nominating Gessen as vice-director lay with him, and that he in no way regretted this because Gessen deserved the post. He further said he did not believe in Gessen's guilt, that he had no evidence of such guilt, that anyone who said he possessed such knowledge was lying, and that he would not himself add to that lie. "To try to pass over in silence any accusations against me constitutes a lie," he said. Repudiating his opponents' tactics of character assassination, he declared, "It is impossible to prove that you don't know anything" (27–29).

For his part, Igor Tamm, who was a close friend of Gessen for many years, stoutly insisted, "I vouch for my brother. I trust my brother. I trust Gessen." The honesty and bravery of Landsberg and Tamm were very perilous. The Soviet regime considered such statements to be themselves tantamount to treason and might well have acted on that basis. It also has to be appreciated what a critical time this was for the whole institute. As director, Sergei Vavilov had to strive to defuse the incident and protect the institute from being totally hijacked by political decisionmaking. By their actions these three men saved the institute and their own self-respect from a dangerously destructive attack.

Beginning in the late 1940s, Soviet attacks on "cosmopolitanism," as I discussed in Chapter 1, were mainly screens for the regime's anti-Semitism. Jewish scientists were the biggest targets. In 1948 the Minister of Higher Education organized a special committee for a forthcoming all-union (that is, all-USSR) conference of physicists to discuss how "Soviet patriotism" could defeat idealism, cosmopolitanism, and "non-Party science." *Idealism* referred to the quantum mechanics of Schrödinger and the gravity theory of Einstein, which were criticized as not being matter-based theories and therefore as not being grounded in dialectical materialism, that is, in Marxism-Leninism. Therefore, those theories of physics had to be wrong, and anyone who espoused them had to be against the Soviet system. But most physicists, including those labeled as cosmopolites, doubted the applicability of dialectical materialism to theories in physics.

The reader can clearly see the absurdity of the regime's demands and state-

---

3. The quotations used in connection with this episode are from A. S. Sosin, *Physical Idealism* (Moscow: Publishing House of Physical-Mathematical Literature, 1994). Page references appear in the text.

ments. But this was again a dangerous situation for physics research in the Academy of Sciences. The physicists of Moscow State University zealously voiced the party line and attacked the physicists of the academy as idealists and cosmopolites. Had the all-union conference taken place as scheduled, physics research in the Soviet Union might have suffered devastating damage. Trofim Lysenko used an all-union conference of biologists to gain a stranglehold on biological research and to attack scientists who disagreed with his harebrained ideas. Remember that Sergei Vavilov's brother Nikolai was one of Lysenko's victims. Biological research in the USSR was derailed for a dozen years or more. Even without an all-union conference, the "war" of physicists brought dreadful results. Let me tell about some of them connected with Mandelshtam, who was Jewish.

In 1949, in one such session of that special committee, physicists from Moscow State University accused Mandelshtam and Papalexi of being German spies. The distinguished physicist Alexander Andronov said at that session, "There can be nothing but disgust toward that speech. It was a dirty, trouble-making speech. The accusation of Papalexi and Mandelshtam of being German spies . . . is an unsubstantiated, slanderous accusation" (135). During another session of the committee concerning cosmopolitanism, Landsberg spoke only about the necessity of good education in physics and about the significance of physics in general. Andronov also spoke only about the lack of good teaching in physics and about the importance of good teachers, saying, "My teacher, the Russian physicist Mandelshtam, was a brilliant lecturer and teacher . . . [and] a great scientist." He continued, "I did not make a slip when I said that Mandelshtam—he was a Jew—is a Russian physicist. It seems that we have to consider it as the following. Composer Anton Rubinstein—a Jew—is a Russian musician. Painter Levitan—a Jew—is a Russian artist, and Mandelshtam is a Russian physicist. If any Jew tells me that Mandelshtam is a Jewish physicist, I shall reply to him that he, himself, is a Jewish nationalist. If any Russian tells me that Mandelshtam is a Jewish physicist, I shall tell that Russian, that he is a Russian nationalist and chauvinist" (149). It was a clever and ironic speech against the origin of cosmopolitanism.

Fortunately, the all-union conference did not take place. How it was canceled is not known. Perhaps someone convinced Stalin that the meeting could be fatal for the atom bomb project. It was said that Stalin's chief overseer on the atom bomb project, the KGB leader Lavrentiy Beriya, once asked the manager of that project, the academician Igor Kurchatov, "Is it true that relativity theory and quantum mechanics are idealism and they should be rejected?" Kurchatov's reply was, "If we produce the atom bomb, its action will be based on both relativity theory and quantum mechanics. If we reject them, we could reject the bomb" (161). Perhaps Beriya told that to Stalin, who then canceled the all-union conference. In any case the horrible event did not take place. But the campaign against cosmopolitanism continued.

That campaign included more attacks on the idealism of Mandelshtam, in particular, against volume 5 of his *Collected Works,* which contained his lectures on quantum mechanics and relativity theory. After a terrible scandal, that volume appeared in 1950 only because Sergei Vavilov rescued it. But on 28 January 1952, roughly a year after Vavilov's early death, a session of physicists titled "On the subjective idealism of Mandelshtam" was convened. And in 1953 a paper, "The philosophical mistakes of Mandelshtam," appeared in the journal *Uspekhi Phizicheskikh Nauk.* Furthermore, *The Course of Physics,* edited by Papalexi, *Mechanics,* by Semyon Khaikin, and some papers of other disciples of Mandelshtam were criticized as based on Mandelshtam's mistakes.

The board of directors of PhIAN and some of its senior members condemned the mistakes of Mandelshtam and organized a commission to examine the methodological problems of his works. Igor Tamm gave a very hard speech against the philosophical accusation against Mandelshtam. He and Grigoriy Landsberg said that the charges against Mandelshtam were in contradiction with many parts of his book. In 1953, however, the commission duly condemned Mandelshtam at a session of PhIAN's scientific council. Mikhail Leontovich immediately denounced the conclusions of the commission. Among other things he said, "Well, Mandelshtam's opinions are not consistent from the point of view of dialectical materialism. However, even more, they cannot be of that kind, and nobody gave them out to be so. As for the problems connected with the basis of the relativity theory and quantum mechanics, I think that such a canonical point of view does not and cannot exist at present." Regarding that commission he said, "It follows that the serious physicists of that commission are dealing with general philosophical problems and involuntarily gave way to the fetishism of words which characterizes many of the comrades who are philosophizing about physical problems. . . . I continue to think that it was to my credit to publish the fifth volume of Mandelshtam . . . some comrades of that commission were against it . . . the late Sergei Vavilov solidly supported it" (157). The statements of Leontovich were firm and brave indeed. The members of the commission simply denounced Leontovich's speech and published their conclusions against Mandelshtam.

With this I finish my brief remarks about the scientific school of Mandelshtam and some of the attacks on it. Those physicists were both distinguished scientists and people of high moral and civic responsibility. Above I spoke of my dismay at the behavior of some other notable Soviet physicists both in the 1960s, 1970s, and 1980s, when it was necessary to manifest civic courage to defend freedom and truth, and at this crucial time for Russia, a time of transition when it is no longer dangerous to manifest human self-respect and civic responsibility. Nobody will now be arrested and sent to the Gulag for that.

To speak again about such disappointing events is, in a sense, to force open a door. In the end, the different civic and moral behaviors of people reveal basic differences in human temperament and character. Unfortunately, during recent years more than a few physicists, particularly those who fled Russia after the collapse of the USSR, have shown that they do not care about their civil duties. They put their own interests above everything. What is unforgivable is that in public talks and publications these physicists misrepresent the sad pages of history of Soviet physics. Such people exasperated Mandelshtam.

17

How We Settled in the United States, 1988–2000

Vienna

Our last meeting with our familiars in Moscow took place two days before our departure with our enormous allotment of foreign currency: $299. We arrived in Vienna on 24 December 1987 physically and emotionally devastated.

The Hebrew Immigration Aid Service (HIAS) arranged for our room and gave us a small stipend—enough to survive on while we were in Vienna. Later they bought us plane tickets to the United States, which we repaid after our arrival. The HIAS was founded in the United States in 1880 by Jewish émigrés from tsarist Russia, who wanted to help other Russian Jews to come to America.

Soon we forgot the ill treatment we had received at the airport from the representative of Sokhnut (a Jerusalem-based international body representing the World Zionist Organization), the purpose of which was to assist Jews emigrating from the Soviet Union to settle in Israel. He knew that we were not going to Ladispole, Italy, which was a transfer city for emigrants who were going on to Israel. By a special decision of U.S. officials we were to be allowed to go directly to the United States from Vienna. Later we learned that the man from Sokhnut was also routinely rude to other emigrants from the USSR who did not plan to go to Israel. Notwithstanding that, we are most grateful to the administrators of HIAS and Sokhnut for the help and support these organizations gave us.

Although the United States was our next, and ultimate, destination, we were not allowed to go there immediately. For fifty-five days we remained in Vienna, awaiting visas. During that time we were grateful for the hospitality of several people who treated us to meals and showed us the sights: a young couple, the biologist Nadya Fratzle and the physicist Peter Fratzle, and Professor Volker Kirrint and his wife, Helda, all friends of Joel Lebowitz, who told them of our arrival in Vienna; Leon Zelman, chair of the Jewish Committee of Vienna; and Reinhart Leitinger, secretary of one of URSI's radio commissions, and his wife, Dorti. I also met and had many interesting long discussions with Warren Zimmerman, the head of the U.S. delegation for Negotiations on Security Collaboration. I had heard about that respected person, who was also involved in human rights activities, in Moscow.

While we were waiting for permission to go to the United States, Owen Storey sent me the royalties from the sale of books of mine that had been published by Cambridge University Press. Storey had generously acted as my trustee and kept the money in a bank account for me.

Finally the special jury committee of the American embassy in Vienna asked us to come to them. Svetlana and I had been there for several minutes, chatting with the committee, when a handsome man came in. Although he was dressed in civilian clothes, I understood immediately from his bearing and manner that he was a security agent of some kind. He sat down and after a few minutes he said, "Yakov, why did they give you permission to leave to go to America? You were so close to Sputnik work and to other secret projects."

"Ask them," I said. For what else could I say? I had no idea why, at this point in my life, after they had interrupted my scientific work for twelve years, the Soviet authorities had decided to grant me an exit visa.

"Yes, yes, I understand," the man said. He was very polite. I did not mind the delay or the questions. We live in a complicated world, and the United States should be careful.

America and First Scientific Sojourns

I am pleased to write now how our circumstances were favorably arranged during our years in the United States. We think that it must be a matter of simple good fortune. Indeed, fortune is a real factor in our lives. Still, as a wise person told me recently, one needs to know how to have good luck. In any case, we have been completely satisfied with these years, and that is the important thing.

On 18 February 1988 we arrived in Boston, where we would make our new home. The first weeks we lived in Medford, a suburb of Boston, where we rented an apartment across the street from Eugene and Marina Chudnovsky. They and Mario Grossi helped us very much in the first weeks after our arrival in Boston. We received visits from many people. Among them were Joel Lebowitz, David Gross, and Arno Penzias from New Jersey, Owen Storey from Washington, and the physicists George Bekefi and Robert Jaffe from MIT.

We learned that an agreement had been made with the National Aeronautics and Space Administration (NASA) for a six-month research grant for me at the Harvard-Smithsonian Astrophysics Observatory. Owen Storey and Mario Grossi had arranged this. Owen worked at NASA then, and Mario had worked for dozens of years at the observatory. I am sad to tell here that Mario, an excellent human being, died on 11 January 1999, one day after his seventy-fourth birthday.

Svetlana and I decided to take time to rest. In April we had our first vacation in the United States and spent ten days at Fort Lauderdale, Florida. In the evenings I began making notes about my plans for research in the United States. Before that, however, and soon after our arrival in Boston, the Space Research Department of Boston University arranged a reception for us. We received a kind letter from Senator Edward Kennedy congratulating us on our arrival in the United States. I also had a nice meeting and talk with Elie Wiesel.

Our first trip in the United States was to New York at the beginning of March 1988. There we attended a special session of the Committee of Concerned Scientists (CCS). On that occasion a dinner was held at the apartment of the physicist Miriam Sarachik. We stayed in New York at a luxurious hotel in a two-room suite. Svetlana and I were bewildered at being in such a large and expensive suite. We thought that the CCS could not possibly pay such a lot of money for us to stay there. I asked the manager of the hotel to move us to a cheaper and more modest room. He was astonished and could not comprehend my request. Soon he smiled and told me that everything had already been paid for!

We visited Washington for the first time in May 1988. We were there again in June and November 1988, and I was also there alone in 1989 and later. David DeVorkin of the Smithsonian Institution's National Air and Space Museum interviewed us for the museum's oral history archive, and he twice came to Medford to continue the interviews. The tape-recorded interviews amounted to about five hundred pages of typescript plus one hundred pages of photographs and supporting documents.

In May 1988, when I was already seventy-seven years old, I presented my first talk at a scientific conference in the West at the annual meeting of the American Geophysical Union in Baltimore. Svetlana and I were there together. My paper was scheduled to run for forty minutes but continued for more than an hour because there were many questions. My talk was a review of my investigations of the ionosphere and radio wave propagation, as well as about the work of other scientists in the USSR. In truth, it was a talk on science and life.

To England and California, 1988–1989

In 1959, as I mentioned in Chapter 2, I had been awarded a year's Overseas Visitor status at St. John's College, Cambridge, but the Soviet authorities would not allow me to go there. Almost thirty years later, Kenneth Budden initiated a new visiting professorship for me. I was delighted to be able to accept this honor, but for various reasons we decided to spend only three months in Cambridge. We lived there in one of the residences owned by Cavendish Laboratories. I also had an office at Cavendish, where I continued my research on nonlinear waves in the ionosphere. Budden created a computer program for my research, and we worked together a great deal.

While in Cambridge we had interesting encounters and social dinners. There was always a solemn and spiritual atmosphere during mealtime in the large hall at St. John's College, which is about five hundred years old. Candles lighted the hall, and dinner began with a prayer. The physicist David Schoenberg involved me in an event that stands out in my mind. Together we went to see the private room of Isaac Newton at Trinity College. I held Newton's walking stick in my hands and realized that he was a diminutive man.

At Cavendish it was a pleasure to have several meetings with Nevil Mott, a Nobel laureate in physics, who was chair of Cavendish Laboratories from 1954 to 1971. It was Neville Mott who had invited me to Cambridge in 1959. He was eighty-three years old in 1988, but he was still very active. Budden, Mott, Schoenberg, and other Cambridge scientists stood outside Cavendish with me in a group photograph taken just before our departure. The photographer for Cavendish Laboratories said that he had never before been able to gather so many distinguished scientists for a photograph.

An astonishing thing happened to me in Cambridge. Walking along the corridors of Cavendish Laboratories and looking at the many photographs on the walls, I saw a group picture of the physics research students of 1907 posing with the physicist John Thomson, who did research at Cavendish and won the Nobel Prize in physics in 1906 for the discovery of the electron. Among the students was the twenty-seven-year-old Nikolai Papalexi. Thus, I "met" Nikolai Dmitrievich at Cavendish eighty-one years later. The events of our lives are truly unpredictable! This was an unexpected and pleasant event for me.

Another event at St. John's College was meeting the physicist Roald Sagdeev. He was there to attend the Chapman Conference on Aurora Physics. One day I was greeted in the lobby with, "Yakov Lvovich, I am so glad to see you!" I turned and saw Sagdeev running toward me. I immediately said, "But I am not happy to see you."

"Why not?" he asked. I replied that it was because of his behavior during the difficult past (see Chapter 11 and appendix C). Despite my unwelcoming attitude, he did not go away but remained and spoke to me about various things for a long time. Later, he often demonstrated publicly that he was friendly with me, although we had never been friends. Such were the actions of Roald Sagdeev.

A surprise invitation to come as a regent lecturer to the University of California at Los Angeles and to the San Diego campus for six weeks, from January to March 1989, was most pleasant. The invitation was initiated by the physicists Margaret Kivelson, a space researcher from UCLA, and Henry Booker of UCSD. But Booker died before my arrival in California, and James Arnold, a chemist at UCSD, became my host in San Diego. I had regularly received reprints of scientific articles and preprints from Kivelson and Booker in Moscow. Arnold and his wife, Louise, visited us there in October 1979. The invitation was not only in recognition of my achievements in research; I believe it was also the act of people of good will who wished to lend us financial support during our first months in the United States. In fact, the most generous income I ever received in the United States was the honorarium given by UCLA and UCSD. It was most needed then, and it enabled us to buy a car.

During those six weeks we visited museums, Disneyland, the San Diego Zoo, Hollywood, and other places. On Hollywood's Walk of Fame we were amazed to catch sight of the name Alpert among such names as Sophia Loren and Elizabeth Taylor. Later we learned that Alpert is the name of a well-known American musician, Herb Alpert. I covered his first name by sitting on it, and Svetlana took a picture.

Our Visit to Moscow, 1990

The first two years after our arrival in the United States were saturated with activity and manifold impressions. The third year began with a one-week visit to Moscow in January 1990. I had been invited for the celebration of the fiftieth anniversary of IZMIRAN, where I had worked for twenty-seven years. I began my talk "Science and Life" at the scientific conference of that celebration by relating the circumstances that had taken me to that institute from PhIAN. My colleagues from the institute heard the story for the first time. I also spoke with emotion about the recent situation in the USSR. After my talk, the director of IZMIRAN, who chaired the session, said, "We would never have known these extraordinary stories if Yakov Lvovich had talked only about his research. His was a remarkable talk."

My former colleagues told me that Valadimir Migulin had strenuously opposed inviting me to the celebration. It was curious to see Migulin in the audience at my talk and know that he had tried to keep me away.

As part of the festivities my young colleagues organized a party for me in my old office. For the party we used desserts and refreshments that we had brought to give to our friends in Moscow. We had also brought souvenirs and gifts for many people. About two weeks before our trip to Moscow we prepared a souvenir and gift matrix consisting of forty lines of different items and twenty columns of people's names. The spectrum of 121 gifts on that list was diverse: woolen jackets, shoes, chocolate, coffee, sausages, shirts, jeans, and so on. We were afraid that the Moscow customs officers would not allow those things to come into the country. As it turned out, however, the customs officers did not even ask us to open our suitcases.

Naturally, Svetlana spent a lot of time visiting her mother, and I met with Irina twice. We also spent memorable evenings with Katy and Anatoly Pokrovsky. Twice we were with Lyalya and Lev Gor'kov and with Lev and Lyuba Pitaevsky. Other friends came to see us at our hotel.

For the entire trip the Academy of Sciences provided me with a car, a Volga, and we had no transportation difficulties. The trip to Moscow was exciting. We returned to the United States with many mixed, contradictory feelings. We were hopeful that the changes in Russia would be for the good, but we also understood that our motherland was in deep trouble.

Seeing the World and Putting Down New Roots

As we gradually became used to living in the West, we greatly enjoyed our new freedom to travel, whether simply on our own, to visit friends, or to attend scientific conferences. It was an enormous change in our lives. We still had restraints on our movement — the normal ones of time, money, energy, and so on — but they were light ones compared to the Soviet bureaucracy. It was a great treat, for example, to visit San Francisco, which Svetlana had dreamed of seeing since she was a young girl and her older sister Lida had gone there with the Bolshoi Ballet. In the past decade we have visited California, Hawaii, France, Italy, Belgium, Scandinavia, Canada, Jamaica, and Japan, often in connection with scientific conferences. After being completely banned from accepting invitations to the West during my career as a Soviet scientist, I take a special pleasure in the free exchange of ideas and viewpoints at these conferences.

There are sometimes surprising encounters at these events. For example, in October 1992 we went to Belgium, where I presented a talk in Brussels at the scientific AGARD NATO meeting on radio propagation and system aspects. My talk was titled "Theoretical calculations of focusing radio waves in the ionosphere." I was told that I was the first scientist from the USSR to attend a scientific meeting at NATO. During a farewell party, when I was introduced to the commander-in-chief of the organization and began to tell him about myself, he smiled and said, "We know everything about you."

In November 1993 Svetlana and I became citizens of the United States. We lost our citizenship in the USSR when we emigrated. The judge who conducted the citizenship ceremony approached us on leaving the stage after his speech. He congratulated us and shook my hand.

Let me add that from 1990 to 1995 I was a consultant at AT&T Bell Laboratories and also had some small contracts with NASA until 1994. In May 1989 Svetlana found a good position at the Department of Mathematics at Harvard University. She enjoys working with students and with nice, friendly people. Since August 1994 I have received a Social Security pension. Thus, we settled well in the United States.

1991 and 1996: Eightieth and Eighty-fifth Birthday Parties

At the beginning of March 1991 the New York Academy of Sciences organized a reception and dinner on the occasion of my eightieth birthday, as I mentioned in the introduction. It was a memorable evening in the beautiful halls of the New York Academy with many dozens of friends and well-wishers. In 1996 the Committee of Concerned Scientists arranged a dinner in New York on the occasion of my eighty-fifth birthday. (We also celebrated Svetlana's fifty-fifth and my eighty-fifth birthday — both our birthdays are in March — at Lake Louise in the Canadian Rocky Mountains. There we walked a lot and visited mountains designated for skiing.)

In New York, we stayed with Eugene and Marina Chudnovsky. The dinner took place at the large and comfortable apartment of Miriam Sarachik in Manhattan, who offered her apartment for the dinner so that there would be an intimate atmosphere, like a family party. Many friends were invited; some sent their congratulations through the committee. Joseph Birman, Eugene Chudnovsky, Dorothy Hirsh, Joel Lebowitz, Louis Nirenberg, Yuri Orlov, and others proposed moving, heartfelt toasts that they made with humor and without any "eulogizing." Birman read the congratulations of friends: the

Тот, кто чувствует собственное достоинство, поймет свои обязанности к другим людям и обществу.

Тот, кто не живет для других, не живет для самого себя.

Каждому своя обязанность - таково наше главное призвание, и для него мы живем в мире.

. . .

He, who feels self-respect, will understand his duties to other people and to the community.

He, who does not live for others, does not live for himself.

Everyone has his duty - this is our principle mission - and for that we exist in the world.

Michel de Montaigne (1533-1592)
Essays, 1580-1588

I believe in intuition and inspiration ...Sometimes I feel I being on a right way but I cannot explain my confidence. When the Polar Eclipse of 1919 confirmed my conjecture, I was not at all surprised. I would have been surprised if it had not happened... ...Imagination is more important than knowledge, for knowledge is limited, whereas imagination involves all in the world, stimulates progress and promotes its evolution... ...Strictly speaking, imagination is a real factor in scientific research...

Albert Einstein

14. The passages from Montaigne and Einstein that the author distributed at his eighty-fifth birthday party

Ginzburgs in Russia, the Cartans and the Storeys in France, the Buddens and the Schoenbergs in England, Inga Fisher in Sweden, Bott and Taubes at Harvard, Langer in Santa Barbara, and many others.

To that dinner I brought for all the guests copies of Michel de Montaigne's statement of his humanistic principles, published in his essays, and Einstein's famous statement about the role of imagination, intuition, and inspiration in science. In my talk I spoke about the crucial times of my life and how those statements had struck me on reading them for the first time dozens of years ago. Those ideas have always been closely related to the demands of my spirit. The guests were astonished and delighted to have those copies. Many asked me to sign the sheets, but I said, "It would be wrong for me to sign my name after the name of Einstein." I have already quoted Einstein's words above, in Chapter 5; they are the words I posted on my office wall at IZMIRAN. Here I would like to show a copy of what I handed out at the party (figure 14).

Finita la commedia, or, Ende gut alles gut

Before concluding this chronicle of events I must also tell that in 1995 I completed research into the basic electromagnetic oscillating nature of the background of the magnetosphere. I had worked hard on that problem for four or five years. I published three papers on the subject together with Dr. Louis Lanzerotti of Bell Labs. My small monograph on the subject, *The Resonance Nature of the Magnetosphere,* is in press with the journal *Physical Reports.* I am content with that study and trust that the future will show that work to be an important contribution to the physics of the magnetosphere.

On 22 March 1999, I presented an invited paper at the centennial meeting of the American Physical Society in Atlanta. The title of my paper was "Refusniks' Seminar — Unofficial Collaboration," and I gave it as part of a symposium titled "Physics Cooperation in Cold War and Post–Cold War Eras." That talk concluded an important and memorable part of my life, and it was a pleasure and honor for me to give it.

Finally I would like to repeat, we settled well in the United States, we were fortunate. Of course, we experienced hard and unpleasant times here too. But no one's life is without such events. During the past few years I have come to know a new world and the imperfections of its moral character and to recognize the extent to which all of humanity's systems are flawed. What then is our choice in life? To try to see things as they are and to be honest about what we see, to work and work, and to remember, *nil admirari,* or more optimistically, *per aspera ad astra.*

Epilogue

These recollections do not make an autobiography. They do not amount to an emotional narration of the successive events my life. Here I have described only some of the events of that long period of time that is my life; I am writing these words now having just turned eighty-nine years of age. Our homeland has changed greatly in the years since Svetlana and I parted from Moscow. But the whole world has changed, too. We love Russia, and our homeland is always in our thoughts and hearts. I often think about the world and Russia and about the fate of mankind in the twenty-first century. But to explore those thoughts would require another book.

The greatest pursuit of my life has been radio and space plasma physics research. For the nearly fifty-five years of my work in Moscow, my PhIAN and IZMIRAN colleagues devotedly helped me. Together we realized many projects. Some of those involved in these projects worked with me for thirty or thirty-five years. During that time these colleagues became fathers and mothers and even grandparents. I would like especially to mention here my collaborators Dora Fliegel and Vyacheslav Sinelnikov and our uncommon and extremely good laboratory assistants, Vera Krayushkina and Vera Morozova. For their help and fruitful collaboration, I hold in my heart deep gratitude to them all and to the other members of my laboratory.

I have not deeply analyzed the evolution of my political views or the reasons why I acted as I did in the episodes I have related. It often surprised me to hear people say of me, "Yakov Lvovich is acting against himself." By this they seem to have meant, "Yakov Lvovich is acting against the interests of his career." The fact is that I have always found it difficult, even impossible, to behave in such a way as to be in contradiction with myself, to be at odds with my own conscience. I am aware that such a stance can lead to conflict with others, and in fact, it did lead to conflicts in my life. But such is my nature. It brought many unfortunate consequences, but sometimes it also helped me to be strong in difficult situations. It helped to save my self-respect. I have worked hard all my life and still work hard now. I am still very involved in my scientific interests and research. What I say here can also be an answer to those in the West who often have asked me, "How did you save yourself? What is your secret?"

Many aspects of my life are not presented in this book. For the most part I have related only the outward aspects of the stories of my years, largely un-colored by the feelings, contradictions, beliefs, and doubts that accompany all of us during our lives. Yet to present the account of my life as I have here was my intention.

In conclusion I am pleased to say again that from 1944 to 1969, Irina Chernysheva was my wife and good, close friend. Ira and I spent twenty-five good and interesting years together. We always understood each other. I am very grateful to her for those years.

Svetlana and I have been together for almost thirty years. Although certainly not without its contradictions and difficulties, our life together has been a bright, intense, and interesting one from the very beginning. Without her help this book would not exist. To her I express my love and deepest gratitude for her help and devotion.

Appendix A: Memorandum on High-Altitude Atom Bomb Explosions

Memorandum
Ionosphere and Other Geophysics Effects
Created by High-Altitude Atom Bomb Explosions
Ya. L. Alpert, IZMIRAN
Contents

Appendix B: Roster of the
1959 Conference in Geneva

CONFERENCE ON THE DISCONTINUANCE
OF NUCLEAR WEAPON TESTS

PRIVATE
GEN/DNT/HAT/INF.1
22 June 1959
ORIGINAL: ENGLISH

TECHNICAL WORKING GROUP ON THE DETECTION AND
IDENTIFICATION OF THE HIGH-ALTITUDE NUCLEAR EXPLOSIONS

List of Members of the Working Group

A. *Members of the Delegation of the Union of Soviet Socialist Republics*

Head of Delegation
Mr. E. K. Fedorov   Professor, corresponding member of the Academy of Sciences of the USSR

Members of Delegation
Mr. A. M. Sadovsky   Corresponding member of the Academy of Sciences of the USSR

Mr. J. L. Alpert   Professor, corresponding member of the Academy of Sciences of the USSR

Mr. O. I. Leipunski   Professor, Doctor of Physics and Mathematics

Mr. A. I. Ustyumenko   Member of the Scientific Staff of the Academy of Sciences of the USSR

Mr. O. A. Grinevsky   Third Secretary at the Ministry of Foreign Affairs of the USSR

B. *Members of the Delegation of the United Kingdom of Great Britain and Northern Ireland*

Head of Delegation
Mr. Henry Hulme   Technical Adviser, Ministry of Defence
Members of Delegation
Mr. I. Maddock   Technical Adviser, Ministry of Defence
Dr. R. Press   Technical Adviser, Conference on the Discontinuance of Nuclear Weapon Tests, Ministry of Defence

C. *Members of the Delegation of the United States of America*

Head of Delegation
Dr. Wolfgang K. M. Panofsky   Director, High Energy Physics Laboratory, Stanford University, Stanford, California

Members of Delegation
Dr. Stirling A. Colgate,   Technical Advisor, Physicist Staff Member, Lawrence Radiation Laboratory, Livermore, California
Dr. Allen F. Donovan,   Technical Advisor, Vice-President and Director Astrovehicles Laboratory, Space Technology Laboratory, Los Angeles, California
Dr. Alvin C. Graves,   Technical Advisor, Physicist and Division Leader, Los Alamos Scientific Laboratory, Los Alamos, New Mexico
Dr. Spurgeon M. Keeny, Jr.,   Advisor, Office of the Special Assistant to the President for Science and Technology, Washington 25, D.C.
Dr. Richard Latter,   Technical Advisor, Chief, Physics Division, Rand Corporation, Santa Monica, California
Colonel Dent Lay,   Technical Advisor, Assistant Director, Technical Operations Division, Advanced Research Projects Agency, Department of Defence, Washington 25, D.C.
Dr. Allen M. Peterson,   Technical Advisor, Head, Propagation Laboratory, Stanford Research Institute, Stanford, California
Dr. Kenneth M. Watson,   Technical Advisor, Professor Physics, University of California, Berkeley, California

Appendix C: *Tempora and Mores of Soviet Physicists*

Now that the U.S.S.R. no longer exists, the expression "Soviet physicist" has become part of history. Those for whom that was formerly an honorable title are now being seen quite differently. Some physicists changed only their descriptor, "Soviet," while others have changed their profession entirely. Everyone, however, has their own relationship with the past, whether they now entirely ignore it, try to comprehend it, spit upon it, or alter it to suit their own convenience.[1] It is actually a wonder that anybody is ready to admit at least their own moral responsibility for what happened in their homeland. Nonetheless, the old-fashioned question of "Science and Morals" does exist and will exist forever.

The Soviet physicist Andrei Sakharov dealt with this question openly, in full view of the eyes of humanity. As for his colleagues, among whom he used to live and work, their actions were and are often ambiguous and even sinister. In the Soviet

These pages were submitted to *Physics Today* on December 21, 1994. I print the original, unedited document here. Only a much-shortened version was eventually published in *Physics Today*, in the Letters section of the July 1995 issue. A full version was published in Russian in the journal *Priroda* in April 1995. The editor of each journal privately told me of pressure not to publish the material in any form; the editor of *Priroda* also informed me that the April 1995 issue was one of the journal's best-sellers.

1. A. Abrikosov's interview, *Izvestia,* 5 May 1993; *New York Times,* 15 July 1993; Yakov Alpert and A. Migdal's articles, *Vremya I My* 122 (1993) (in Russian).

Union of 1981, in an article written while in exile in Gorky, Sakharov characterized his colleagues:

> Every true scientist should undoubtedly muster sufficient courage and integrity to resist the temptation and the habit of conformity. Unfortunately, we are familiar with too many counterexamples in the Soviet Union, sometimes using the excuse of protecting one's laboratory or institute (usually just a pretext), sometimes for the sake of one's career, sometimes for the sake of foreign travel (a major lure in a closed country such as ours)."[2]

This is just a general description. For those who did not participate in the social life of Soviet physics, and have no personal knowledge of the Soviet mechanics of conformism, only concrete facts about the actions of specific scientists could be convincing. Based on these facts one can understand why so few Soviet scientists, with their privileged social status, practiced independent judgment within the social reality that prevailed in the U.S.S.R.

Recently an autobiographical book by Roald Sagdeev has appeared, and its title promised to answer the question, "how a Soviet scientist was made."[3] The lengthy book and its foreword by the well-known American astronomer Carl Sagan have resulted in two strikingly different perceptions.

On the one hand, an American physicist, Richard Garwin, in his review published in Physics Today, presents this quotation from Sagdeev's book:

> "Many, despite the pressure of mundane life, stay firm in their selfless service to science. God help them to do so with the same grace, tenacity and integrity that distinguished that special breed of scientists, 'the keepers of the flame,' that were Kapitsa and Landau, Leontovich and Sakharov."

Then Garwin concludes, "I have no doubt that Sagdeev also belongs on this list."[4]

On the other hand, Russian scientist Alex Gurshtein, who worked under Sagdeev in the Soviet Institute of Space Research (IKI) for many years, expresses a very different opinion of Sagdeev in his review of the book:

> "Sagdeev strives to create an image of a moralist with a suit free of spots. All negative stories are out of his memory. But as a scientific feudal member of the House of Lords, he ruined hundreds of careers . . ."

Gurshtein notes that Sagdeev describes his working relationship as director of IKI with his deputy, Colonel Georgy P. Chernyshev, the KGB security commissar at IKI, "but he never mentions how often he ordered Chernyshev to discredit his oppo-

2. Andrei Sakharov, "The Social Responsibility of Scientists," *Physics Today,* June 1981, 29.

3. Roald V. Sagdeev, *The Making of a Soviet Scientist: My Adventures in Nuclear Fusion and Space from Stalin to Star Wars* (New York: John Wiley & Sons, 1994).

4. Richard Garwin, " A Courageous Odyssey Through Soviet and Post-Soviet Science," *Physics Today,* October 1994.

nents. . . . No doubts, no repentance — these emotions are out of the author's reper-
tory."[5]

What is behind the divergence of these reviews? To answer this question it is
necessary to confront the past truthfully and to analyze the behavior and psychology
of the community of Soviet physical scientists. That would be a large undertaking.
However, in this article I limit myself to presenting only a few highly revealing facts,
leaving judgment of these facts to the reader.

Unequivocal Facts

In past years a number of articles on the subject of science and morality,
including some in *Physics Today,* have bewildered me. For more than 50 years I
worked in the Soviet Academy of Sciences, meeting and talking on different subjects
with Sakharov, Leontovich, Landau, and many other physicists mentioned in Sagdeev's book. The problem in question was an urgent one for me during many years,
especially after 1968 when Soviet tanks entered Prague, and after 1975, when I
became a refusnik and an active participant in an unauthorized scientific seminar.[6]

I hoped that post-Soviet time itself would eliminate distortions in Western understanding of "who was who and how did it happen" in Soviet physics. But what has
happened? To place Sagdeev in the same rank as outstanding physicists and personalities such as Kapitsa, Landau, Leontovich and Sakharov is a gross distortion of
historical reality — a complete devaluation of moral standards.[7] This shocking, naive conclusion of the eminent American physicist Richard Garwin has forced me to
try to clarify the real historical situation. Let us examine the facts.

In 1978 "The First Joint U.S.-U.S.S.R. Workshop on Laser Plasma Interaction"
took place in Zvenigorod, not far from Moscow. Each country was represented by a
few dozen scientists. Two Americans, Frederick Mayer (then director of fusion
experiments at KMS Fusion Inc.) and Eli Yablonovitch (then at Harvard University),
visited our unauthorized seminar of refusniks. It was arranged that 10 to 12 American scientists would attend the next seminar and give a few talks.

By noon on the arranged day some thirty Russian scientists, refusniks, and dissidents had come. Sakharov was among them. Two hours later Mayer and Yablonovitch appeared, and Eli Yablonovitch related the following:

> "This morning Sagdeev summoned us and, in the presence of other Russian and
> American physicists, told us: 'You should not go to the seminar. There are no

5. Alex A. Gurshtein, "The Most Famous Tatar Since Ulugh Beg," *Sky and Telescope,*
December 1994.

6. "The New Brain Drain, Soviet Watch," *Discover,* March 1991.

7. Yet more, a strange but scandalous statement appeared recently in *Breaking Free*
(New York: Farrar Straus & Giroux, 1995), a book written by Sagdeev's wife, Susan
Eisenhower. When she learned of Sakharov's death, she writes, "I knew there would be
great pressure on him [Sagdeev] to assume Sakharov's mantle."

scientists at the seminar. Besides, to go there is dangerous'. And he had added: 'Don't think that I am an anti-Semite, my wife is Jewish.' "

Having read Garwin's review, I called these physicists, 15 years after our short meeting at the refusnik seminar. I wanted to check whether they remembered the old event. They more than remembered it! Both were upset, and they urged me to set the record straight. They told me that after their return from the U.S.S.R. they published accounts of the incident in the U.S. media. Dr. Fred Mayer also sent me part of the report to the National Academy of Sciences about their meetings in Moscow.

> The report says that on the morning of the seminar the "Soviet workshop host, S. Anisimov. . . arranged for . . . Dr. R. Sagdeev, together with about eight other Soviet scientists to have a political discussion with the U.S. delegation. . . . Sagdeev appeared to be answering questions truthfully about the numbers of 'refusniks' . . . and the level of anti-semitism in the U.S.S.R. We later learned he had been distorting the truth. He gave the U.S. delegation the strong implication that if we were to visit the 'refusniks' . . . we would be jeopardizing his and Anisimov's careers in physics. . . ."[8]
>
> "Dr. Sagdeev suggested that the visit to the refusniks and the ensuing 'political noise' could jeopardize future exchanges, . . . he discussed the reports of a Jewish quota at Soviet universities. . . . He said there was not a quota . . . Sagdeev was able to dissuade most of the American delegation. . . ."[9]

The report goes on to note that the refusnik seminar included

> many very highly respected scientists and engineers, some of whom were 're-fusniks' and some dissidents, including the most famous Academician A. Sakharov. The first paper to be delivered at the seminar was a paper of Y. Orlov read by Y. Golfand. Orlov's paper was recently published in the West. This contradicted a statement made at our meeting with Sagdeev, where it was stated that 'Orlov was only a politician,' not a scientist. Many such contradictions came out in our discussions with the seminar attendees, making it clear that our meeting with Sagdeev had a considerable number of distortions of the facts.[10]

And the Americans said that the seminar was "one of the most remarkable events of [their] life."[11] Joel Lebowitz, then president of the New York Academy of Sciences, wrote about this seminar in 1979, "If you are going to the U.S.S.R., I urge you not to pass up the opportunity to attend one of these sessions; you will be doing an extremely important good deed and you will find it rewarding, too, both personally

8. "Political Meetings," trip report to Dr. Gershon Sher, the National Academy of Sciences of the United States, 1978.

9. "U.S. Fusion Researchers Conduct a Seminar of Soviet 'Refusniks,' " Soviet Visits, *Laser Focus*, November 1978; see also "U.S. Physicist visits 'refusniks,' " *Boston Globe*, 27 September 1978.

10. Trip report to Dr. Gershon Sher.

11. Laser Focus.

and scientifically. The audience is eager and the discussions are most stimulating. (Nobelist A. Penzias says it was his best audience.)"[12]

James Langer (at present the Director of the Institute of Theoretical Physics in Santa Barbara) wrote in *Physics Today* that the "seminar has been host to more than two hundred visiting Western scientists, and has been the occasion for discussion of some of the most exciting developments in modern research. Most recently, Arno Penzias came directly from Stockholm to Moscow to repeat his Nobel lecture at the Seminar."[13]

It is appropriate to say a few words about the refusnik seminar. It was initiated in 1973 by physicists Mark Azbel, Benjamin Levich, and Alexander Voronel. After all of them emigrated to Israel, the seminar moved from Azbel's home to the home of mathematician Victor Brailovsky. After he was arrested in 1980 (because of this activity), the seminar began to operate at my home until 1987, when I and my wife, engineer Svetlana Alpert, were permitted to leave the U.S.S.R. The seminar was attended by scientists from England, Denmark, France, Norway, Sweden, the U.S.A., etc. In 1980–1987 we had more than 300 visitors, including about 170 scientists. Five volumes of the proceedings of the seminar were published by the New York Academy of Sciences, with the help and editorship of Joel Lebowitz.[14]

Dr. Sagdeev never attended our seminar. Then who informed him that "There are no scientists at the seminar"? It is well known that in the U.S.S.R. virtually every aspect of life, such as meetings with foreign scientists, was regulated by the KGB.

The facts of this episode are clear enough. However, to understand better the whole picture, let us review some other publications from that time to the present.

The Soviet Academy of Sciences as a "political opponent" of the Soviet regime

In 1984 Dr. Timothy Toohig, after having visited the Physical Institute in Dubna, wrote:

> "I tried to understand the dissident situation. Regret was expressed about Sakharov, though it is stated he is no longer a physicist. Whether by this is meant his bomb work cut him off from the general research fraternity, I could not determine. Orlov '. . . [is said to be] crazy. He molests the women he works with. He should be in jail.'"[15]

12. Joel Lebowitz, "Letter from the President: Moscow Sunday Seminar," *The Sciences,* May–June 1979, 15.

13. James Langer, "Journey to an Unauthorized Scientific Meeting," *Physics Today,* June 1979, 9.

14. *Reports of the Moscow Refusnik Seminar,* ed. Joel Lebowitz. Annals of the New York Academy of Sciences 337 (1980); 373 (1981); 410 (1983); 452 (1985); 491 (1987).

15. Timothy Toohig, "View from the Volga — Updated," *Physics Today,* January 1984.

Isn't this political line consistent with what Dr. Sagdeev told American physicists in 1978?

Dr. Valentin Tourchin, the Soviet mathematician who spearheaded Amnesty International activity in the Soviet Union, called Toohig's remarks "rare in their meanness":

> "They are directed against two men to whom I do not know equal in nobility: Andrei Sakharov and Yuri Orlov. . . . Who are Toohig's sources? He says that he had 'frank discussions' with them and adds, 'For reasons of prudence, I will omit direct attribution.' This is a sheer hypocrisy."[16]

Now let me leap to a 1992 article by Roald Sagdeev in *Physics Today*. He wrote in this article,

> The Soviet Academy of Sciences was in many ways an heir of the Russian Academy [i.e. before the 1917 revolution] . . . The Academy was in the first row of political opponents of the Soviet regime. . . . The scientists (myself among them) were bringing up all the issues of perestroika that would later become official policy.[17]

Eugene Chudnovsky and Alex Vilenkin responded to that paper; both these physicists were out of jobs for many years because of the "Jewish quota" denied by Sagdeev, who told visiting American physicists, "there was not a quota." Chudnovsky and Vilenkin wrote that some of Sagdeev's statements gave

> a rather distorted picture of reality. Soviet scientists, and physicists in particular, were an elitist and politically passive group. . . . objectively they were supporting the regime . . . Members of the Academy were granted enormous privileges . . . Calling this 'surviving under the Soviet system' sounds like a joke.[18]

It is obvious how Sagdeev tries to present his moral makeup for the West. And many people have apparently believed him. For example, Carl Sagan wrote that Sagdeev "instituted glasnost before Gorbachev. . . . It is a fair reflection of an extraordinary man and an extraordinary career. I wish there were more people like him to the right hand of every national leader."[19]

Generally speaking, I am pleased to see how Western scientists trust their colleagues. They trusted also the Soviet ones who visited them. However, often they were not aware who these visitors were, and how they were selected for their travel abroad. Thus, it is good to trust, but President Ronald Reagan had indeed sound reasons to like the Russian saying, "Doveryay, no proveryay" — "Trust, but verify."

So, let's verify a little. On January 27, 1980 the official newspaper *Izvestiya*

16. Valentin Tourchin, "Fellow Travelers," *Physics Today,* January 1984.

17. Roald V. Sagdeev, "SOS! Save Our Science," *Physics Today,* May 1992, 22.

18. Eugene Chudnovsky and Alex Vilenkin, "Soviet Scientist, Apolitical Pasts," *Physics Today,* December 1992.

19. Carl Sagan, foreword to Roald V. Sagdeev, *The Making of a Soviet Scientist.*

published a memorandum, "In the presidium of the Academy of Sciences," that stated,

> The presidium of the Academy of Sciences noted that despite its reproach, Academician Sakharov continues to carry out the actions directed to undermine the Soviet state system and, in fact, to counteract the Soviet policy of peace. . . . Sakharov is approving the politics of the most reactionary, aggressive, imperialistic circles, for example, of Senator Jackson.

That is how the Soviet people learned the Academy's opinion on Sakharov. After that an avalanche of articles against Sakharov followed, particularly in *Izvestiya,* describing him as "Slanderer and Pharisee" (January 30, 1980) and endorsing his being sentenced to internal exile ("A just decision," February 23, 1980). On February 15, 1980 an article in *Literaturnaya Gazeta,* "Caesar did not come true," tried to justify Sakharov's exile by asserting, "With all of his blasting actions of the spiritual apostate and provocateur Sakharov put himself in the status of a traitor of his people and country."

Three years later, four of the most influential members of the Academy expressed their opinion on Sakharov. They were the Nobelist Alexander Prokhorov, the director of the Physical Institute and the head of the Department of Physics and Astronomy; Georgy Skryabin, the Foreign Secretary of the Academy; and Anatoly Dorodnitsyn and Andrei Tikhonov, the directors of two other major institutes of the Academy. Soviet people could read in their article in *Izvestiya* of July 2, 1983:

> What kind of man is he to fall so low morally, to come to hate his own country and its people? We see in his actions a violation of the norms of humanitarian and decent behavior which we suppose to be obligatory for every civilized person . . . We know that Sakharov is very popular with those Americans who would like to wipe our country and socialism off the face of the earth. . . . in contrast to Sakharov, who calls for nuclear blackmail directed against his own country and for making possible a nuclear first strike against us, the Rosenbergs were not simply innocent persons . . . They had spoken out for the destruction of lethal weapons. And they were completely honest, humane people.

That is how the Soviet Academy of Sciences was "in the first row of political opponents of the Soviet regime" and how it "was bringing up all the issues of perestroika."

Now it is well known that the Academician who did bring up all the issues of perestroika was Andrei Sakharov, who enunciated them in his 1968 essay, "Reflections on Progress, Peaceful Co-existence, and Intellectual Freedom."

An Outrageous Episode

Another episode also bears telling. In 1983 the American mathematical physicist Norman Zabusky attended an international conference in Kiev. On his way to Kiev he was in Moscow and we arranged that on his way back he would present a talk at the seminar of refusniks. The prominent Russian physicist Eugene Lifshitz called Zabusky and invited him, his wife, and daughter to come for a dinner at the Lifshitz home when Zabusky came back from Kiev to Moscow.

However, soon after Zabusky came back to Moscow, on 1 November, Dr. Lifshitz called him to say that he had to cancel the invitation for the dinner. This was Zabusky's "first inkling that all was not well." Indeed, on 2 November, he was called by an official from the Academy and was informed that as a persona non grata he had to leave Moscow. *Physics Today* described the events:

> According to a State Department source, the science attaché at the US Embassy was telephoned on 2 November . . . that Zabusky's conduct was 'inconsistent with his status as a guest of the Academy.' Zabusky would have to leave by noon Saturday, 5 November[he was to deliver his talk at the refusniks' seminar in the afternoon that day].
>
> The US Academy's Foreign Secretary, Walter Rosenblith of MIT, sent a cable on 5 November to Georgy K. Skryabin, his counterpart at the Soviet Academy, asking for additional information. A month later, Skryabin replied, repeating the original one-sentence charge in essentially the same words . . .";[20] "Norman Zabusky . . . was recently expelled from the USSR for agreeing to lecture at a 'Saturday Evening Seminar' [of refusniks][21]

However, why did Dr. Lifshitz cancel his invitation? Such an outrageous action excited me a lot. Lifshitz used to be my intimate friend for many years. I soon learned that Dr. Sagdeev had visited Dr. Lifshitz and urgently "advised" him to cancel the invitation of Zabusky.

Thus Sagdeev had been aware about the decision of the Soviet "competent bodies" concerning Zabusky at least one day before him. Who asked Sagdeev to go to Lifshitz? Sagdeev's answer to this question would be very revealing.

"For a variety of reasons"

There is another question that Dr. Sagdeev has not answered. In 1988 he proposed Sakharov to be elected to the Presidium of the Academy. Carl Sagan wrote in his foreword to Sagdeev's book, "He refused election . . . in favor of the celebrated dissident physicist Andrei Sakharov." And in the words of Dr. Garwin, "Sagdeev's integrity and courage led him to refuse . . . election to the Academy's presidium, proposing Sakharov instead."[22]

Sagdeev is silent about this deed in his book. But Sakharov recounted in *Gorky-Moscow and Beyond,* "In October 1988 . . . Sagdeev himself called . . . adding that

20. "Soviets Expel Zabusky Before Lecture to 'Refusnik Scientists,' " *Physics Today,* January 1984.

21. Harold Davis, "Restoring U.S.-Soviet Communication in Science," *Physics Today,* March 1984.

22. Garwin, "Courageous Odyssey,"

he had been nominated to the Presidium but for a variety of reasons could not serve and wished to propose my candidacy instead."[23] Well, what was the variety of reasons?[24] It seems that one can draw the answer to this question from Sagdeev's book. He writes in the Acknowledgement, "The very idea to write this book on a now 'extinct species' was suggested by my wife, Susan Eisenhower. . . . The early work on a first draft started in the end of 1988 . . . I had moved to Maryland (it was not the result of brain drain, but rather a 'heart drain')."

Not long before that time, Roald Sagdeev and another academician, Georgy Arbatov, appeared on American television news programs to endorse the Soviet leadership. I remember how Dr. Carl Sagan also campaigned for the Soviet cause on Soviet television. And when he was invited to attend the refusnik seminar, he declined the invitation, explaining that he was afraid to wreck the careers of his Soviet colleagues. Whose career? Sagdeev's?

Sagdeev, who had done good work in plasma physics, appeared later on the political stage. In his book he describes his activity in a group of four academicians — Arbatov, Primakov, Velikhov, and himself — who advised Gorbachev. With disarming self-deprecation he refers to the group as "the Gang of Four" and "political call girls of the Soviet delegation." Sadly, "Gang of Four" rings truer for Sagdeev than the company of "the keepers of the flame, Sakharov, Landau, Leontovich, Kapitsa." To be exact, however, I should say that Arbatov, Primakov, and Velikhov served much more and are still serving their homeland.

The picture is rather unequivocal, and it is not pleasant to have to present it for the readers of *Physics Today,* a journal which deals so much with the subject "Science and Morals." But to let the abuse of the name of Andrei Sakharov go uncontested would have been too great a sin.

23. Andrei Sakharov, *Gorky-Moscow and Beyond* (New York: Alfred A. Knopf, 1991).

24. Susan Eisenhower writes in *Breaking Free,* "Roald told me that he and Sakharov planned this maneuver for almost a week . . . 'but even Andrey doesn't know the deepest motivation,' he whispered." Indeed, Sagdeev maneuvered with Sakharov: he did not tell him the truth.

Appendix D: The Moscow Refusniks' Physics-Mathematics Seminar

Table 1. Activity of the Moscow Refusniks Seminars, 1980–1987

---

350 Visitors from different countries, including:

Scientists

USA	40 physicists, 7 mathematicians, 6 cardiologists
Denmark, Norway, Sweden	35 physicists, 6 mathematicians, 9 biologists and physicians
England	9 physicists, 3 mathematicians, 5 biologists and physicians
France	18 physicists, 5 mathematicians, 15 biologists and physicians
Total	158

Congressmen and Members of Parliaments

USA	11
Canada	2
England	4
Norway	2
Sweden	16
Total	35

Proceedings of the Refusniks Seminars
Annals of the New York Academy of Sciences, ed. Joel Lebowitz*

Volume	Year	Pages
337	1980	213
373	1981	233
410	1983	365
452	1985	411
491	1987	273
Total		1,495

*The proceedings include sixty-one papers of foreign scientists and eighty-six papers and fourteen posters of refusniks, including papers by scientists who never visited the seminars.

Table 2. Physicists, Members of the APS, Participants, and Visitors of the Moscow Refusnik Seminar in 1977–87

1977	James Langer, Institute of Theoretical Physics, Santa Barbara
1978	Leo Kadanoff, University of Chicago
	James Langer, Institute of Theoretical Physics, Santa Barbara
	Joel Lebowitz, Rutgers University
	Frederic Mayer, KMS Fusion, Inc.
	Arno Penzias, Bell Laboratories
	Eli Yablonowitch, Harvard University
1979	James Arnold, UCSD
	Joseph Birman, CUNY
	Arno Bohm, Texas University
	Frank Estabrook, Caltech, Pasadena
	Victor Granatstein, Naval Research Laboratory
	Martin Kruskal, Rutgers University
	Joel Lebowitz, Rutgers University
	Jacob Trombka, Goddard Space Flight Center, Md.
	Robert Wagoner, Stanford University
	Hugo Walquist, Caltech, Pasadena
1980	Freeman Dyson, Princeton University
	Joel Lebowitz, Rutgers University
	Norman Zabusky, Rutgers University

Table 2. Continued

1981	Gordon Hamilton, Magnetic Fusion Lab, Livermore
	Miriam Sarachik, CUNY
	Barry Simon, Caltech, Pasadena
1982	Joseph Birman, CUNY
	Adi Eisenberg, McGill University
	Mitchell Feigenbaum, Cornell University
	Oliver Penrose, Open University, U.K.
	Arthur Yelon, Ecole Polytechnique, Canada
1983	Sidney Bludman, Pennsylvania University
	Arno Bohm, Texas University
	Daniel Friedan, University of Chicago
	David Gross, Institute of Theoretical Physics, Santa Barbara
	John Kogut, Illinois Laboratory, Urbana
	Geoffrey West, Los Alamos National Laboratory, N.M.
	Edward Witten, Princeton University
	Norman Zabusky, Rutgers University
1984	Mitchell Feigenbaum, Cornell University
	Daniel Friedan, University of Chicago
	Douglas Henderson, IBM Research Laboratory, CA
	Michael Mauel, Plasma Fusion Center, MIT
1985	Joseph Birman, CUNY
	Arno Bohm, Texas University
	David Book, Naval Research Laboratory
	Herman Cumming, CUNY
	Hans Fraunfelder, University of Illinois
	Melvin Kalos, CUNY
	Arthur Rosenfeld, UC, Berkeley
1986	Lawrence Abbot, Brandeis University
	Edward Farhi, MIT
	David Gross, Institute of Theoretical Physics, Santa Barbara
	Robert Jaffe, MIT
1987	Joseph Birman, CUNY
	Arno Bohm, Texas University
	Dominique Gressilon, Ecole Polytechnique, France
	Robert Jaffe, MIT

Table 3. Selected Talks of Scientists from the West at the Moscow Refusnik Seminar, 1978–1986

17 December 1978	Arno Penzias (Bell Laboratories) The Origin of the Elements (Nobel Prize lecture)
27 December 1978	James Langer (Carnegie-Mellon University) Snow Crystal Growth Joel Lebowitz (Rutgers University) Recent Developments in Equilibrium Statistical Mechanics
2 November 1979	Owen Storey (CNRS, Orleans, France) Magnetic Confinement of a Flowing Plasma
28 November 1979	Joseph Birman (CUNY, City College) Optics of Spatial Dispersive Media
13 April 1980	Norman Zabusky (University of Pittsburgh) Ionospheric Plasma Clouds Dynamic via Regularized Contour Dynamics
8 May 1982	Gudrun Hageman (Niels Bohr Institute, Copenhagen) Pairing in Rapidly Rotating Nuclei
12 November 1982	Claude Bardos (Ecole Normale Supérieure, Paris) Eigenfrequencies and Trapped Rays for the Wave Equation
20 November 1982	Inga Fisher (Vice-President of the Royal Swedish Academy, Stockholm) Micropolar Phenomena in Ordered Structures
28 November 1982	Louis Michel (IHES, Bures-sur-Ivette, France) Symmetry in Physics
11 December 1982	Mark Davis (Imperial College, London) Nonlinear Filtering Bernard Shutz (University College of Cardiff, England) Statistical Approach to Radiation Reaction
21 January 1983	Seneor Roland (Ecole Polytechnique, Palaiseau, France) On Infrared Problems in Field Theory
7 February 1983	Paul Kessler (College de France, Paris) Discovery of a New Particle Boson W
26 February 1983	Mari Mehlew (Institute of Physics, Oslo) Solar Energy for Heating Houses
12 March 1983	Edward Witten (Princeton University) Supersymmetry and Morse Theory
2 April 1983	Daniel Friedan (University of Chicago) Chiral Fermions of the Lattice
16 April 1983	Eric Karlson (Uppsala University, Sweden) Plasma in a Very Inhomogeneous Magnetic Field

More than 260 talks were presented: 110 by scientists from the West; 150 by refusniks.

Table 3. Continued

21 May 1983	Arno Bohm (University of Texas) Hadronic Rotational Bands
26 June 1983	David Gross (Princeton University) Unified Field Theories John Kogut (University of Illinois) The Phases of Lattice Gauge Theory
13 September 1983	Sidney Bludman (University of Pennsylvania) Cosmic Ray Neutrons
12 November 1983	Jens Larsen (Niels Bohr Institute, Copenhagen) Charge Exchange Reactions and Gamov-Teller Transitions
3 December 1983	Ives Quéré (Ecole Polytechnique, Palaiseau, France) New Development in Radiation Damage on Solids
7 January 1984	Tomas Fried (Research Institute of Physics, Stockholm) Surface Multicharged Ion Interactions at Low Energies Leonard Berkovitz (Purdue University) Differential Games
9 May 1984	Mark Fellows (Institut Pasteur, Paris) Genetics of Sex Determination Herlund Markovich (Institut Pasteur, Paris) Do Cells Age?
19 May 1984	Hanno Essén (Institute Theoretical Physics, Stockholm) Kaluza Klein and Other High-Dimensional Unified Field Theories
26 May 1984	Michel Green (Queen Mary College, London) String Theories
29 September 1984	Rolf Stabell (Institute of Theoretical Astrophysics, Oslo) Realistic Models of the Universe
17 November 1984	Georg Witt (Stockholm University, Sweden) Optical (Spectroscopy) Probing of the Atmosphere
19 January 1985	Bertel Laurent (Stockholm University, Sweden) Is There Gravity in Flatland?
23 February 1985	Martin Ettinger (Copenhagen University) Aspects of Chemistry of Natural Products
9 March 1985	Gunnar Tibell (Uppsala University, Sweden Production of Heavy Hyper-Nuclei: Antiprotons from LEAR at CERN
28 April 1985	Kjell Mark (Trondheim University, Norway) Radiative Corrections to Two Photon Physics
25 May 1985	Arno Bohm (Texas University) Twenty Years of Dynamic Groups

Table 3. Continued

28 September 1985	Frank Laloe (Laboratoire de Physique de JENS, Paris) Bifurcation Period Doubling and Chaos in Clarinet-Like Systems
2 November 1985	Gunnar Berq (Uppsala University, Sweden) Exotic Infrared Radiation Sten Kayser (Uppsala University, Sweden) Minkowski Sums in the Plane
14 December 1985	Jean Verdier (Ecole Normale, Paris) Classical Solutions of Σ-models
18 January 1986	Bernard Shutz (Cardiff University, London) Gravitational Radiation: New Window in Astronomy
25 January 1986	Mawas Clawoe (Director of INSERM, France) Recent Advantages in Bone Marrow Transplants
15 February 1986 (Maimonides seminar)	Alexander Gribanov The Life and Philosophy of Maimonides Vlad Dachevsky About a Classical Rambat Solution: A Jurisprudence Treatise Jens Larsen (Niels Bohr Institute, Copenhagen) Niels Bohr Century in Copenhagen Øyvind Gron (Oslo University) Inflationary Cosmological Model

Index